THE INFECTION OF THOMAS DE QUINCEY

A Psychopathology of Imperialism

JOHN BARRELL

YALE UNIVERSITY PRESS
NEW HAVEN AND LONDON 1991

FOR JACQUELINE

Set in Linotron Bembo by Excel Typesetters Co., Hong Kong
Printed and bound at the Bath Press, Avon, Great Britain

Library of Congress Cataloging–in–Publication Data

Barrell, John.
    The infection of Thomas De Quincey/John Barrell.
        p.   cm.
    Includes bibliographical references and index.
    ISBN 0–300–04932–3
    1. De Quincey, Thomas, 1785–1859 – Knowledge – Orient.   2. De
Quincey, Thomas, 1785–1859 – Biography – Psychology.   3. Authors,
English – 19th century – Psychology.   4. Psychoanalysis and
literature.   5. East and West in literature.   8. Imperialism in
literature.   7. Orient in literature.   I. Title.
PR4538.074B37   1991
828'.809 – dc20

                                                            90–49489
                                                               CIP

Contents

Illustrations

Preface and Acknowledgements

Thomas De Quincey was born in 1785 and died in 1859. He made a slow start as a writer: his first success, *The Confessions of an English Opium-Eater*, was not published until 1821, when he was 36; and he did not become a consistently prolific writer for another ten years or so. By far the majority of the essays which fill the 14 volumes of his *Works* were written in the reign of Victoria, which began when he was in his early fifties. But De Quincey remains, for the general reader, a writer of the Romantic period, an identity fixed by his acquaintance, more or less intimate, with the first generation of Romantic writers, the Wordsworths, Lamb and Coleridge, and by the nature and date of his most famous work: when the *Confessions* first appeared, all the famous writers we think of as 'Romantic' were still alive and active, with the single exception of Keats. Most of the best criticism we have of De Quincey's writing treats him as a Romantic writer, and approaches him in terms of the epistemological questions – the questions about Romantic subjectivity – that have shaped and reshaped our understanding of Wordsworth, or Coleridge, or Shelley.

Occasionally, however, the questions of subjectivity raised by De Quincey's writings have been differently situated, in the context of the concern of the British in general, and of De Quincey in particular, with the nature and development of their Empire – a concern which, to judge by the volume of writing in which it finds expression, became much more intense in the 1820s and 1830s than before. This is where my book situates him too. It examines a fear that is repeated throughout his writings, and which runs back and forth between the most private space of his own childhood and the most public terrain of the British Empire in the East.

I am indebted to the Trustees of the British Museum for permission to reproduce figures 1 and 3. Figures 2 and 4 are reproduced from photographs supplied by the British Library. Figure 6 is reproduced by kind permission of Mrs Rosemary Blok, from a photograph supplied by the Trustees of the Wordsworth Museum, Dove Cottage, Grasmere.

Eight people read my manuscript at one stage or another before it was finished: Homi Bhabha, David Glover, Stephen Heath, Geoff Hemstedt, Cora Kaplan, Nigel Leask, Colin MacCabe and Jacqueline Rose, and I am very grateful indeed for the encouragement they all gave me. Geoff Hemstedt's reading was so careful and creative that I began to worry that he should have written this book, not me. My debt to Nigel Leask is enormous: he allowed me to read the draft of his own superb essay on De Quincey in his book *Romanticism and the Interest of Empire*, forthcoming from Cambridge University Press; he supplied me with a stream of information, bibliographical and historical; and he kept me in touch with my own past, as a historian of literature, when I seemed to be in danger of losing it. The influence of Tony Tanner on my manner of reading De Quincey's prose is very apparent to me: of all literary critics I covet his skills the most, and the shortcomings of this book will show why. My biggest debt is to Jacqueline Rose. Without her support and advice this book would never have been started; without her continual rereading, rethinking, redrafting, it would never have been finished. Among those I have never met who have written on De Quincey, my largest debt is to Grevel Lindop, whose various researches, bibliographical, biographical, critical, editorial, have made De Quincey newly accessible, and even more fascinating than before. Thanks finally to the staff of the London office of Yale University Press, always a pleasure to work with, and especially to Rosemary Amos and John Nicoll.

John Barrell
May 1990

Abbreviations

All references in the form (for example) 7: 329, or 14: 82, are to the volume and page numbers of *The Collected Writings of Thomas De Quincey*, edited by David Masson, 14 vols, Edinburgh (Adam and Charles Black) 1889–90.

All references in the form (for example) VII: 245, or XIV: 13 are to the volume and page numbers of *The Standard Edition of the Complete Psychological Works of Sigmund Freud*, edited by James Strachey and Anna Freud, 24 vols, London (The Hogarth Press and the Institute of Psycho-Analysis) 1966–74.

All references in the form (for example) 1803 43 are to page numbers in works by De Quincey listed by date in the bibliography.

All references in the form (for example) B20 1826 844 are to the volume number, year of publication, and page number of the periodicals designated by the initial letters listed below.

References preceded by initial letters are to the following:

B   *Blackwood's Edinburgh Magazine.*
E   *Edinburgh Review.*
H   *Hogg's Instructor.*
J   *The Posthumous Works of Thomas De Quincey*, ed. Alexander H. Japp, 2 vols, London (William Heinemann) 1891–3.
L   Grevel Lindop, *The Opium-Eater. A Life of Thomas De Quincey*, London (J.M. Dent) 1981.
P   H.A. Page (pseudonym of A.H. Japp), *Thomas De Quincey: His Life and Writings. With Unpublished Correspondence*, 2nd edn, 2 vols, London (John Hogg) 1879.
Q   *Quarterly Review.*
T   *Tait's Edinburgh Magazine.*
U   *The Uncollected Writings of Thomas De Quincey*, ed. James Hogg, 2 vols, London (Swan Sonnenschein) 1890.
W   *Westmorland Gazette.*

From *Confessions of an English Opium-Eater*

May 1818. – The Malay has been a fearful enemy for months. Every night, through his means, I have been transported into Asiatic scenery. I know not whether others share in my feelings on this point; but I have often thought that, if I were compelled to forgo England, and to live in China, among Chinese manners and modes of life and scenery, I should go mad. The causes of my horror lie deep, and some of them must be common to others. Southern Asia, in general, is the seat of awful images and associations. As the cradle of the human race, if on no other ground, it would have a dim, reverential feeling connected with it. But there are other reasons. No man can pretend that the wild, barbarous, and capricious superstitions of Africa, or of savage tribes elsewhere, affect him in the way that he is affected by the ancient, monumental, cruel, and elaborate religions of Hindostan. The mere antiquity of Asiatic things, of their institutions, histories, – above all, of their mythologies, &c., – is so impressive that to me the vast age of the race and name overpowers the sense of youth in the individual. A young Chinese seems to me an antediluvian man renewed. Even Englishmen, though not bred in any knowledge of such institutions, cannot but shudder at the mystic sublimity of castes that have flowed apart, and refused to mix, through such immemorial tracts of time; nor can any man fail to be awed by the sanctity of the Ganges, or by the very name of the Euphrates. It contributes much to these feelings that South-eastern Asia is, and has been for thousands of years, the part of the earth most swarming with human life, the great officina gentium. Man is a weed in those regions. The vast empires, also, in which the enormous population of Asia has always been cast, give a further sublimity to the feelings associated with all oriental names or images. In China, over and above what it has in common with the rest of Southern Asia, I am terrified by the modes of life, by the manners, by the barrier of utter abhorrence placed between myself and them, by counter-sympathies deeper than I can analyse. I could sooner live with lunatics, with vermin, with crocodiles or snakes. All this, and much more than I can say, the reader must enter into before he can comprehend the unimaginable horror which these dreams of oriental imagery and mythological tortures impressed upon me. Under the connecting feeling of tropical heat and vertical sunlights, I brought together all creatures, birds, beasts, reptiles, all trees and plants, usages and appearances, that are found in all tropical regions, and assembled them together in China or Hindostan. From kindred feelings, I soon brought Egypt and her gods under the same law. I was stared at, hooted at, grinned at, chattered at, by monkeys, by paroquets, by cockatoos. I ran into pagodas, and was fixed for centuries at the summit, or in secret rooms; I was the idol; I was the priest; I was worshipped; I was sacrificed. I fled from the wrath of Brama through all the forests of Asia; Vishnu hated me; Seeva lay in wait for me. I came suddenly upon Isis and Osiris: I had done a deed, they said, which the ibis and the crocodile trembled at. Thousands of years I lived and was buried in stone coffins, with mummies and sphinxes, in narrow'chambers at the heart of eternal pyramids. I was kissed, with cancerous kisses, by crocodiles, and was laid, confounded with all unutterable abortions, amongst reeds and Nilotic mud.

    Some slight abstraction I thus attempt of my oriental dreams, which filled me always with such amazement at the monstrous scenery that horror seemed absorbed for a while in sheer astonishment. Sooner or later came a reflux of feeling that swallowed up the astonishment, and left me, not so much in terror, as in hatred and abomination of what I saw. Over every form, and threat, and punishment, and dim sightless incarceration, brooded a killing sense of eternity and infinity. Into these dreams only it was, with one or two slight exceptions, that any circumstances of physical horror entered. All before had been moral and spiritual terrors. But here the main agents were ugly birds, or snakes, or crocodiles, especially the last. The cursed crocodile became to me the object of more horror than all the rest. I was compelled to live with him; and (as was always the case in my dreams) for centuries. Sometimes I escaped, and found myself in Chinese houses. All the feet of the tables, sofas, &c., soon became instinct with life: the abominable head of the crocodile, and his leering eyes, looked out at me, multiplied into ten thousand repetitions; and I stood loathing and fascinated. So often did this hideous reptile haunt my dreams that many times the very same dream was broken up in the very same way: I heard gentle voices speaking to me (I hear everything when I am sleeping), and instantly I awoke; it was broad noon, and my children were standing, hand in hand, at my bedside, come to show me their coloured shoes, or new frocks, or to let me see them dressed for going out. No experience was so awful to me, and at the same time so pathetic, as this abrupt translation from the darkness of the infinite to the gaudy summer air of highest noon, and from the unutterable abortions of miscreated gigantic vermin to the sight of infancy and innocent human *natures.*

(3: 441–3)

1

Introduction: This/That/the Other

A 'compromised' person is one who has been in contact with people or things supposed to be capable of conveying infection. As a general rule the whole Ottoman empire lies constantly under this terrible ban.

A.W. Kinglake, *Eothen*, 14n.

He described the present state of Syria as perfectly impracticable for travellers, or at least highly dangerous, from the united obstacles of marauders and pestilence. He saw a party of deserters marched in near Damascus, chained to each other, and occasionally a man free from plague joined hand in hand with one who was infected.

The Hon. Mrs Damer, *Diary of a Tour*, 1: 22.

I

Thomas De Quincey became a 'regular and confirmed' opium addict in 1813; before that, for ten years, he had used the drug, usually if not invariably in the form of laudanum, on a weekly rather than on a daily basis. When in London he would take it on Saturday nights, and with the idea of indulging in one of two competing pleasures. He went to the opera; or he became a *flâneur* for the evening, a watcher of the poor in their hours of relaxation. Most people, he acknowledges, 'are apt to show their interest in the concerns of the poor chiefly by sympathy with their distresses and sorrows', but 'I at that time was disposed to express mine by sympathising with their pleasures'. Saturday night was the best time for experiencing this sympathetic pleasure, for then the poor, released from the bondage of labour, would congregate in family parties to 'purchase their Sunday's dinner' (so Mayhew explains) at the great street-markets of the metropolis. De Quincey's 'sympathy' was such that on Saturday nights he too began to feel that he was 'released from some yoke of bondage, had some wages to receive, and some luxury of repose to enjoy'. He would, accordingly, knock back his laudanum and 'wander forth, without much regarding the direction or the distance', to all those parts of London where this Saturday night spectacle could be enjoyed (3: 392; Mayhew 1: 10).

This early account of the pleasures of the *flâneur* communicates a very specific sense of the developing modern metropolis. Those that De Quincey calls the 'poor' are the working poor, probably largely employed as outworkers, and paid only on Saturday afternoons or evenings when they take their work to the warehouse. The market-traders must therefore work late on Saturday nights (and also on Sunday mornings) if the poor are to be able to purchase the necessities of life. It is the regularity and uniformity of the working week – regular even in its irregularities, its St Monday, its Friday-night 'ghoster' – that produces this sudden and regular visibility of 'the poor' at a certain time in certain places – and that offers De Quincey the opportunity of 'witnessing, upon as large a scale as possible' this 'spectacle' of early nineteenth-century metro-politan life.[1]

No less interesting is the nature and scope of what De Quincey represents as his sympathy with the poor. 'If wages were a little higher,' he writes, 'or were expected to be so – if the quartern loaf were a little lower, or it was reported that onions or butter were falling – I was glad; yet, if the contrary were true, I drew from opium some means of consolation' (3: 393). There is no pretence that this is a general concern for the well-being of the poor; their pleasures he could use, but he had no need of their sadness. Their job, there-fore, was to remain cheerful and acquiescent even in adversity; and to a mind soaked in laudanum, they readily gave the impression of being so:

> sometimes there might be heard murmurs of discontent: but far oftener expressions . . . of patience, of hope, and of reconciliation to their lot. Generally speaking, the impression left upon my mind was that the poor are practically more philosophic than the rich; that they show a more ready and cheerful submission to what they consider as irremediable evils or irreparable losses.   (3: 392–3)

The consolations provided by these Saturday nights, it seems, were as much political as personal, and they are consolations familiar to those brought up within the class structure of Britain. The pleasure is not at all to pretend to be *one of* an inferior class; it is to pretend to be *like* them, fundamentally the same, but different in all that really concerns one's sense of identity and self-esteem. The search for a common human nature becomes the search for a means of reassurance, of making safe what seems to be threatening in the poor, in the 'masses', in the enormous numbers of the working class that the timetable of modern life sometimes permits to congregate together. Especially at those moments it becomes important to believe, as De Quincey puts it, that 'the most hostile sects unite, and acknowledge a common link of brotherhood' (3: 393).

De Quincey's own fear of the working class is elsewhere very evident. They were 'Jacobins' – he could still use the word in the 1850s to describe those whom he had first recognised as the inferiors and enemies of his own class when he was an eight-year-old schoolboy during the Terror. Grevel Lindop describes how in 1842 De Quincey wrote to Blackwood, of *Blackwood's Magazine*, about an essay he was writing on revolutionary movements and the working class. He had kept the 'working poor' under surveillance, he explained, for many years. He had listened carefully to what they said; he had taken every opportunity to encourage them into 'the express manifestation' of their 'true secret dispositions'. 'To a man I look upon the working poor, Scottish or English, as latent Jacobins – *biding their* time' (L345). In the article 'On the Approaching Revolution in Great Britain', a jeremiad published in 1831 in anticipation of the passing of the Reform Bill, he disclosed that he had also been keeping his eye on the class of 'petty shopkeepers', who were just as bad:

> I have observed them much, and long . . . no symptom has escaped me for the last sixteen years . . . the result of my observations is, that, with the exception here and there of an individual, bribed, as it were, to reserve and duplicity, by his dependence on some great aristocratic neighbour, this order of men is as purely Jacobinical, and disposed to revolutionary counsels, as any that existed in France at the time of their worst convulsions. (B30 1831 323)

And in an essay of uncertain date, on Judas Iscariot, he writes of the same class:

> They receive, and with dreadful fidelity they give back, all Jacobinical impulses. . . . In times of fierce political agitation these are the men who most of all are kept *au courant* of the interior councils and policy amongst the great body of acting conspirators. (8: 182n.)

This is the other side of the jovial *flânerie* amongst the families of the poor, the market-traders, the small shopkeepers of London: a fearful suspicion, a paranoia, that in the apparently routine and good-natured transactions of a Saturday-night shopping trip, con-spiratorial words are being whispered, glances exchanged. While De Quincey is watching the poor, they are watching out, for the moment to strike; and as they have no real grievances, the revenge they are contemplating is stimulated by nothing but a 'plebeian envy', a 'low-minded jealousy against the aristocracy' (B30 1831 324).[2]

The need to denounce these petty shopkeepers may have been influenced by the habit, noticed by De Quincey, of referring to them in Scotland as *'merchants'*. De Quincey's father, a member of high bourgeois society in Manchester, had described himself as a merchant, and Thomas himself had announced, in the *Opium-Eater*, his pride in being the 'son of a plain English merchant'. But the devaluation of the term in Scotland, where Thomas spent the last half of his life, was a threat to whatever degree of social distinction he had inherited as his birthright. That birthright had always been problematic, however, and in England especially, where the disdain for 'trade', however lucrative, and however much an unacknowledged component of the fortunes of those who passed as 'landed', had always represented the De Quinceys as inferior to the polite and leisured classes that he and his mother wanted so badly to be part of. It was those ambitions that had led De Quincey's mother to decorate the family name – originally plain 'Quincey' – with what he calls 'the aristocratic *De*'. When even she had abandoned it, he retained it, as if to reassure himself that, though apparently a hack writer, permanently on the run from his creditors, he was a member of some *noblesse de plume* (8: 182n.; 1971 61; 1: 30; 3: 459).

The double vision that for De Quincey seems to have characterised the spectacle of the poor is clear enough in the *Opium-Eater* itself, where he describes his happy and hazy wanderings. He begins that description by assuring us that 'the pleasures of the poor . . . can never become oppressive to contemplate', but by the very next paragraph they have become precisely that: to the 'opium-eater, when in the divinest state incident to his enjoyment . . . crowds become an oppression'. The more opium he took, the more the spectacle of mass society produced the fears he had been trying to make safe; and if they disappeared in the evening, they were to return, years later, in a different but still recognisable form at night. There may seem to be a vast geographical and psychic distance between the cheerful bustle of a London street-market on a Saturday night, and the terrifying oriental imagery of the opium dreams, but De Quincey saw in one the representation and displacement of the other. Whatever else they were, the dreams were dreams of the terrors of 'mass society', which De Quincey often rationalised into a fear of popular Jacobinism – of those 'myriads of murderous levellers', for example, who had emerged from the 'dark recesses' and 'gloomy dens' of Paris, and 'wallowed in the blood of illustrious victims' (3: 392, 394; B28 1830 705).

'The human face tyrannised over my dreams'; this tyranny, a kind of dream-dictatorship of the proletariat, was the result not only of the wandering from market to market, but of the continual search, when De Quincey was in London, to find, among the endlessly multiplied faces of the metropolitan crowd, the one face of Ann, the prostitute and 'pariah' who had befriended him on his first trip to London as a teenager, and with whom he had then lost touch.[3] 'I suppose that, in the literal and unrhetorical use of the word *myriad*, I must, on my different visits to London, have looked into many *myriads* of female faces'; and the search 'pursued in the crowds of London', was pursued also 'through many a year in dreams'. On the last occasion that he saw Ann, he had been worried about the difficulty of attempting to find her again in 'the great Mediterranean of Oxford Street', and his later dreams literalised for him the expression 'a sea of faces' (3: 394, 375, 222, 368). As a result of this 'searching for Ann amongst fluctuating crowds' (*fluctus*, a wave), he writes, the 'human face began to reveal itself' upon the 'rocking waves' of an ocean:

> the sea appeared paved with innumerable faces, upturned to the heavens; faces, imploring, wrathful, despairing; faces that surged upwards by thousands, by myriads, by generations: infinite was my agitation; my mind tossed, as it seemed, upon the billowy ocean, and weltered upon the weltering waves. (3: 441)

This sense of the sheer terrifying numberlessness of the world's population, of its 'hunger-bitten myriads', of 'surplus' or 'redundant' people (7: 257–8), re-emerges in the preamble to the opium dreams as a terror inspired by 'the enormous population of Asia'. 'The difficulty in India is in individualizing your man', wrote the Baptist missionary Joshua Russell (265); and De Quincey like most other Europeans conceived of Asia beyond the Tigris as a place where people seemed to run into each other, to replicate each other, to compose one mass without divisions or features. 'South-eastern Asia is, and has been for thousands of years, the part of the earth most swarming with human life, the great *officina gentium*. Man is a weed in those regions'. The phrase '*officina gentium*', 'factory where people are made', is also used by De Quincey, in an incident we shall look at later, to describe a factory, full of 'Jacobins', that frightened him in childhood. Differently construed, it is probably this phrase that Disraeli had in mind when, in 1838, he described England's aspirations to be 'the workshop of the World'; and the phrase may once have proposed a kind of equivalence between the 'mass society' of the industrial nations, and an idea of Asia as '*swarming* with *human* life' – with human beings who are evoked only to be dehumanised.[4] In a late essay on China, De Quincey found in Canton, a city where the myriads were oriental, a final realisation of his nightmares:

Canton, the city where Englishmen are 'cut to pieces' whenever they wander out alone; and the city which, as De Quincey acknowledged, was the creation of Europe, and of the European 'factories' there, as the trading warehouses were called (3: 442; 1857 7).

This terror of society in the mass, of what he calls in an earlier essay on China the 'monstrous aggregations of human beings . . . in the suburbs of mighty cities', is certainly not, as De Quincey sometimes suggests, the whole of what is displaced and represented as oriental in the description of the opium dreams and its elaborate preamble (B50 1841 688). It was the bit, perhaps, that he could most easily own up to, could acknowledge to himself, at the time when he was writing the *Opium-Eater*. Nor were humans growing like weeds, or swarming like ants or bees, the only 'unimaginable horror' to take on an oriental character in De Quincey's writing about his dreams. The turbaned 'Malay' who had once called in at Dove Cottage; the imagery of Hindu theology; the Hindu caste system; the vastness of space and time in India and China; the fauna of everywhere from Egypt to China, but chiefly snakes and crocodiles; pagodas, pyramids, forests, reeds, mud, the Ganges, the Nile, the Euphrates, and so on and so on – all these came together to form, in De Quincey's head, an eclectic visual style he described as the 'barbaresque', a cabinet of oriental curiosities, partly terrifying just because its contents were so unpredictably miscellaneous (14: 48–9, 55–9).

At one point De Quincey himself represents his 'oriental imagery' as composing, precisely, a *collection*:

> under the connecting feeling of tropical heat and vertical sunlights, I brought together all creatures, birds, beasts, reptiles, all trees and plants, usages and appearances, that are found in all tropical regions, and assembled them together in China or Hindostan. From kindred feelings, I soon brought Egypt and her gods under the same law.   (3: 442)

What is being evoked here is perhaps not so much the random collection of oriental curios in the haphazard way of the mid-eighteenth-century virtuoso; it is the beginnings of the large-scale, scientific collecting of the nineteenth-century museum age, with its aspiration to represent *everything* – '*all* creatures . . . *all* trees and plants' – in its galleries and in its botanical and its zoological gardens.[5] Just as the experiences of urban society which find expression in this dream imagery speak to us of a very specific moment in the economic, social and cultural history of Britain, so does that imagery itself. The 'barbaresque' Hindu divinities, for example, had been elaborately depicted in Thomas Maurice's *History of Hindostan* (1795–9) and Edward Moor's *Hindu Pantheon* (1810). In rather less elaborate form they had illustrated Sir William Jones's essay 'The Gods of Greece, Italy, and India' in the *Asiatic Researches*, which De Quincey had read when a boy, and in which he would have read the first serious essays of British orientalists in India. The antiquities collected by the Napoleonic expedition to Egypt – hitherto regarded as too inhospitable a country for regular collectors – were confiscated by the British in 1801 and brought to England in 1802, to form the real basis of the collection of Egyptian antiquities in the British Museum. The Chinese imagery, more generalised, seems to derive from the *chinoiserie* of eighteenth-century garden design and interior décor: pagodas, and tables and sofas 'instinct with life' because carved with the heads and feet of animals.

In short, this oriental imagery is the imagery of an early but well-established imperialist culture, an imagery which had been collected and become familiar to the British imagination, to this degree and in this combination, only in the very last years of the eighteenth century and the opening decades of the nineteenth. Its availability depended on the combination of military, naval, mer-cantile and scholarly endeavours and acquisitions which was especially typified by the activities of the Asiatic Society in Bengal around 1800; but the increase of British 'interest' in Asia further east than India, for example, and the increasing awareness in Britain of the Ottoman Empire as sick but surviving competitor in the Near East, were contributing their own ingredients to this miscellaneous oriental soup. These ingredients did not come only or mainly as material objects – animals, ornaments, exhibits; they came as narratives too, circulated by newspapers, by engravings, and by melodramas, pantomimes and plays. At the centre of these narratives was a succession of oriental characters drawn from fictions such as the *Arabian Nights*, or from barely less fictionalised accounts of history and politics – Nadir Shah, Siraj-ud-daula, Haider Ali, Tipu Sultan, Ali Pacha, Runjeet Singh – 'oriental despots' who were the forerunners in the European imagination of Khomeini, Ghadaffi, and Saddam Hussein – all individualised by the different ferocities imputed to them, but more or less identical to each other in their power to thrill the nursery and the theatre, and to enrage the drawing-room and the club.

The various ingredients, material and immaterial, of the oriental soup, had only two things in common. They were images of an exotic world east of the Mediterranean and still only haphazardly penetrated, not to put too fine a point on it, by western European power; and they were especially serviceable, as forms, images, ideas which could be used to represent 'unimaginable horrors', precisely because the East entered the western European imagination as an unknown, empty space – empty of everything, that is, except its appropriable resources, imaginative as well as material. Of all those resources, the abundantly decorated surfaces of the artefacts of Turkey, Egypt, Persia, India and China, intricately abstract or flamboyantly figurative, were perhaps particularly valuable and easy to appropriate. So crowded, to western eyes, were the surfaces of oriental objects, covered with decoration and imagery not under-stood and not thought worth understanding, that they could become the very opposite of what they appeared to be – blank screens on which could be projected whatever it was that the inhabitants of Europe, individually or collectively, wanted to displace, and to represent as other to themselves.

II

In De Quincey's writing, however, there is often a particular process or scheme of displacement at work, one which suggests that a simple binary model, of self and other, might not always be adequate for thinking about the uses and dangers of the oriental to the western imagination. An especially interesting example – interesting because it seems to occur playfully, anecdotally, as if nothing very much is at risk – occurs in his discussion of the highly differentiated topography of John Palmer's mail-coaches, in the first section of the long essay 'The English Mail-Coach'.[6] The essay either records or invents a fascinating moment in the history of class division, the moment when – according to De Quincey – it became a fashionable, a sparkish thing to do, for young gentlemen to travel on the outside of the coach, next or near to the coachman, rather than on the inside, the traditional and more expensive refuge of the genteel. The fashion took hold, according to De Quincey, at some time in the first decade of the nineteenth century, when he was an undergraduate at Oxford. Before that time, the relation between the division of space on the coach and the division of class among the passengers had apparently been unambiguous; those on the outside were, precisely, outsiders, 'Pariahs' as De Quincey puts it. When the fashion became established, and young gentlemen took to travelling on the outside, the insiders attempted to behave as if the usual etiquette which governed the behaviour of the two types of passenger at inns and staging-posts, and which kept them apart at meal times especially, could still universally be applied. This attempt was strongly resisted by the sparkish young gents.

The division was reinforced by the simple binary terminology in which it was described. In addition to 'insider' and 'outsider', the politics of the first decade of the nineteenth century made available the terms 'aristocrat' and 'democrat'. And because since the early and middle 1790s to be a 'democrat' was to be allied, in the eyes of 'aristocrats', with the un-English, Francophile, and therefore treasonous politics of revolution, De Quincey can describe the relations between insiders and outsiders in terms of treason and the suspicion of treason. No insider would have dreamed, he tells us, of exchanging one word of civility with an outsider: 'even to have kicked an outsider', he writes, 'might have been held to attaint the foot concerned in that operation, so that, perhaps, it would have required an act of Parliament to restore its purity of blood'. If outsiders attempted the treasonous act of breakfasting with insiders, the act would have been so incomprehensible as to be regarded as 'a case of lunacy . . . rather than of treason'. Though the outsiders were 'gownsmen', they were 'constructively', by virtue of where they sat, 'raff' or 'snobs' – varsity slang for (mere) townsmen – there is a reference here to the controversial crime of 'constructive treason', and a suggestion that, by sitting outside, the young Oxford gentlemen 'lose caste'. In spite of all this, however, the young gentlemen managed to effect 'a perfect Revolution' in mail-coach society'.[7]

Characteristically, or so it will soon appear, De Quincey attempts to heal the breach between insider and outsider by treating it, in the first place, as not really a breach at all, there being no real class difference between the two varieties of passenger; and then by looking round for a third object which both the first two can agree to regard as other to themselves. He remembers a coach from Birmingham, some 'tawdry', 'plebian', 'jacobinical' '"Tallyho" or "Highflyer"', which once had the temerity to race against the mail. 'The connexion of the mail with the state and executive government' enables him to argue that for 'such a Birmingham thing . . . to challenge us . . . has an air of sedition'; and for it actually to win would have been 'treason'. It is not enough, however, to represent the 'poor Brummagem brute' as plebeian, even as Jacobinical; to complete the processes of identification and abjection in which he is engaged, the rival coach must be orientalised. It had, noted De Quincey scornfully, 'as much writing and painting on its sprawling flanks as would have puzzled a decipherer from the tombs of Luxor'. The accusation of un-Englishness, expressed in the terms 'pariah' and 'traitor', and originally used to distinguish between insiders and outsiders on the Royal Mail, is now used to unite them, by being levelled at the oriental and treasonous 'Brummagem coach'. It is a characteristic of true Englishness, we are reminded – of the Englishness of the polite classes – that they practise understatement, by contrast with the plethora of meaningless signification which characterises the East, and which has come to be connected, somehow, with the tawdry, the gimcrack, and with whatever other vulgarities are conjured up by 'Brummagem'. The connection of all these terms – pariah, vulgar, traitorous, un-English – is finally underlined when the triumph of the English mail-coach, in leaving the Birmingham vehicle far behind, is enjoyed by all except 'a Welsh rustic', who for the playful purposes of the essay can be regarded as a true, because foreign and plebeian, outsider (13: 273–83).

The process we have been observing begins by identifying an apparently exhaustive binary: there is a self, and there is an other, an inside and an outside, an above and a below. The self is constituted by the other, and it requires that other to mark out its own limit, its own definition; yet the two are implacably hostile, and their confrontation appears unavoidable, for there is no third term, no other identity conceivable, nowhere else to go. This is the situation we are presented with at the start of 'The English Mail-Coach', and if De Quincey himself starts off on the outside, and so apparently in the place of the other, that is only an early indication of how easily the distinction is about to be, not abolished exactly, but accommodated. The scheme of this accommodation is given in the title of this chapter: the terms self and other can be thought of as superseded by 'this' and 'that', in a narrative which now says, there is *this* here, and it is different from *that* there, but the difference between them, though in its own way important, is as nothing compared with the difference between the two of them considered together, and that third thing, way over there, which is truly *other* to them both.

I could borrow Gayatri Spivak's distinction here between a 'self-consolidating other' and an 'absolute other', for what is involved is precisely an act of consolidation of the self. If I prefer my own way of putting it, that is because it seems to dramatise how what at first seems 'other' can be made over to the side of the self – to a subordinate position on that side – only so long as a new, and a newly absolute 'other' is constituted to fill the discursive space that has thus been evacuated. In an essay on the mutiny, rebellion or war of independence in India in 1857, De Quincey describes his writing as a matter of 'putting this and that together'; and the phrase seems to make the point that to talk of 'this' and 'that' is always to suppose or to require 'the other', a continually reinvented third term which acknowledges that whenever two things have been 'put together', something else has been pushed aside (Spivak 1985b 131; U1: 311–12; 1: 102).[8]

There is a whole historical and geopolitical system in De Quincey's works which is constructed by using the same spatial scheme as is at work in 'The English Mail-Coach'. There is a 'this', and there is a something hostile to it, something which lies, almost invariably, to the east; but there is an East beyond that East, where something lurks which is equally threatening to both, and which enables or obliges them to reconcile their differences. The translation of the London poor, experienced as oppressive, into 'the enormous population of Asia', may already have provided an example of the process used to make safe more serious threats than the one offered by the 'Brummagem thing' to the genteel mail-coach. It may be the representation of the poor as oriental, when they are experienced as 'oppressive', that enables them to be experienced also as 'sympathetic': whatever is bad about them is characterised as exotic, as extrinsic, as not really them at all, with the effect that they are separated from, and contrasted with, their own representation as oriental. There are the cities of London and Westminster; there is the East End; and there is the East. It is by this means that the limited class solidarity essential to an imperial power, and especially to its ruling class, is produced, for it enables the differences between one class and another to be fully acknowledged, and then represented as almost trivial, when compared with the civilisation they both share, but which is emphatically not shared by whatever oriental other, the sepoys or the dervishes, is in season at the time (see Kiernan, 316–17). Here are some more examples.

French History

The village where Joan of Arc was born, Domrémy, stands on the Meuse, which divides France from the territories of the Dukes of Bar and Lorraine. Despite its significance as a political frontier, the river did not divide the populations; it was crossed by bridges and ferries, there was a good deal of intermarriage between the left bank and the right, and so, 'like other frontiers, it produced a *mixed* race, representing the *cis* and the *trans*'. 'The Dukes of Bar and Lorraine had for generations pursued the policy of eternal warfare with France on their own account, yet also of eternal amity and league with France in case anybody else presumed to attack her'. This river was a frontier, therefore, only when no third party was to be taken into consideration. There was however another frontier, to the east – the mountains of the Vosges, covered with vast, impenetrable and mysterious woods. This formed the true 'eastern frontier' of France and Lorraine alike, the dividing line between two Empires of East and West, not unlike 'the desert between Syria and the Euphrates' (5: 390, 394–5).

Greek History

In the time of Herodotus, Persia was the sole enemy of Greece, and at that time the whole of the known world consisted of the Persian

Empire, and of the countries more or less within the orbit of Greek civilisation or knowledge. In that sense the known world was divided between Greece and Persia, and it is easy to think of the 'terrific collisions' between the two as engrossing all that there then was of history and the world. But if the Greeks, seen in this light, had an interest in the defeat of Persia, they had still greater interest in the stability of the Great King and his Empire. For in another light Persia was 'a great resisting mass interjacent between Greece and the unknown enemies to the north-east or east'. The sense of uncertainty, caused by ignorance of what 'fierce, unknown races' lay eastwards of Persia or in the easternmost reaches of the Persian Empire, meant that the Great King could also be seen 'as a common friend against some horrid enemy from the infinite deserts of Asia', though to be sure he appeared more often to the Greeks as an enemy than as a friend (10: 176–7).

Roman History

The garden of Greenhay, a small country house to the south of Manchester, was divided from the surrounding countryside by the Cornbrook, a stream crossed by a small bridge at the front gate of the garden. The territory on one side of this stream belonged to Romulus, on the other side to his scornful brother Remus, and the two territories may have corresponded to the kingdoms of Gombroon and Tigrosylvania. The brothers were engaged in continual conflict with each other. The northern boundary of the area formed by their two conjoint territories was the River Medlock, and the bridge over this river was held at one time or another by Carthaginians and by various other enemies of Rome – Goths, Vandals – in equal need of deletion. In their long-continued war with these peoples, the Roman brothers were always if uneasily united (1: 69–117).

Byzantine History

Because of the habit of regarding the Roman Empire as in a state of more or less permanent decline from as early as the reign of Commodus, and because of the hostility of the refined and effeminate Byzantine Court to the simple and manly Crusaders, 'we have all been accustomed to speak of the Byzantine Empire with scorn'. This is a great mistake; for though in many respects western Christendom and the Byzantine Empire appear as binary opposites, masculine and feminine, Roman and Greek, in another light they must be seen as united in their resistance to the formidable powers of the further East. However effete the Byzantine Empire may have been, its forces were capable in the seventh century of crossing the Tigris deep into Persia; more recently, it has been the 'capital bulwark' against the forward march of 'Mahometanism', the 'great aegis', indeed, of western Christendom (7: 255–6).

The History of 'Frankistan'

But then again, and in yet another light, Christendom and the 'Mahometan nations' should not be seen as in all respects exhaustively and irrevocably antagonistic. Both have this in common, that they subscribe to true religions; 'true', not in the sense that both have equal access to the absolute truth, for when all is said and done, Christians are Christians and masculine, and Muslims are emasculated infidels. But the religions of both are, truly, *religions* and not mere superstitions: they are both, as the Muslims say, 'religions of the book'; they are monotheisic, and they consist in a body of doctrine and of moral teaching, and not simply in a set of ritual observances. And even if we do think of Christendom and Islam as ineluctable opposites, and as connected only by their hostilities, they have become familiar to each other, even companionable, by that very opposition. This is true, at least, of the Ottomans, Arabs and Moors. To these peoples, and to European Christendom, we might apply the collective name *Frankistan*, to differentiate them from the peoples of southern and eastern Asia, whether the effeminate 'Mohammedans' of Bengal, or the 'Hindoos' and Buddhists, for example, with their 'foul', 'monstrous idolatries', and (especially) the 'pollution' of 'Hindoo polytheism'. This process of *rapprochement* between Christendom and western Islam has been accelerated in the nineteenth century, as a result of the decay of the Ottoman Empire (according to De Quincey, 'cancered', 'crazy', and 'paralytic'), and the growth of steam power, science, and European travel and trade to the Levant. 'Asia Minor, Egypt, Syria – all that lies west of the Tigris', is coming 'within the network of Christian civilisation', and has been 'taken under the *surveillance* of the great Christian powers' (1: 373; 7: 275; 8: 207–43, 308; J1: 41, 290; J2: 12n.; 7: 212; B48 1840 559–62).[9]

III

The kind of imaginary geography represented by De Quincey's 'this/that/the other' formula had its historical equivalent in British imperial policy or (for they were not always the same thing) the policy of the East India Company: the attempts to 'play off' Muslim against Hindu, or Sikh against Muslim, are obvious examples, and so is the tortuous policy of the Company towards Afghanistan. Here is the *Edinburgh Review*, pronouncing on imperial policy in 1840:

It is of vital importance to British India that Afghanistan should be interposed as an effectual barrier between the great Mahomedan power of Central Asia – urged on by Muscovite intrigue, and supported, whenever a favourable opportunity may offer, by Muscovite troops – and all that is inflammable within the peninsula.
(E71 1840 339)

The 1838 invasion of Afghanistan – the country to which the terms 'barrier-state', 'buffer-state', were first applied – was only the clearest instance of that 'monomaniac' zeal which, as Henry Lushington pointed out, could entertain no other conception of the country than that its destiny was to be a 'barrier to British India' (Lushington 55).[10]

In Afghanistan, indeed, to which between 1840 and 1844 De Quincey devoted no less than three essays, two competing 'systems of diplomatic calculation' were kept from colliding with each other only by the buffers interposed by the inhabitants and the geography of that country: it was here that in the 1830s and early 1840s British imperialism met itself coming back, as it were. For as it gazed eastward from Britain, the Tigris appeared as the last ditch between a manageable and an entirely hostile other; but as it gazed westward from India, the Indus became the 'river of separation' between a vulnerable and over-extended empire and the fantasised rapacity of Persia and Russia. In two essays from the early 1840s, by no means untypical of mid-century writing on the imperial theme, De Quincey attempts to 'arrange', to 'settle and determine the idea of Persia' – the other large country, besides Afghanistan, between the Tigris and the Indus – not according to any Persian notion of that country, but according to what it might be convenient for a version of British foreign policy to believe. 'The Turkish or western chambers' of 'Southern (or Mahometan) Asia,' he announces, 'may be viewed as reaching to the Tigris; the middle, or Persian part, from the Tigris to the desert on the west frontier of Affghanistan; the third or Affghan chamber to the Indus'. The Indus is thus proclaimed as 'the true natural eastern boundary of Cabul or Affghanistan'; and the same river, before the annexation of Sind and the Punjab carried the frontier still further west, was often represented as the 'natural boundary' of India – the more natural because one of its other names, the 'Attok', so the traveller G.T. Vigne explained, 'is derived from Atkana, or Atukna, signifying in Hindustani, *to stop*; no pious Hindoo will venture to go beyond it of his own accord, for fear of losing caste' (B52 1842 280; B48 1840 562; E71 1840 355; Vigne 1840 30).[11]

This is not the occasion to attempt a discussion of the effects on the imperial imagination of these complementary yet also competing systems of geography – systems which at times the British sought to impose by force on the imaginations of others. But the attempt to annex Afghanistan, and the continued anxiety about the security of the North-West frontier, must have contributed much to that sense of divided positionality which – as Homi Bhabha in particular has argued – became a characteristic of the British in the mid-nineteenth century, in Britain as well as in India. De Quincey, who shared Tory doubts about the wisdom of sending the expeditionary force to Kabul, probably suffered less than many from this particular symptom of ambivalence, the dis-orientation produced by the discovery of enemies to the west as well as to the east. He attacked the Afghanistan campaign on the grounds that it was an attempt to raise 'a powerful barrier' against 'enemies who might gather from the *west*' (my emphasis), but who had never been clearly identified (B56 1844 139). His own horror of the Orient was so great that for him the primary geopolitical significance of the Indus was probably as an additional line of defence, keeping the Hindus where they belonged. 'Such is the wonderful attachment to the British uniform', wrote Vigne, 'that in the late expedition to Afghanistan, the native Sepahis [sepoys], many of them Rajpoots, cheered loudly when they saw the British flag flying at Bukkur, and passed the bridge over the Indus with enthusiasm' (Vigne 1840 30–1). That image alone is enough to explain De Quincey's hostility to the Afghanistan adventure: the image of Hindus, in arms, crossing the Forbidden River, advancing towards the Tigris and Frankistan, and threatening to reclaim *that* barrier state for the *other*.

IV

The scheme we have been examining has clear affinities to the rhetorical figure Barthes described, in relation to the politics of class, as 'inoculation'. This consists in 'admitting the accidental evil of a class-bound institution the better to conceal its principal evil'. His more general, supplementary description of inoculation is for our purposes more useful: 'one immunizes the contents of the collective imagination by means of a small inoculation of acknowledged evil; one thus protects it against the risk of a generalized subversion' (Barthes 150). The apparently mixed metaphor here, which seems to identify political opposition and disease, is particularly appropriate to De Quincey's scheme, which figures the oriental as infection, and also as rebel, mutineer or subversive immigrant. De Quincey's life was terrorised by the fear of an unending and interlinked chain of infections from the East, which threatened to enter his system and to overthrow it, leaving him visibly and permanently 'compromised' and orientalised. 'It is well known', he writes, that the very reason why the Spanish beyond all nations became so gloomily jealous of a Jewish cross in the pedigree was because, until the vigilance of the Church rose in ferocity, in no nation was such a cross so common. The hatred of fear is ever the deepest. And men hated the Jewish taint, as once in Jerusalem they hated the leprosy, because, even whilst they raved against it, the secret proofs of it might be detected amongst their own kindred; even as in the Temple, whilst once a Hebrew king rose in mutiny against the priesthood (2 Chron. xxvi. 16–20), suddenly the leprosy that dethroned him blazed out upon his forehead.   (13: 210)

The 'oriental leprosy', 'oriental cholera', 'oriental typhus fever', the 'plague of Cairo', the 'cancerous kisses' of the Egyptian crocodile: the fear and hatred projected on to the East kept threatening to return in one such form or another, as in dreams they did return; and it is against these that De Quincey inoculates himself, taking something of the East into himself, and projecting whatever he could not acknowledge as his out into a farther East, an East *beyond* the East.[12] The Eurocentric nomenclature of imperialism is absolutely to the point here, in its definitions of a treacherous but sometimes manageable 'Near East', a terrifying 'Far East', and between them an ambiguous and hard to locate 'Middle East', which seems (like the Middle West in America) to wander around the continent on its own tectonic plate, turning up here or there according to need – a kind of itinerant barrier or buffer between what can possibly be allowed in, and what must be kept out at all costs.

The process of inoculation we have been examining in De Quincey's geopolitical schemata is rather less successful, however, than Barthes suggests. It never *immunises* against the infections of the East; at best it enables the patient to shake them off for a time, or gives him the illusion of having done so, but always with the fear that they will return in a more virulent form, as supergerms now themselves immune from the attacks of antibodies. The process of inoculation involves simultaneously protecting someone against a disease and infecting them with it, and the troubling ambiguity of this process is often visible in the very language in which it is described. 'The finished and accomplished surgeon', writes De Quincey, explaining why he refused to pick a quarrel with one, 'carries a pocket-case of surgical instruments, – lancets, for instance, that are loaded with *virus* in every stage of contagion. Might he not inoculate me with *rabies*, with *hydrophobia*, with the plague of Cairo'? (5: 353). To be inoculated *against* the disease is at the same time to be inoculated *with* it, and in De Quincey's case the process was accompanied by a higher than usual degree of risk; for he already had the disease he was attempting to immunise himself against. As we will see, the disease was always an external materialisation of an internal psychic anxiety, something first projected and rejected, then taken back in; and there was no guarantee that he might not rediscover that disorder in the East he had ingested as well as in the East he had thrown away.[13]

A case in point is his use of opium. To begin wth, the phrase 'English Opium-Eater' itself can be read as an example of inoculation. The use of opium was associated in the English imagination with every Asian country from Turkey, through Persia and India, to China, but to describe oneself as an 'eater' of opium was to claim kinship with a recognisably Turkish identity – a kinship qualified, however, and hopefully made safe, by the adjective 'English' (L249). At one point in the *Opium-Eater* – we can worry about the precise point later – De Quincey playfully describes his long experience of 'East Indian and Turkish' opium as a sequence of medical experiments conducted 'for the general benefit of the world'. He tells us of various surgeons who for the purposes of research had inoculated themselves with cancer, plague, and hydrophobia. Like these, De Quincey had 'inoculated' himself 'with the poison of eight thousand drops of laudanum per day', in search of 'happiness', and against the return of the 'misery', the 'blank desolation', the 'settled and abiding darkness' which had first made him a habitual user of the drug. By day the opium drove the misery away; by night it returned, by the agency of the opium itself, and more virulent than ever (3: 406, 231).

It cannot have helped that the practice of inoculation itself, no less famously than the practice of taking opium, had been borrowed from the Turks – the method of protecting oneself against the oriental was itself oriental – and no one knew better than De Quincey that his inoculations rarely provided the immunisation they promised. The opening section of 'The English Mail-Coach', his most light-hearted rehearsal of the 'this/that/the other' scheme, seems to function as the architectural plan for a system of fortification which is normally to be found only as an archaeological ruin, as the trace of an overwhelming defeat at the hands of a persistent and ferocious invader. We have seen how, in the first part of the essay, insiders and outsiders are brought together by the identification of something truly outside, plebeian and oriental. But no sooner has this rearrangement been managed, than De Quincey discovers (we shall see how later) that the coachman perched up beside him on the box of the mail-coach itself, loyally dressed in the King's livery, has been transfigured into an Egyptian crocodile, quite close enough to threaten De Quincey with his 'cancerous kisses' (13: 289).

Likewise, the vast sea of the metropolitan poor, the 'myriads' of human faces that tyrannised over De Quincey's dreams, were transformed at one stage in the description of the opium dreams into the 'abominable head of the crocodile . . . multiplied into ten thousand repetitions' – and this at the point where the crocodile takes over from the Chinese as the worst possible thing to find yourself next to, and to be forced to live with. Or still worse, the coachman appears as the very proof of the dangers of inoculation – part man, part reptile, a horrifying mixture of human and inhuman, English and oriental, a crocodile grafted on to a man, the product of 'the horrid inoculation upon each other of incompatible natures'. In botany, 'inoculation' can involve the grafting of one genus or species on to another, and that is exactly what has happened here. The appearance of the coachman as crocodile is one *mise en scène* – one of many, as we shall see – of De Quincey's horrified discovery that his is (to use Homi Bhabha's term) a *hybrid* identity; that his relation with an imaginary East, like that of an imperial power with its colonial 'dependencies', is a relation (at best) of symbiotic inter-dependence, and can no longer be thought of in terms of a safe transaction between a self and an other (3: 443; 13: 291n.; Bhabha 20–2).[14]

The continual attempt to create places of safety, the continual return of an 'alien nature' which has been so carefully expelled, the repeated rediscovery of hybridity, of cultural/racial impurity, is described by De Quincey in these terms

> The dreamer finds housed within himself – occupying, as it were, some separate chamber in his brain – holding, perhaps, from that station a secret and detestable commerce with his own heart – some horrid alien nature. What if it were his own nature repeated, – still, if the duality were distinctly perceptible, even that – even this mere numerical double of his own consciousness – might be a curse too mighty to be sustained. But how if the alien nature contradicts his own, fights with it, perplexes and confounds it? How, again, if not one alien nature, but two, but three, but four, but five, are introduced within what once he thought the inviolable sanctuary of himself? These, however, are horrors from the kingdom of anarchy and darkness, which, by their very intensity, challenge the sanctity of concealment, and gloomily retire from exposition.   (13: 92n.)

An 'alien nature', once its presence within one has been suspected, can sometimes be represented, it seems, as a repetition or a 'double' of one's own nature, not the self, exactly, but not the other, either – a 'that' to one's own 'this'. To treat it like this is to produce a psychic economy which is bearable, but barely so; the self may still be a kind of sanctuary, though hardly an inviolable one. It may be, however, that the 'alien nature' is so very alien as to be the enemy of one's own, in which case it will have to be represented as beyond the *cordon sanitaire* which defines what can be accepted as one's own nature, and which constitutes that nature. But what if it won't go quietly? or what if it has the power of reproducing itself infinitely, so that as each alien nature is tamed, domesticated, recuperated, another appears in the very place, the very chamber of the brain, the very sanctuary which has just been swept, swabbed down, disinfected, fumigated?[15]

The oriental is for De Quincey a name for that very power, that process of endless multiplication whereby the strategy of self-consolidation, of the recuperation or domestication of the other, always involves the simultaneous constitution of a new threat, or a new version of the old, in the space evacuated by the first. The Orient is the place of a malign, a luxuriant or virulent productivity, a breeding-ground of images of the inhuman, or of the no less terrifyingly half-human, which cannot be exterminated, except at the cost of exterminating one's self, and which cannot be kept back beyond the various Maginot lines, from the Vosges to the Tigris, that De Quincey attempts to defend against the 'horrid enemy from Asia'. In the *Opium-Eater* he speaks of the Chinese and 'the barrier of utter abhorrence placed between myself and *them*', but though the abhorrence was real enough, there was no barrier at all, and no 'between'. Clive, writes Macaulay (1: 508–9), 'was no sooner matched against an Indian intriguer, than he became himself an Indian intriguer'. De Quincey was all the figures from the Orient that appear in his writings. He *was* Chinese; he *was* the Malay that haunted his dreams; he *was* the crocodile. In one of his essays on Roman history he repeats the story told by a late Roman historian – he treats it as absurd, as an example of the 'anecdotage' of Rome in decline – of how Julius Caesar so enjoyed tickling the 'catastrophes' (the posteriors) of crocodiles (presumably he had some in a pool) that he 'anointed himself with crocodile fat, by which means he humbugged the crocodiles, ceasing to be Caesar, and passing for a crocodile, swimming and playing amongst them'. Like Caesar, De Quincey had become smeared with the fat of crocodiles, the mud of the Nile, the oil of opium, with whatever varieties of slime the Orient afforded, and so he had ceased to be *himself* (6: 439).

V

So far, the question of what anxieties, fears, terrors are figured by the oriental in De Quincey's dream narratives has received only one answer – his fear of the urban poor. He himself, however, gives other answers to the question: the visions, he suggests in the final preface to the *Opium-Eater*, are expressions of a fear of losing a woman, or they are repetitions of the story of how she is already lost. In this light, as we have seen, the myriads of faces seem to have meaning only as the manifestation of some 'shadowy malice' which occludes the sight of the 'lost Pariah woman' – 'Ann the Outcast'; a nightmare vision self-consciously repaired in De Quincey's 'Auto-biography', where the early death of his sister Elizabeth is repre-sented as her absorption, 'high in heaven', into 'a gleaming host of faces'. In other discussions of the origin and meaning of his dreams, he acknowledges that 'some of the phenomena developed in my dream-scenery, undoubtedly, do but repeat the experiences of my childhood; and others seem likely to have been growths and fructifications from seeds at that time sown'. At another time there seems to be no content in the dreams worth considering that is not a displacement of De Quincey's 'nursery experience', as he calls it, or his 'nursery afflictions' (3: 222; 1: 50; 1985 92; 13: 339–40).

I have offered, in this introductory chapter, to write an account of De Quincey's fear of the Orient, and of the means by which he attempts to cope with that fear. What I have actually written, it will soon be apparent, is largely an account of his 'nursery afflictions', or of the mythic melodrama he created from his childhood memories and his adult fantasies. Only in the last five chapters will we discover De Quincey turning his attention to various 'Eastern Questions' – the recent history of the Ottoman Empire, the Opium Wars, the first Afghan War, the Kandyan wars in Sri Lanka, the Indian 'mutiny' – as matters of general public concern. It is, I hope to show, especially but by no means exclusively in the myth of his own childhood, as it is elaborated in his autobiographical writings, and as it re-emerges – by way of repeated patterns of imagery and structures of narrative – in his stories and essays, that most of the material is to be found which is pertinent to an account of De Quincey's terror of almost all things oriental. The scenery of that mythic melodrama is as much and as eclectically oriental as the scenery of the opium dreams themselves: the corpses that litter the stage are discovered against a backdrop of various eastern landscapes, from an orientalised East End to a demonised Far East; behind every palm-tree lurks an eastern assassin, human, animal or microbiological. The cast are all members of De Quincey's own family, some appearing as the terrified victims of the Orient, and some as its terrifying embodi-ment.

But this fear of the oriental, which at times will appear as a displacement of some primal and private terror, is also just what it appears to be: a fear of the 'modes of life', the 'manners', of a vaguely differentiated but universally abhorrent Asia. De Quincey himself seems to suggest that this fear, just because it is 'deeper than I can analyse' (3: 442), must be standing for the fear of something else; but this book will avoid (I hope) the attempt to establish a hierarchy of precedence, an organisation into the manifest and the latent, the surface and the depth, among the various objects of fear his writings disclose. One part of my argument will be that in De Quincey's writings the guilt of childhood is ·made over to a troop of wild animals and assassins who are especially terrifying because they are oriental; and that the peoples of the Orient – the Kandyans, the Hindus, the Chinese, the Malays – become especially objects of terror to De Quincey, just because they are used to represent the bogeymen and bogeywomen of his earliest years. It is equally possible, however, to conceive of the guilt which finds expression in the narratives of De Quincey's childhood as a fully social guilt, a guilt at his own participation in the imperialist fantasies that become so all-pervasive in the national imagination from the 1820s and 1830s, and which, because it cannot be avowed, can find a voice and can be rationalised only by being displaced. It seems best, indeed, to think of the relation between childhood and the oriental in De Quincey's writings as a relation between two forms of guilt, personal and political, in which each can be a displaced version of the other, and in which each aggravates the other in an ascending spiral of fear and of violence.

VI

Some final words on the texts I have used, and on the ordering of the chapters that follow. There is no definitive edition of De Quincey's writings, and no possibility of producing one. Most of his writings of substance exist in two more or less distinct forms – the original version, written for periodical publication, and a revised version, produced for inclusion in the first collective edition of his writings, which appeared in the 1850s. In the case of the most directly autobiographical writings – the *Opium-Eater*, 'Suspiria', and the various essays that came to make up the 'Autobiographical Sketches' or 'Autobiography' – the textual history is considerably more complex.[16] This book, for the convenience of writer and reader alike, is based mainly on the texts published by David Masson in what was the last attempt to produce a collected edition; these can be regarded, in most but not all cases, as De Quincey's final versions. But I have not hesitated to refer to earlier versions, and to writings De Quincey chose not to revise and reprint, wherever I have found it useful to do so.

I make no apology for this eclectic choice of texts. In most of the chapters that follow, I am attempting to reconstruct what I have called De Quincey's myth of his own childhood. The narratives in which the myth is characteristically embodied can provisionally be thought of as divided into what I will call narratives of trauma and narratives of reparation, though that distinction will be progressively harder to maintain as the argument of this book develops. On many occasions the process of rewriting involves the invention of narratives of reparation which replace, which supplement, or which even anticipate narratives of trauma. We will see, for example, how an anguished story of the public exposure of a secret guilt – a story involving a vast quantity of books – which appeared in 1845 in the group of essays known as 'Suspiria', did not find its way into the first collective edition; while in that same edition a story was added to the *Opium-Eater*, again about a quantity of books, in which a secret guilt is successfully kept secret. The story in 'Suspiria' is paired with a story from the *Arabian Nights* about the detection, by a magician, of a young man guilty of intruding where he had no right to intrude. This too is absent from the first collective edition, in which however we find another story from the *Arabian Nights*, about the detection, by a magician, of a boy who is described as 'innocent'.

But if some of these texts are subject to large-scale revision, it does not therefore follow that the myth itself is changing. It is more likely, indeed, that it was the very persistence in De Quincey's imagination of the narratives of trauma that produced the need for so many narratives of reparation. Nor are reparative narratives produced only in the process of revision: they may follow hard on the heels of narratives of trauma, in the same version of a text, as we shall see when we examine the account of a sequence of murders committed in the East End in 1812. The point I am trying to make is that we can make no assumptions about the relation between the chronological order of De Quincey's writings and rewritings, and the development of his psychic life – as if the appearance of a narrative of reparation should tell us of some act of recognition, of acceptance, or of negation he has performed. If his psychic wounds had responded to treatment as easily as that, they would not have needed treating so often, or in so many different ways. It is this profusion of narratives of reparation which justifies my own treatment of De Quincey's writings, in which they are read as constituting together a synchronic myth whose different versions are not themselves easily susceptible of narrativisation, or not of that sort of narrativisation which can distinguish the stages of a case history or the phases of a neurosis.

The synchronic form in which this myth is available to us does not make it easy to divide it into a sequence of self-contained chapters, and in the pages that follow I have found it convenient to recount the myth in two different ways at once. On the one hand, I have attempted to isolate what I take to be its two primary narratives of trauma, and to explore, in these two narratives, the identity of the victims and then of the aggressors. I discuss some examples of narratives of reparation, and their repeated failure to do the work of reparation assigned to them. I examine, finally, some of the more violent effects of that failure, both for De Quincey's private concerns, and for his view of imperial history and imperial policy. But shadowing this account of the myth is another, complementary version, in which the traces are visible of the process of my own discovery of how the two primary narratives of De Quincey's myth might have been related. According to this second way of proceeding, each chapter knows less of the story than the chapter which follows it, and an account may be offered, at one stage, of a passage or an event, which at a later stage may come to seem short-sighted or one-sided. I have thought of rewriting the book, and of allowing each chapter an equality of knowledge concerning the direction the story is taking. In the end I decided against this, not because I want to keep my readers in suspense, but because the story that eventually emerges is so disturbing (at least I find it so) that I would not ask anyone to believe it who had not watched it come together from the hints and fragments scattered across the most disparate range of texts.

The variety of De Quincey's writings is one of the most remarkable things about them: they include novels, short stories, translations of fiction mainly from the German, works of literary theory, autobiographical writings in various modes, biographical essays, essays critical, essays economic, geographical, historical, philological, philosophical, political, scientific, and so on. But perhaps the most remarkable thing, in turn, about these various texts is that, in whatever direction they seem to travel, towards whatever different goal, they arrive, time and time again, in the very same place. That place is, at times, a literal place, an upper chamber of a house where an appalling act of violence is imagined and believed to have been perpetrated; though it may not always be clear just which room – whose room – it was, or just what has been done to whom. Just as often, the place is represented as some other bedroom, somewhere else; or else it is 'a chamber of the brain', in one of De Quincey's favourite phrases; or it is not a chamber at all, but is still a place constructed by the same words and images that we find attached to the other scenes of uncertain horror. De Quincey's texts return compulsively, to that place; they return in horror, certainly, but also in pleasure, to the redescription and refiguration of what is imagined to have happened there. De Quincey is at once haunted by a hateful memory, and actively colluding with the ghost.

This book is an attempt to think about these compulsive returnings, and to ask what it means that texts on such disparate matters as going for walks with Wordsworth, the siege of Smolensk, and a breakthrough in nebular astronomy, should all converge on the same scene of imagined domestic violence. But to ask that question, the book is itself compelled to return to that scene almost as often as De Quincey does. The result, I know, is *too much* – the book is excessive in its own representation and refiguration of violence. I do not think it could make its point if it were not; and if I thought I could have written it some other way, I would certainly have done so, rather than lay myself open to the charge I have levelled at De Quincey, of returning to that central and repeated scene as much in pleasure as in horror.

2

Hydrocephalus: The Death of Elizabeth

Many small houses in Cairo have no apartment on the ground-floor for the reception of male visitors, who therefore ascend to an upper room; but as they go upstairs they exclaim several times, 'Destoor!' ('Permission!'), or 'Yá Sátir!' ('O Protector!' that is, 'O protecting God!'), or use some similar ejaculation, in order to warn any woman who may happen to be in the way to retire or to veil herself.

E.W. Lane, *Manners and Customs of the Modern Egyptians*, 188.

It is indeed a most striking scene; an awful stillness, a lifelessness pervades the ruins, . . . no huts encumber them, no filthy Arabs intrude on you . . . and, at sunrise, at sunset, in the morning glow, or in the evening calm, wandering among those columns, so graceful in themselves, so beautiful in their sisterly harmony, I thought I had never seen such loveliness – such awful loveliness! – lovely and yet awful; at times you almost feel as if Palmyra were a woman, and you stood by her corpse, stilled in death, but with a sweet smile lingering on her lip.

Lord Lindsay, *Letters on Egypt, Edom, and the Holy Land*, 323–4.

I

Thomas De Quincey was the fourth of eight children. The eldest, William, was born late in 1781 or early in 1782; Elizabeth, Thomas's favourite sister, was born in 1783, and Mary in 1784. Then came Thomas himself in 1785, three and a half years younger than William and rather more than two years younger than Elizabeth. In the following year Jane was born; she died in 1790. There were two other brothers, and then one more sister, born after the death of Jane, and named after her. Whether from simple lapse of memory or for some other reason, De Quincey in his autobiographical writings altered this chronology in a number of small ways. William, he says, was more than five years older than himself, whereas in fact he was more like three and a half years older. Elizabeth he makes three years his senior, and he represents the first Jane as two years his senior, instead of a year his junior; so that when he tells us (correctly) that she died at the age of three and a half, he gives his own age at the time as 'one and a half, more or less by some trifle that I do not recollect' (1: 29n., 33, 37).

On June 2nd 1792, Elizabeth died: 'according to my recollection', writes De Quincey, she 'was just as near to nine years as I to six', though in fact he was nearly seven (1: 37). In the various autobiographical writings published by De Quincey from the 1830s through to the 1850s, the death of Elizabeth is represented as the most important psychic event of his life, the event which effectively originates the myth of his own childhood.[1] This myth is written and rewritten through the final three decades of his life, in the form of narratives which refer sometimes directly, sometimes obliquely, to Elizabeth herself. Many of the other girls and young women whom he encounters, in his waking life or in dreams, seem to become re-visions or surrogates of Elizabeth, and the deaths they die or seem to be in danger of dying are experienced as repetitions of her death. Elizabeth died of hydrocephalus, or water on the brain, and on at least two later occasions De Quincey persuaded himself that he was suffering from hydrocephalus. This hypochondria seems to have been the symptom of an overwhelming sense of guilt that came to be attached to the death of Elizabeth, a guilt which finds expression in two different narratives, the traces of which can be discovered throughout his writings.

In the first narrative, De Quincey's guilt consists in the fact that he feels himself to have been somehow indirectly responsible for his sister's death. He has allowed her to die, through his own lack of courage in failing to confront whatever it was that killed her. In his account of Elizabeth's death, he writes of his 'morbid sensibility to shame', and represents it by a recurrent fear

> that if I were summoned to seek aid for a perishing fellow-creature, and that I could obtain that aid only by facing a vast company of critical or sneering faces, I might, perhaps, shrink basely from the duty. It is true that no such case had ever actually occurred; so that it was a mere romance of casuistry to tax myself with cowardice so shocking. But to feel a doubt was to feel condemnation; and the crime that *might* have been, was in my eyes the crime that *had* been.   (1: 45)

This is certainly not said as an admission that in some sense he had indeed failed to protect his sister from 'perishing'; the point of saying it, indeed, is to reassure himself that 'no such case had ever actually occurred', and that this very fear was obliterated by his grief for

Elizabeth, at least 'for anything that regarded my sister's memory'. But as we shall see, the fear of being or being held responsible for the death of a young female remained a repeated theme of De Quincey's.

As Grevel Lindop has pointed out, De Quincey was subject to 'a recurring dream about meeting a lion'. He is required to 'face' the lion as one faces a difficulty; to 'stand up' to it; instead, he lies down before it without a struggle.[2] He may do this with a sense of being helpless, of being 'disarmed' into 'languishing impotence', of being 'spellbound' in a moment of 'abysmal treachery' which 'publishes the secret frailty of human nature – reveals its deep-seated falsehood to itself' (L2; 3: 316; Jordan 87; 13: 304). In the portion of 'Suspiria de Profundis' that describes the Brocken-spectre, and which De Quincey later described as a 'dream-echo' of the events surrounding the death of his sister, something like this dream seems to have become a way of expressing the guilt of having failed to prevent the death of Elizabeth.[3] He attempts to discover whether the spectre – who is a shadow of himself, for that is the nature of the apparition – has also, in childhood, 'suffered an affliction that was ineffable'. This ineffable affliction is not, however, the death itself or the grief it caused, but the sense that 'when powerless to face such an enemy, you were summoned to fight with the tiger that couches within the separations of the grave' (1985 155–6).

The second story is still more ineffable. Obscurely and unbearably, De Quincey connects his last sight of his dead sister with some appalling sexual sin and pollution. On the day after Elizabeth's death, he found he could 'steal up into her chamber' by way of the back stairs. The expedition is cloaked in secrecy and saturated in excitement: 'I reached the chamber-door; it was locked but the key was not taken away. Entering, I closed the door so softly, that, although it opened upon a hall which ascended through all the stories, no echo rans along the silent walls.' De Quincey's extraordinary account of what happened next in Elizabeth's bedroom, a sequence of memory, trance, hallucinations auditory and visual, digressions that are not digressions, is brought to an end when 'there was a foot (or I fancied so) on the stairs'. He was alarmed, he explains, because

if anybody had detected me, means would have been taken to prevent my coming again. Hastily, therefore, I kissed the lips that I should kiss no more, and slunk, like a guilty thing, with stealthy steps from the room. Thus perished the vision, . . . thus mutilated was the parting which should have lasted for ever; tainted thus with fear was that farewell sacred to love and grief, to perfect love and to grief that could not be healed.   (1: 42)

The parting was mutilated and tainted, or so De Quincey assures us, by the haste of his departure, but that haste was in turn caused by a guilty fear of discovery – the ghost in *Hamlet*, on hearing the cock crow, 'started like a guilty thing Upon a fearful summons'; and the phrase also recalls a line from Wordsworth's 'Immortality' ode, 'Did tremble like a guilty thing surprised'. This fear of discovery is very clearly related to the 'taint' of a sexual guilt, in spite of De Quincey's immediate insistence that love between two children is '*altogether holy*' (his emphasis). He speculates that, when he dies, the 'clouds of death' may be illuminated by the memory of 'this final experience in my sister's bedroom, or some other in which her innocence is concerned'; the sentence seems to be an attempt to represent the bedroom experience as an *innocent* experience, but all too clearly the syntax invites a reading which opposes Elizabeth's previous innocence to De Quincey's guilty experience of her death.

The 'taint' associated with this scene is one version of the infection, or of the many infections, by which De Quincey felt himself to have been compromised and morally debilitated. 'Did you ever read', he writes in his journal in 1844,

> of leprosy as it existed in Judea, or – and that was worse – as it existed in Europe during the dark ages? Did you ever read of that tremendous visitation in the early days of Judaism, when if the poor patient would have hushed up his misery in silence, the walls of his house whispered of his whereabouts. Horrible! that a man's own chamber – the place of his refuge and retreat – should betray him!   (P1: 329)

The sound that betrays guilt, the 'chamber' as a secret place of guilt – both are to be found again, in a scene in the *Opium-Eater* which is strikingly similar to the account of Thomas's last visit to his sister's bedroom, and which will give a sense of how complex were the meanings that came to be attached to that real or imagined event. As he stood for the last time in his Manchester room before absconding from school, he 'dreamed ominously with open eyes' of a time when, two years earlier, he had visited the Whispering Gallery. This visit is misremembered: the gallery, he recalls, took hold of the merest whispers and returned them as thunder, making public to all what was confided in utmost secrecy – as if the secret kept by the 'unechoing walls' of Elizabeth's bedroom had there been broadcast to the world. It was, he says, 'a hateful remembrance'; but once recalled, it forces him to listen to the whispers, and then to 'the volleying thunders', of his own conscience. 'Once leave this house', it threatened, 'and a Rubicon is placed between thee and all possibility of return'. Then, just as in Elizabeth's room, 'a sudden step upon the stairs broke up my dream . . . I prepared myself for a hasty farewell' (3: 295–7). On the wall of his room was the picture of

> a lovely lady . . . the eyes and mouth of which were so beautiful, and the whole countenance so radiant with divine tranquillity, that I had a thousand times laid down my pen, or my book, to gather consolation from it, as a devotee from a patron saint. . . . I went up to the picture, kissed it, then walked gently out, and closed the door for ever. (3: 297)

The woman in the portrait, with her 'sweet Madonna countenance', was never identified by De Quincey, but evidently enough the image of Elizabeth, in what seems to be a repetition of the scene of her death, has been displaced by another idealised picture of femininity, still benign and tranquil, divine and transcendent, but now *maternal* (3: 297).[4]

On leaving Manchester, Thomas began a walking-tour in Wales, during which he imagined himself, according to the *Opium-Eater*, as the Wandering Jew. He attributes to himself the same identity ('O Ahasuerus, everlasting Jew!') in the 'Autobiography', immediately after speaking of the events in Elizabeth's bedroom. The apparent reason for this apostrophe is to maintain that the grief of Ahasuerus on hearing his 'doom of endless sorrow' could be no greater than De Quincey's own sorrow on passing for ever from his sister's room. But in fact the narrative suggests that he was fully expecting to be able to visit her room again, and tried to do so; and the comparison between himself and Ahasuerus may be based as much on a sense that both are equally tainted, and equally cursed. The act of kissing Elizabeth becomes a deed of the same kind and seriousness as the act of reviling Christ – or, if it comes to that, of kissing him. These crimes seem enormous only because other people think them so; they deserve to be forgiven just because the memory of them causes the criminal so much pain. Judas, as we shall see, has been entirely misjudged; so has Thomas (3: 329; 1: 43).

Throughout De Quincey's autobiographical writings, he takes to himself the identity of Wandering Jew, and so also of pariah, in the apparent belief that pariahs were outcastes, and even confusing them (or so at times it seems) with untouchables.[5] The role of Wandering Jew, adopted after he ran away from school, facilitated his identification with the prostitute Ann, by an associative logic which transforms Wandering Jew into pedestrian, into peripatetic philosopher or 'walker of the streets', into peripatetic as 'street-walker', into Ann 'a lost Pariah woman', untouchable except by those willing to be polluted, and except by fellow-pariahs, fellow-untouchables. With Ann too, the sense of being a pariah is associated with a guilty kiss, or rather with a kiss which is represented as innocent in spite of appearances, for to De Quincey, Ann's lips 'were not polluted', and indeed he had never held himself 'polluted by the touch or approach of any creature that wore a human shape' (3: 222, 329, 342, 359–60, 445). If this seems to be protesting too much , so in a sense is the whole acceptance of the identities of Wandering Jew and pariah, and so too is the interest, everywhere evinced in De Quincey's writings, in those who suffer 'under some dreadful taint of guilt, real or imputed' (1: 101). This interest, and that acceptance, may represent an attempt to come to terms with – to negate, in some sense, by affirming – a sense of guilt and self-hatred which at times (as we shall see) does not produce a sympathetic identification with other outcasts and outsiders, but an extraordinary verbal violence against them.

II

A mode of relation between these two stories of guilt (the failure to save, the sexual taint) is offered in De Quincey's anonymous novel, originally attributed to him by Mortimer Collins, *The Stranger's Grave*.[6] Edward Stanley and Sarah Franklin, it is assumed by both their families, will one day marry. Both are young; Edward is an attractive, intelligent, romantic, impulsive young soldier, Sarah is 'modest, retiring, bashful', 'the prettiest and most sweet-tempered girl in the whole countryside'. When Edward returns from his first tour of active service, he finds that his niece Emily Gordon, a good-natured atheist and, like himself, thoroughly impulsive, has come to live in the family home; she is only two years younger than Edward. To begin with, Edward's relations with the two girls are similar, and similarly free from guilt. With Sarah, Edward is 'as intimate, and as innocently so, as with a sister'; and he and Emily behave 'as brother and sister'. Soon, however, uncle and niece become more warmly attached, and the clearest sign of this is the way they kiss on meeting each morning: 'They met . . . with an eagerness of delight. . . . The salutations which they freely gave each other were longer and more sweet than those offered by any other member of the family'. It is clearly time for Sarah to go (1823 103, 132, 107, 97,100).

The three go boating together, and their skiff is overturned. Edward seizes Sarah, who happens to be next to him, and is making with her towards land, when he sees that Emily is in difficulties, and, leaving Sarah to sink or swim, he rescues his niece instead. Sarah is drowned. That Edward had sacrificed Sarah to save Emily becomes a guilty secret known only to the survivors, and it torments them both. For even though 'it was extremely natural, that an uncle should preserve his niece in preference to a stranger, in circumstances where it was impossible to save both, still the consciences of Edward and Emily reproached them as if they had been in some degree responsible for their friend's death'. Put that way, of course, the guilt seems manageable enough; but it can also be put another way – a way the text seems to know it should be put: that Edward preserved one sister, and allowed the other to die, because he wanted to sleep with one and not the other. Put like that the guilt seems rather harder to bear. A few pages later they are obliged to admit that 'our love is not that of brother and sister', and despite their mutual exhortations to virtue – 'let us not be guilty' – the 'wretched culprits' first make love in a bower near where Sarah was drowned (1823 134, 139–40).

The Stranger's Grave is a transparent *roman à clef*, in which Edward Stanley (S——ley, as it might have been written by the satirists of the previous century) stands for Percy Shelley, and Emily Gordon (Go——n) for Mary Godwin. It was written in 1823, the year after Shelley had died, and is composed in the monitory spirit of *Adeline Mowbray*, Amelia Opie's novel about the life and death of Mary Wollstonecraft, Mary Godwin's mother. Shelley could be thought of as having allowed one woman to drown in order to conduct a relationship with another, who, like Emily, was the daughter of an impoverished freethinker; and like Edward, Shelley had been forced to conduct that affair abroad. In an essay of 1845–6 Shelley is compared by De Quincey with 'his own Wandering Jew'. He may have been thinking of Shelley's juvenile poem *The Wandering Jew*, versions of which had been published in 1829 and 1831; or of Ahasuerus in *Hellas*; but more likely he had in mind the character of Ahasuerus as he appears in the notes to *Queen Mab* (11: 371).[7]

If De Quincey's version of the life of Shelley provides two places to be inhabited by sisters – so that the sister who dies is separated from the sister whose innocence is violated – there are also two places in the novel available to be inhabited by surrogates of De Quincey himself. He can find himself in Edward Stanley, of course: in 1803 he had confided to his journal the belief that there was 'no harm in sexual intercourse between a brother and sister (commonly termed *incest*)' (1928 206). But he can find himself in another character in the scene where Sarah's body is eventually pulled out of the river. Her father, Colonel Stanley, 'threw himself upon her bosom, and covered her livid cheek with kisses'. The text – allegedly written by Edward himself – dwells on the desire to 'lay us down beside the corpse of our beloved one, to share with it the dark bed in which it must slumber', and this passage would later be reworked by De Quincey, in his autobiographical writings, into a description of his feelings at Elizabeth's funeral (1: 44). As if polluted by that desire, or by the kisses he has showered on his daughter's corpse, Colonel Stanley leaves the district immediately after the burial, and (again like Ahasuerus) he 'became a wanderer upon the face of the earth, and found no resting-place till he found it in the grave' (1823 128–31). After Emily's death, Edward too longs to join her in the grave, and he too becomes a wanderer, a stranger upon the earth.

III

The knot of ideas or images that constitutes the story of sexual guilt attached to Elizabeth's death – the closed door, the footfall on the stairs, the motionless woman, the kiss, the Wandering Jew – together compose what De Quincey called an 'involute'. The word suggests an intricately coiled or interwoven manifold, and though De Quincey claimed the word as his own coinage, it was already familiar to conchologists, for example, who used it to describe the tightly whorled shells of some gastropods. 'Far more of our deepest thoughts and feelings,' he writes, 'pass to us through perplexed combinations of *concrete* objects, pass to us as *involutes* . . . in compound experiences incapable of being disentangled than ever reach us *directly*, and in their own abstract shapes'. De Quincey's thought, wrote Baudelaire, was 'naturally spiral'; and the idea of a shaped vacancy enclosed by an open-ended spiral of concrete objects, by a shell which – like the shell of the Arab in *The Prelude* (De Quincey knew the passage by heart) – is also a book, seems to provide the materialist De Quincey with an equivalent for the soul; or with as many such equivalents as there were involutes in his memory or imagination (1: 39; Baudelaire 1: 515; 2: 268–9; Wordsworth 140, 142).[8] 'Man is doubtless *one*', he writes, with a grudging orthodoxy in the chapter of the 'Autobiography' describing Elizabeth's death and burial,

> by some subtle *nexus*, some system of links, that we cannot perceive, extending from the new-born infant to the super-annuated dotard: but, as regards many affections and passions incident to his nature at different stages, he is *not* one, but an intermitting creature, ending and beginning anew; the unity of man, in this respect, is co-extensive only with the particular stage to which the passion belongs.   (1: 43)

Another involute came to attach itself to, and to stand for, the story of De Quincey's guilt for having failed to prevent Elizabeth's death, and it represents that death as a specifically *oriental* event. This relation of the oriental with what De Quincey offers as the inaugural moment of the history of his life thus offers a new explanation for the ubiquitous presence of oriental imagery in his writing, and for the terror it produced. In the *Opium-Eater* the oriental functioned, or so De Quincey seems to have believed, as a displaced representation of the urban poor. In the later autobiographical writings, De Quincey suggests that images of the oriental became attached more or less fortuitously to the scene of Elizabeth's death, but that once that attachment was made it could not be broken. The fear of the oriental is therefore apparently over-determined – reinforced, or even produced, by some of the most visible and public aspects of early nineteenth-century society in Britain, and by the most secret places in De Quincey's private world.

When De Quincey gained entrance to Elizabeth's bedroom, he found that the bed had been moved, so that where he looked to find her face, he saw instead 'one large window, wide open, though which the sun of midsummer at mid-day was showering down torrents of splendour'. Thereafter the midday, and sometimes specifically the tropical, sun became attached to the idea of death, or to the idea of the death of young girls. This was the result, he argues at first, of the 'antagonism between the tropical redundancy of life in summer, and the frozen sterilities of the grave' (and see 11: 316); but he goes on to argue that summer, and the summer sun, had for him 'connected itself' with death, 'not merely as a mode of antagonism, but also as a phenomenon brought into intricate relations with death by scriptural scenery and events' (1: 38, 40).

This happened, he suggests, as a result of the habit of sitting in the nursery, with his three sisters and a favourite nurse, looking by firelight at the pictures in an illustrated bible. These represented images of death in an 'oriental' climate – 'the passion of death in Palestine' and 'the cloudless sunlights of Syria'.[9] The involute includes also 'the very name of Palm Sunday', or the complex image the name conjures up, a name which, says De Quincey, 'troubled me like an anthem'. '"Palms!" what were they? *That* was an equivocal word; palms, in the sense of trophies, expressed the pomps of life; palms, as a product of nature, expressed the pomps of summer' (1: 39–40; see below p. 198, n. 6). The word, indeed, seems rather more equivocal than De Quincey suggests – on the very next page he describes 'the stiffening hands' of the dead Elizabeth, 'laid palm to palm'; and the palm-tree figures in a third involute which is repeatedly invoked in his writings, and which seems to be capable of expressing both versions of his guilt in relation to Elizabeth. It is the image of a Roman coin which, according to his account of it, depicts Judaea – the Roman province – in the form of a veiled woman, sitting under a palm-tree, weeping (see Figure 1).

1   Sestertii of the Emperor Vespasian (AD 71).

No less equivocal, perhaps, was the word 'Sunday' itself: 'what was *that*?' he asks. His answer, that it was 'a day of peace which masked another peace deeper than the heart of man can comprehend' seems inadequate, however dead an Evangelical English Sunday may have been. As the narrative of Elizabeth's death suggests but does not spell out, the sun was not only an observer, or in some vague way a concomitant, of Elizabeth's death. She died (or so De Quincey would have us believe) as a result of drinking tea in a labourer's cottage, and then walking home through damp meadows on a Sunday evening; 'the sun had set', but its 'fervent' heat had caused the meadows to reek with dewy exhalations which, together with the tea, condensed (I presume) inside Elizabeth's head, and formed water on the brain. But more troublingly, I suggest, the notion that the 'sun' killed Elizabeth became, or stands for, the notion that Elizabeth was killed by the 'son' – and by a tropical, or an 'oriental' son; and as we shall see in Chapters 4 and 5, the question of who that might be is one of the most crucial issues addressed if not answered by De Quincey's myth of childhood.

These three involutes sometimes reappear separately in De Quincey's writings, but often each of them seems to evoke one or both of the others, and so immediately as to suggest they are best thought of as a complex triple knot – not as the *same* involute, because 'man is . . . an intermitting creature', but still as related and

conjoined structures gathered around 'fixed determined centres', so
that the orthodox notion of a transcendent 'human unity' is not, De
Quincey suggests, 'greatly . . . violated' by his reluctant, even
anguished belief in the discontinuity of the self (L389).[10] As we
encounter and re-encounter these involutes in the course of this
book, they will seem to constitute together an apparently primal
scenery – a setting for that moment, or narrative, described by Freud
in which the child first confronts or represents to itself the question
of its sexual origins and destiny – the moment in which the child first
acknowledges the difference between the sexes, out of which he
himself (supposing him a boy like Thomas) was engendered, and in
terms of which he must eventually find his own sexual identity and
place. For Freud this moment was traumatic, taking the form, if only
in fantasy, of the child's thrilled and horrified witnessing of the
sexual act. For the boy, that thrill and that horror centres explicitly
on the body of the mother, in his recognition of her body as
different, a difference which he can only understand as a violence on,
or threat to, his own body, his most fundamental, physical, integrity
of self. Freud's account therefore places in the most intimate relation
a set of elements – illicit sexual discovery, spectacle, violence – all of
which we will see recurring over and over again in De Quincey's
writings, but with this crucial difference, that it is the body of the
dead Elizabeth or her surrogates which seems to occupy the mother's
sexual place. Incest is thus compounded with incest and violence is
taken to its furthest extreme. It is hard not to read in this recurrent
narrative a particularly grotesque version of the primal scene, but
particular only in so far as it makes explicit and (as we shall see)
almost literalises the horrors latent within the story that Freud both
discovered and described.

The full inventory of this scenery is much longer than I have so far
suggested. It includes frost, clouds, lawn,[11] an upper chamber,
anthems – the name 'Palm Sunday' is one such 'anthem' we have
encountered; and the halo – the image of Elizabeth herself, according
to De Quincey, presents itself to him as with 'a *tiara* of light or a
gleaming *aureola*' around her 'ample brow' – ample, because swollen
with hydrocephalus. There is the corpse of Elizabeth like a statue of
marble in oriental surroundings – not unlike the marble columns of a
Greek city in a Syrian landscape, in Lindsay's fantasy of Palmyra as a
dead woman which stands as an epigraph to this chapter. These and
other related images will be discussed further as and when we need
them. But there are two other images in this complex knot which
occur so often that they had better be noticed here. One is the image
of Elizabeth and/or death as the dawn, as Aurora, connected no
doubt with the 'aureola' that surrounded her head, and with the

thought of Christ's death, which 'slept' upon the minds of the children reading the bible in the nursery 'like early dawn upon the waters'. The second image is of Elizabeth, and the other girls and young women with whom she is associated, as flowers: in particular as roses. In fact, in his description of Elizabeth's death, roses are associated with the death of Jane, and his childish hopes for her resurrection. 'Summer and winter came again – crocuses and roses; why not little Jane?' (1: 39, 35). But Jane may best be regarded here as a type of Elizabeth, or as a type of which Elizabeth is the paradigm, and it is her death, in June, which may particularly have attached to her the image of the rose. There is a recurrent narrative, indeed, in De Quincey's writings, which casts itself in the form of one of Wordsworth's Lucy poems, 'Strange fits of passion', though usually in a peculiarly elliptical form.[12] The narrative begins as Wordsworth's poem begins –

> When she I lov'd, was strong and gay
> And like a rose in June, –

and then ends immediately, even more abruptly than Wordsworth's version –

> 'O mercy!' to myself I cried,
> 'If Lucy should be dead!'

3

Nympholepsy: Phantoms of Delight

I witnessed here the performances of a professed enchanter. . . . He first knelt and inhaled the smoke of juniper fried in goats' grease (that of no other animal will suffice), and then rolled about the ground as if intoxicated; afterwards, he rose and jumped about in a circle like a madman, then stopped, and pretended to address the fairy whom he saw on the top of the mountains. He said that she had a dog with her.

G.T. Vigne, Travels in Kashmir, Ladak, Iskardo, 2: 326.

To such an absurd pitch do Muslims carry their feeling of the sacredness of women, that entrance into the *tombs* of some females is denied to men . . . and a man and woman they never bury in the same vault, unless a wall separate the bodies.

E.W. Lane, Manners and Customs of the Modern Egyptians, 188.

I

Among De Quincey's first memories, he recorded 'a profound sense of pathos with the reappearance, very early in the spring, of some crocuses'. This reappearance he describes as their 'annual resurrection', and we have just seen that, when Jane died, he expected her, or so he says, to reappear as they did. But the 'pathos', whenever it got attached to the crocuses, seems to tell another story too, of a relation of antagonism, as he would put it, between flowers and Elizabeth, of a failure, or a refusal, to believe that she could come back to life as they had done. There is a passage of the 'Suspiria', excised from the 'Autobiography', in which De Quincey describes the 'recoil', the 'revolt of my feelings' at the funeral service for Elizabeth, 'when I heard those dreadful words . . . "It is sown in corruption, it is raised in incorruption; it is sown in dishonour, it is raised in glory . . . We shall be *changed.*"' He recoiled from St Paul's words, he explains, because he interpreted them as a threat, not a promise; if Elizabeth was 'to come again in beauty and power', he wanted it to be the same beauty, the same power, the same Elizabeth: Elizabeth before hydrocephalus (1985 108–9).

The resurrection of Elizabeth is a continual theme of De Quincey's writings. In one form or another, she is continually reappearing, the object of what De Quincey describes as 'nympholepsy', a frenzy that sometimes comes upon those who 'in Pagan days caught in forests a momentary glimpse of the nymphs and sylvan goddesses'. These 'nympholepts' were 'struck with a hopeless passion': they were 'men under a delirious *possession* by the heavenly loveliness of air-born nymphs'. In a discussion of their complaint, De Quincey refers us to the line from *Childe Harold* which speaks of 'the nympholepsy of some fond despair'; the preceding line, not quoted by De Quincey, makes the object of this frenzied vision 'a young Aurora of the air', the goddess in whom Elizabeth is transfigured.

There is a whole series of girls and young women in his writings, 'phantoms of delight' but also of terror, who are represented, consciously or otherwise, as re-visions, repetitions, resurrections of Elizabeth, and who become the nymphlike objects of his 'hopeless passion'.[1] The nymphs were 'beings whom it is not lawful to see and live', and so the victims of nympholepsy, according to legend, were 'doomed' to die. Curiously, however, it is not De Quincey that comes to be threatened with death as a result of seeing these nympholeptic visions. It is the nymphs themselves, who seem to bring Elizabeth back to life only to repeat her death or to threaten to repeat it. It is as if Elizabeth's resurrection offers De Quincey a new chance to save her from death, or threatens him with a new chance to fail to do so (7: 219–20; 8: 438, 442).

The death that threatens these surrogates of Elizabeth repeats her death in this way especially, that it is often imaged as an *oriental*, a 'near-Eastern' event – it would be futile, in the case of so Eurocentric a writer as De Quincey, to use anything other than a Eurocentric vocabulary to describe his imaginary geography. When in his essay 'Modern Superstition' De Quincey seems about to write an account of 'the superstitions of the ancients about *Nympholeptoi*', what he offers instead is a series of anecdotes of European travellers in the East who had died as a result of seeing the phantom forms, or hearing the phantom sounds, of caravans or other groups of Arabs in the desert. 'To see them, or to hear them, even where the traveller is careful to refuse their lures, entails the certainty of death in no long time.' This eastern superstition, of death presumed to be at the hands of mysterious Arab phantoms, is twice compared by De Quincey with nympholepsy (8: 438–42).

But nympholepsy was connected with Elizabeth in more than one way. In the first version of 'Suspiria', when De Quincey returns to the question of Elizabeth's resurrection, he represents the morbid hope of joining the departed in the grave – the hope which, as we have seen, was connected in his mind with the kiss of death and the Wandering Jew – as nympholepsy (1985 119); and in a posthumous fragment of the 'Suspiria', he writes of the child as capable of developing 'a passion for the grave as the portal through which it may recover some heavenly countenance, mother or sister, that has vanished. Through solitude this passion may be exalted into a frenzy like a nympholepsy '(J1: 13). Those who have once seen the nymph Elizabeth, and now can see her no more, have nothing to hope for but death. There is no question here of Elizabeth's resurrection, perhaps rather of being assured that she is truly dead, and can breathe no word of what is imagined to have taken place in her bedroom. In this context the promise of St Paul, that Elizabeth will arise from corruption and dishonour, is especially a threat – the kind of thing to be expected from a saint so committed to the breaking of confidences that he has a gallery, at his cathedral in London, consecrated to that very purpose.

II

'Little Kate Wordsworth'

The most hallucinogenic of Elizabeth's surrogates is the Wordsworths' daughter Kate, who was a great favourite of De Quincey's when he was living at Grasmere, and whose death produced in him an especially severe 'frenzy' of 'nympholepsy'. As Kate was 'not above three years old when she died', and as she died in June, she became for De Quincey a type of Wordsworth's Lucy, who was 'like a rose in June ', and lived or 'grew' for three years only. She is one of a number of girls and young women who participate in the involute which links death with roses: Jane, Elizabeth, and others we have not yet met. Kate is one of two pre-pubescent girls with whom, says De Quincey, he shared his bed, as if in a repetition or an 'innocent' reparation of the guilt attached to the bedroom of Elizabeth. 'Little Kate Wordsworth,' he writes, 'returned my love, she in a manner lived with me at my solitary cottage; as often as I could entice her from home, walked with me, slept with me, and was my sole companion' . . . she 'so fascinated my heart that I became blindly, doatingly, in a servile degree, devoted to this one affection'. She died 'just as the first gleams of morning began to appear . . . about an hour, perhaps, before sunrise' (2: 442–3).

> I had always viewed her as an impersonation of the dawn and the spirit of infancy; and this abstraction seated in her person, together with the visionary sort of connexion which, even in her parting

hours, she assumed with the summer sun, by timing her
immersion into the cloud of death with the rising and setting of the
fountain of life, – these combined impressions recoiled so violently
into a contrast or polar antithesis to the image of death that each
exalted and brightened the other.   (2: 443)

After Kate's burial in the churchyard at Grasmere, De Quincey
'often passed the night upon her grave'. And he continued to see her,
usually emerging out of 'wild plants, such as tall ferns, or the purple
flowers of the foxglove' – the purple foxglove, as well as being
poisonous, was a remedy used in the treatment of hydrocephalus.[2]
There is nothing explicitly oriental about the circumstances of Kate's
death, except in so far as she participates so fully in that connection
between death and the summer sun that is so crucial to the
orientalisation of the death of Elizabeth (2: 444; Jordan 263–72).

The Girl in Greek Street

The other girl to sleep with De Quincey was the younger of a
symbiotic pair of females who appear in the London section of the
Opium-Eater. This girl, who lived in the unhappy and neglected
house in Soho where De Quincey camped when he arrived in
London at the age of 17, is described as 'a poor, friendless child,
apparently ten years old; but she seemed hunger-bitten; and
sufferings of that sort often make children look older than they are':
the attempt seems to be to make her the same age as Elizabeth was
when she died.[3] She slept with De Quincey 'for warmth, and for
security against her ghostly enemies' – she believed the house was
haunted (3: 354–5). This girl disappears from the text of the
Opium-Eater when Ann the 15-year-old prostitute is introduced.
Together they form a pair not unlike the pairing of Sarah and Emily
in *The Stranger's Grave*.

Ann of Oxford Street

Or Ann the Outcast. Just as he had made the girl in Greek Street into
a surrogate of his sister by reducing her age, so he describes the
'unhappy women' of the streets as his 'sister in calamity'; and as for
Ann herself, 'I loved her as affectionately as if she had been my sister'
(3: 359, 367). In the opium dream of Ann later in the *Opium-Eater*,
the identification is no less strong. De Quincey finds himself near the
grave of a child he had once tenderly loved, who died in summer. It
is as if a resurrection is imminent: it is 'A little before sunrise', and
it is Easter Sunday, a day to look forward to 'the first-fruits of
Resurrection'. He turns, and suddenly the domes and cupolas of an
oriental city are visible – perhaps Jersualem, he suggests, remem-

bered from a picture seen in childhood. In a repetition of the image of
weeping Judaea, the image on the Roman coin which forms a part of
the involute of Elizabeth's death, he sees a woman sitting on a stone,
'shaded by Judean palms . . . it was – Ann!' She says nothing; but she
seems tranquil, if unusually solemn. He recalls that the last time he
had seen her, when 'her eyes were streaming with tears', he had
kissed her lips ('lips, Ann, that to me were not polluted!').

This kiss is thoroughly ambiguous, and may be at once the agent
of pollution, of cleansing, and of resurrection. Though it is loudly
denied that Ann is at all polluted, the kiss can be read as a repetition
of the kiss by which Thomas was first infected with the moral disease
which, as if it were leprosy, had made him a pariah. It may also be
the means by which he cleanses himself of the pollution he had
sucked from Elizabeth's lips, by passing it on to Ann: the prostitute
as the carrier of male sexual guilt, and shut out from society like the
carrier of an infection. It also allows Thomas to take up the role of
forgiver and comforter, who kisses innocently and kisses things
better: the kiss not as repetition but as reparation. By this reading,
the tears that Judaea sheds, in the description of the coin in the
passage on the Brocken-spectre, are merely the *before* of a before-
and-after narrative, which now ends in resurrection and restoration.
The kiss of death is now a kiss of life; the vision of an oriental Ann
vanishes, but De Quincey finds himself 'in London, walking again
with Ann – just as we had walked, when both children, eighteen
years before' (3: 445–6).

Ann reappears, once again orientalised, in the dream essay 'The
Daughter of Lebanon', added to the *Opium-Eater* in 1856. The
daughter of Lebanon herself is a well-born prostitute, 'a poor ruined
flower', in whom, as De Quincey makes clear, Ann is figured and
transfigured (3: 452, 222). The daughter of Lebanon, driven to
prostitution by a misunderstanding on the part of her princely father,
wishes to be washed clean of her sins and to be restored to her
father's house. 'A great evangelist – one of the four' promises that
within thirty days both these wishes will be fulfilled; the first by her
baptism, the second by her death, when she will be restored not to
her father on earth, but to her Father in Heaven; she will be
resurrected as a 'spiritual body'.

The scene of the baptism and death of the Daughter of Lebanon is
very evidently a repetition or reparation of the scene of Elizabeth's
death. The 'new Christian daughter' is suddenly and inexplicably
represented as suffering from a fever: she has a mild delirium, and
troubled vision, both symptoms of hydrocephalus. Dressed entirely
in white – and thereby 'making proclamation . . . of recovered
innocence and of reconciliation with God' – she lies in bed on the flat

roof of her house, sheltered from the hot noonday sun by an awning. She looks down over 'the rose-gardens of Damascus', tokens of her imminent resurrection as a spiritual body. She is reluctant to die, however: she does not wish to leave behind her virtuous twin sister, whom she had not seen since her disgrace. The evangelist points to the heavens with his pastoral staff; and in the 'infinite chasm' which opens in the sky – a chasm we will encounter again and again in De Quincey's writings – the Daughter of Lebanon sees her twin sister, who has died that night of grief at her sister's departure. The Daughter of Lebanon now agrees to die herself; whereupon 'the evangelist gave the signal to the heavens, and the heavens gave the signal to the sun; and in one minute after the Daughter of Lebanon had fallen back a marble corpse amongst her white baptismal robes'. She dies, it appears, as Elizabeth did, through the agency of the sun, or perhaps the 'Son' – in any case, she is now with Jesus (3: 453–5). The sister who carries the burden of sexual guilt has gone to join the innocent sister who (like Sarah) has been allowed to die first; and that reading may not be incompatible with another, by which not simply Elizabeth but Thomas himself is purged of the guilt of Elizabeth's death and reconciled with God. For if Thomas could imagine himself to be a girl, not a boy – and as we shall see, he certainly could – then he would not be the 'sun' who caused Elizabeth's death, he would be the daughter whose wish to join Elizabeth in death has been fulfilled.

Fanny of the Bath Road

There is a similar pairing of surrogates of Elizabeth in 'The English Mail-Coach'. Fanny, 'the loveliest young woman for face and person that perhaps in my whole life I have beheld', used to meet the Bath coach at a certain spot on the Bath road; the coachman was her grandfather. Fanny is imaged as Aurora – 'Fanny and the dawn are delightful' – and as Wordsworth's Lucy, for the thought of her is inseparable from the thought of a rose in June; each conjures up the other, and they 'come both together . . . roses and Fannies, Fannies and roses, thick as blossoms in paradise' – a poetic thought, unkindly treated by subsequent semantic change. Fanny thus participates in the same involute as Elizabeth and Ann: she is connected at once with the sun, with death, and with roses.[4] The death she evokes is again an oriental event, for the thought of her brings with it, inescapably, a terrifying Egyptian bestiary, compounded with the beasts of heraldry. Whenever the memory of Fanny or a rose in June evoke each other, they call up also a crocodile, in the royal livery of the mail-coach, and with him 'a dreadful host of semi-legendary animals – griffins, dragons, basilisks, sphinxes . . . unutterable

horrors of monstrous and demoniac natures, . . . monstrous creations of darkness'.

According to De Quincey, the association of Fanny with this
horrific bestiary was the result of his making, as it were by chance,
that association between her grandfather, the coachman, and a
crocodile, that we noticed in the first chapter. De Quincey could chat
up Fanny only occasionally, when he was travelling on the Bath
coach, and only briefly, when the coachman's back was turned.
Fortunately, the coachman was very slow in turning round, and this
caused De Quincey to compare him once with a crocodile, which
apparently has the same problem, and which he thinks of as an
Egyptian beast – it comes with references to the Nile, Pharaohs and
pyramids. It was this playful and fanciful linkage, of man and
crocodile, De Quincey suggests, that caused his dreams thereafter to
be infested with images of 'the horrid inoculation upon each other of
incompatible natures'. And so no doubt it was; but had those
terrifying images not found their way into his head by that route,
they would have found it, we may assume, by another; for images of
an oriental death are for De Quincey almost inescapably a part of the
involute which includes young girls, the dawn, and flowers (13:
285–92).

An analogue, possibly a source, of this fantasy appears in some
remarks by Alexander von Humboldt on the crocodiles of the Rio
Apure, which De Quincey had quoted in a review he contributed to
the *Westmorland Gazette* when he was editing that paper at the start
of his literary career.

> The Indians . . . related to us the history of a young girl of
> Uritucu, who by singular intrepidity and presence of mind, saved
> herself from the jaws of a crocodile. When she felt herself seized,
> she sought the eyes of the animal, and plunged her fingers into
> them with such violence, that the pain forced the crocodile to let
> her loose, after having bitten off the lower portion of her left arm.
> The girl, notwithstanding the enormous quantity of blood she
> lost, happily reached the shore, swimming with the hand she had
> still left. (W, March 27th 1819)

The same review quotes Humboldt on the difficulty crocodiles have
in turning round, a notion which Goldsmith, for example, had
dismissed as 'fabulous' (Humboldt 2: 155; Goldsmith 5: 298). I will
have more to say about this anecdote in a later chapter.[5]

The Girl in the Reedy Gig

In a later section of 'The English Mail-Coach', we are introduced to a
young woman – variously described as a 'young lady' and a 'young

girl' – whom De Quincey is suddenly called upon to save from death. In the small hours of the morning – the time of 'the first timid tremblings of the dawn' – the coachman on the Lancaster mail-coach has fallen asleep; the horses have bolted; and a long way off, at the other end of a long 'Gothic aisle' of trees lining the road, De Quincey sees a young man kissing a young lady in a reedy gig, both of whom are too distracted to realise that they are in danger of being overwhelmed by the advancing mail-coach. The two stories of guilt come together in the figure of the young man in the gig: by incurring the sexual guilt of kissing the girl, he risks incurring the additional guilt of failing to prevent her death. But by resourceful action, De Quincey can save her life. Will he be up to it? – or will he, at the risk of being 'self-denounced' as a murderer and traitor, lie down once more before the lion? By shouting aloud, he manages, just in time, to attract the attention of the young man; the responsibility of preventing the death is now fully devolved upon him; and he does just enough, just in time, to save her. Both men have proved they are equal to doing *something* – enough to save the girl's life – but they have not done enough to preserve her from the terrifying 'vision of sudden death' (13: 306–16). As the coach thunders past,

> from the silence and deep peace of this saintly summer night – from the pathetic blending of this sweet moonlight, dawnlight, dreamlight – from the manly tenderness of this flattering, whispering, murmuring love – suddenly as from the woods and fields – suddenly as from the chambers of the air opening in revelation – suddenly as from the ground yawning at her feet, leaped upon her, with the flashing of cataracts, Death the crowned phantom, with all the equipage of his terrors, and the tiger roar of his voice.   (13: 317–18)

Death appears here, as it had done in the piece on the Brocken-spectre, as a tiger, as the animal which for De Quincey, as we will see, represented more fully than any other the fierceness and the violence of the demonised Orient, of India and China imagined as places of unutterable terror.

In the 'dream-fugue' that follows, the identification of the girl in the reedy gig with Elizabeth and the other victims of an orientalised death is confirmed, and not only by her participation in Elizabeth's involute of summer, roses and dawn. By a series of images of resurrection, and by relating the 'Gothic aisle' of trees along the Lancaster road to a cathedral in which a repetition of Elizabeth's funeral appears to be taking place, the girl's survival (at whatever cost to her future sanity) is converted into an image of Elizabeth's resurrection, ambiguously in the body or the spirit (13: 321–7).

Agnes

The heroine, or victim rather, of the novella 'The Household Wreck', also suffers a predictably oriental death. The 'nymphlike' Agnes is made in the image of 'some Hebe or young Aurora of the dawn'; she is the narrator's child-bride, and he feels for her an overwhelming sense of personal responsibility, an anxiety so 'irrational' as to lead him to accuse himself of 'unmanliness and effeminacy'. The last morning they spend together, before her arrest for petty theft and her eventual death, is fixed by an image of husband, wife and young son seated at breakfast near an open window, in 'the golden light of the morning sun'; they are anticipating a walk in the neighbouring meadows, like those which Elizabeth had walked through immediately prior to her illness. To this involute of window, golden sun, breakfast-room and meadow, is added the notion of the 'palm' which had thrown an oriental shadow over the sunlit death of Elizabeth. The death of Agnes is foretold by a Hungarian woman with a 'sultana-like style' of 'Oriental beauty', who reads Agnes's palm and announces to the narrator that 'there is a frightful danger at hand' (12: 165–77).[6]

Agnes dies, in the end, from typhus fever, then taken to be a disease from the Near East. The narrator – her husband – and their son Francis are both attacked by the same disease, and the son dies. But by identifying the disease as 'jail-fever', it is possible for the novel to attribute to the man responsible for Agnes's wrongful imprisonment the responsibility also for her death. He is described, accordingly, as a 'bloody tiger', as a 'tiger from hell-gates that tore away my darling from my heart'; and Agnes is compared with 'a young Christian martyr, in the early ages of Christianity, exposed in the bloody amphitheatre of Rome or Verona to "fight with wild beasts," as it was expressed in mockery – she to fight! the lamb to fight with lions!' (12: 200, 163–4, 204).[7]

III

This inventory by no means exhausts the numerous occurrences of nympholepsy in De Quincey's writings, the vision or the invention of surrogates of Elizabeth, often in circumstances in which they are threatened by an oriental death. One such occurrence we encountered even before the book proper began, in De Quincey's description of his opium dreams. He often awoke from those dreams, he says, in 'the gaudy summer air of highest noon', to find his children standing by his bed – his daughters, he is thinking of – in their 'coloured shoes, and new frocks'. The sight of them does not come as a relief, however, but as a new occasion for awe and pathos, as if their 'infancy' and their 'innocent *human* nature' is as much threatened as he has been by the 'unutterable abortions' of his 'oriental dreams'. The incident makes the point that what we are investigating is not to be regarded simply as a phenomenon of De Quincey's dream-life; it is a phenomenon of his writing in general. What was true of Fanny was true of young women in general – the younger and the more beautiful they are represented as being, the more inevitably are they written into a scenario of imminent and oriental death (3: 443).

Some other instances of nympholepsy will turn up in later chapters; but one – probably the most remarkable – I have held back to the end of this chapter. When De Quincey was 14, the usher at his school accidentally struck him with his cane – he was aiming at another boy. De Quincey made the most of the injury: 'at first,' he wrote, looking back on the affair from the early 1850s,

> it was supposed that my skull had been fractured; and the surgeon who attended me at one time talked of trepanning. This was an awful word: but at present I doubt whether in reality anything very serious had happened. In fact, I was always under a nervous panic for my head; and certainly exaggerated my internal feelings without meaning to do so, and this misled the medical attendants.
>
> (1: 159)

He was kept at home for months, and seems to have believed, or half-believed, that he was suffering from incipient hydrocephalus – he was to suffer a hydrocephalus scare again in 1818, and in the *Opium-Eater* he wonders if his dreams of 'lakes and silvery expanses of water' were manifestations of 'some dropsical state or tendency of the brain'. Throughout his life, as we shall often have reason to notice, he exhibited an extraordinary concern for the health and safety of other people's heads, as well as of his own. 'It is not generally known,' he wrote in 1828 (for example), 'that Lord Grenville retired from public affairs in consequence of a complaint in his head, connected with one singular symptom, viz., an extraordinary thinness of the skull-bone'. 'The Emperor Tiberius,' he notes elsewhere, 'could fracture a boy's skull with a *talitrum* (or fillip of his middle finger)' (L26–7; Jordan 324; 3: 440; 1966 309; B56 1844 138; Suetonius 148).[8]

When De Quincey began to get over his first hydrocephalus scare, he told the whole story to his sister Mary, who was at school in Bristol; and he signed the letter, 'your affectionate sister, Tabitha'. Tabitha was a disciple in Joppa, a woman 'full of good works'. When suddenly she died, her friends sent for Peter, who came over to Joppa from Lydda, and found Tabitha's body lying in 'an upper chamber'.

He sent everyone away, so that he was alone with the body; and, turning to it, he said 'Tabitha, arise,' and Tabitha opened her eyes, and sat up. De Quincey can be found playing both parts in this story: he has apparently become his own sister, who has recovered from hydrocephalus, and been brought back to life by the words of a disciple who, like Thomas, has been left alone with her in an 'upper chamber'. Thomas's assumption of the name Tabitha may therefore have inscribed him within a narrative of reparation; though elsewhere the 'upper chamber', a ubiquitous location in De Quincey's writings, will figure in narratives which seem to be mere repetitions of the story of sexual guilt. In 'The Daughter of Lebanon', for example, a 'festal company of youths' sits 'revelling' in 'an upper chamber'; 'one amongst this dissolute crew' is her companion, the 'wicked lover' who has 'ruined' her. (P1: 36–41; L27; Acts 9. 36–42; 3: 451–3)

In the figures and passages discussed in this chapter, death has been imaged, for the most part, as an oriental event. But as our examination of De Quincey's geopolitical fantasies made clear, the East is for him a very movable East. There are tranquil oriental deaths, which are followed by physical or spiritual resurrections, and which take place in the remembered, elegiac landscape of bible illustration; and there are violent and terrifying deaths which happen in a nightmare landscape of crocodiles and fevers, or at the hands or paws of a roaring tiger. This; that; the other: the strangeness, the alien nature of death is expressed in the oriental character almost everywhere attributed to it; but those deaths which seem to have the function of repairing the tragedy of Elizabeth's death are altogether less alien than those which seem merely to repeat it, in all its original horror. I want to look now in more detail at some of the agents of the more violent oriental deaths. Broadly speaking, they are of two kinds. Some are Turkish or Egyptian, or from some less specific area of the Ottoman Empire. But the worst monsters, the most virulent diseases, the most ferocious killers are from further east, and I want to begin with those.

4

Tigridiasis: Tipu's Revenge

My mind strained eastward, because that farthest shore was the
end of the world that belongs to man the dweller – the beginning
of the other and veiled world that is held by the strange race,
whose life (like the pastime of Satan) is a 'going to and fro upon
the face of the earth'. . . There, on the one side of the river, (you
can swim it with one arm,) there reigns the people that will be like
to put you to death, for *not* being a vagrant, for *not* being a robber,
for *not* being armed and houseless.

A.W. Kinglake, Eothen, 111, 114–5.

Just as my piece went off, the creature sprung from the spot where
he lay, and at one bound vaulted clean over my head . . . and seized
on one of the native troops just behind me. Captain———, with
admirable presence of mind, instantly turned and lodged the
contents of his piece in the body of the tiger, who fell dead upon
his victim. There was a ball found in the animal's shoulder, which
we thought must have been mine, and had perhaps caused that
tremendous spring which cost the poor man his life. On
examining him, we found the bones of his skull literally crushed
by the fangs of the tiger; – commend me to fifty Burmese rather
than one of these gentry! So far as I can learn, the woods around us
are not infested by them, which is a great comfort; farther up they
are known to be numerous.

Mrs Hofland, The Young Cadet, 111–2.

I

One side of the obscure 'blame' that attaches to De Quincey in
connection with his sister is that, though powerless to prevent her
death, he failed to prevent it: he failed to stand between Elizabeth and
the wild beast that killed her. In De Quincey's dream of impotence
that wild beast is imaged as a lion, but much more generally it figures
in his writings as a tiger. This tiger has been revealed to us three
times so far: it was couching 'within the separations of the grave' –

the grave, apparently, of Elizabeth; it was heard in the voice of
'Death the crowned phantom', as the English Mail-Coach careered
past the reedy gig; and it appeared as the wildly malevolent traducer
of Agnes, who caused her wasting death. If De Quincey can identify
this tiger, he can pass the guilt over to where it really belongs; and if
he can represent that assassin as truly ferocious and terrifying, his
own claim to have been powerless to resist it will be vindicated.
There is a form of leprosy known as 'leontiasis', so I gather from the
Oxford English Dictionary, 'in which the face looks somewhat
lion-like'. If there was another form in which it looked somewhat
tigerish, it might be called 'tigridiasis'. This chapter describes De
Quincey's preoccupation with pointing out in others the signs and
symptoms of tigridiasis, perhaps to conceal them in himself.

Until the second half of the eighteenth century, and the enormous
expansion and consolidation of British power in India, the tiger
seems to have stood, in the British imagination, for something
especially ferocious but not very *specifically* so: its ferocity differed
in degree but not in quality from that of other exotic wild animals,
'the rugged Russian bear', for example, or 'the arm'd rhinocerous' –
the beasts which, along with 'th'Hyrcan tiger', were a little less
terrifying to Macbeth than the ghost of Banquo. The tiger's ferocity
rating must certainly have been increased, however, by Buffon's
extraordinary essay on the animal, which represented it as crazy for
blood, as killing for the mere pleasure of killing, and as capable of
destroying even the members of its own immediate family in the
vain attempt to satisfy its appetite:

> With indiscriminate fury he tears in pieces every animal around
> him; and, while thus intent on satisfying the malignity of his
> nature, hardly, however famished, does he find time to appease
> the cravings of his appetite. . . . The tiger . . . has no characteristics
> but those of the most base wickedness, of the most insatiable
> cruelty. For instinct he has nothing but an uniform rage, a blind
> fury; so blind, indeed, so undistinguishing, that not unoften he
> devours his own progeny, and, if she offers to defend them, tears
> in pieces the dam herself. – Would that this thirst for his own
> blood the tiger gratified to an excess! Would that, by destroying
> them at their birth, he could extinguish the whole race of monsters
> which he produces!   (Buffon 1775–6 2: 382)

The sentence about the tiger devouring his own children and even
'the dam herself' is included in the popular abridgements of Buffon
apparently intended for the instruction and edification of youth; and
even in Goldsmith's less sensational (and much reprinted) adaptation

of Buffon's essay, the tiger's reputation for motiveless domestic violence was certainly augmented (Buffon 1791a 173; Buffon 1791b 1: 132; Goldsmith 2: 409–19).

But it was especially as a result, I believe, of the third and fourth Mysore wars (1790–2, 1799) between the armies of the East India Company and Tipu Sultan of Mysore, that the tiger had become the especial symbol of an India imagined as ferocious and in need of taming by means justifiably violent. Tipu (the name is Kanarese for 'tiger') kept live tigers in his palace at Seringapatam; his throne was decorated with tigers' heads and suported on a full-sized gilded tiger; his soldiers were uniformed in *bubri*, a tiger-striped woollen fabric; he owned various weapons decorated with tigers' heads, and some mortars and pieces of artillery in the form of tigers. Most famously of all, he owned a near life-size mechanical toy of a tiger mauling a soldier of the Company, now kept in the café at the Victoria & Albert Museum in London; the tiger's belly housed an organ which emitted a cacophonous duet of snarls and screams. From the early 1790s and for more than thirty years after his death in 1799, a curious cult status was accorded to Tipu in Britain, and he became 'firmly embedded in . . . nursery folklore' as the oriental tiger the British loved to hate.

As Denys Forrest has shown, a remarkable number of paintings and engravings were produced in the 1790s and early 1800s of incidents in the last Mysore wars.[1] In 1800 a panorama by Robert Ker Porter of the storming of Seringapatam, at which Tipu was killed, was exhibited in London. A play about Tipu was staged at Covent Garden in 1791, and the following year two more plays about him were put on at Astley's. Tipu's death inspired a fourth play, performed at Covent Garden in 1799. In 1823 there was a fifth, when *Tippoo Saib, or the Storming of Seringapatam* was produced at the Royal Coburg Theatre, with sets by Clarkson Stanfield and with Kemble as Tipu; a version of this play was marketed for use in toy theatres. In 1829, thirty years after his death, Tipu appeared again at Astley's, in yet another version of the storming of Seringapatam. He also turns up, with his father, in Scott's novel *The Surgeon's Daughter* (1827), and in various other books and poems (Wilks 3: 274; Forrest 214–6, 316–24, 346–61; Hyde 65).

De Quincey, a furious jingoist, was as much exercised by the perverse admiration of the British for Haider Ali and Tipu, as he was by the 'oriental and barbaric pageantry' of the rulers of Mysore, and by their 'insane hatred' and 'diabolic enmity' towards Britain. He could be indulgent towards the famed brutalities of the long-dead

Emperor Babar, or ' "the Tiger" as he is called', who, '*for* a Tiger, is really not a bad Tiger'; but Haider Ali was 'a rabid tiger', and Tipu was a 'very tiger, more than tiger-hearted'. If De Quincey had known – it is not clear that he did – that in 1798 a Jacobin club had been established at Seringapatam, and Tipu Sultan had become Citizen Tipu, it could only have increased his delight that the tiger's 'unparalleled ferocity was settled effectually by one thrust of a bayonet in the hands of an English soldier'.[2] By means of a comparison with the brazen bull of Phalaris, he magnifies the clockwork toy of Tipu into a more than full-size tiger, capacious enough for a living victim to be contained in its belly, so that when it was heated as a furnace, the cries of the victim would appear to be made by the tiger roaring. Since De Quincey would almost certainly have seen the toy – in 1808 it was placed on exhibition in the library at India House in Leadenhall Street, and became one of the sights of London – his exaggeration may not have been unconscious[3]. More generally, De Quincey was a strong advocate of the British duty to tame the tigers of the East, and the tiger-cats – the offensive diminutive by which the image of ferocious little people was conjured up. He thought the 'British bull-dog' certainly superior to the 'Bengal tiger' in courage (1966 36; 3: 116; 5: 389, 172; U1: 306; U2: 35; 7: 102; 4: 197n; J2: 76).

The image of tigerish ferocity is used on numerous occasions by De Quincey without any apparent appeal to this imperialist discourse, but by the middle decades of the nineteenth century the image must always have evoked an obscure and imaginary oriental ferocity. Thus when De Quincey denounces the child murderers Herod, Hecuba and the Macbeths as tigers and tigresses, the effect would certainly have been to give a particularly oriental colour to their violence. And it is no accident, of course, that child-killers bulk large in the catalogue of those he describes as tigers – including, for example, the tigers we came across in the last chapter, hiding in Elizabeth's grave, or indirectly responsible for the death of Agnes's son, as well as the 'Oriental cholera' which attacks infants with its 'tiger-grasp' (8: 319n.; 4: 73; 10: 392; J1: 11).

The notion of the tiger as the quintessence of oriental ferocity was matched in De Quincey's imaginary geography by the notion that the River Tigris (the name is the Greek for tiger) was the definitive, because the easternmost, boundary between the Occident and the Orient. There were all sorts of purposes known to the discourses of imperialism and racism and to the historiography of Christendom which made it convenient for De Quincey sometimes to draw that boundary line further to the west, even as far west as the Vosges; and as we shall see it was certainly possible to imagine that whatever killed Elizabeth originated from an Orient altogether less remote. But the boundary could be pushed no further east than the Tigris, which was what De Quincey describes as 'a river of separation' (7: 443): as we saw on page 13, nothing west of the Tigris was, for De Quincey, absolutely alien to the occidental imagination, and nothing to the east of it could be imagined as anything other than *other*. When in 1840 he turned to the discussion of the first Opium War with China, and sought to represent China as beyond comparison the *most* oriental, in moral and cultural terms, of all the variously detestable oriental countries beyond the Tigris, he may have been gratified to discover that the natural harbour at Canton, the meeting point for the time being of Britain and China, was known to Europeans as the tiger's mouth, the Bocca Tigris (14: 169);[4] and as we shall see, in China too there was a regiment of soliders uniformed as tigers, whom the British encountered at Amoy in 1841.

An important factor, no doubt, in the representation of the Tigris as the clearest of all the demarcation lines in De Quincey's psycho-geography, was its appearance in *Paradise Lost*, a poem in which De Quincey was steeped as deeply as was Wordsworth or Keats. Before it was diverted from its original course by the sin of Adam and Eve, the Tigris flowed into Paradise and ran underground, until it re-emerged as a fountain by the Tree of the Knowledge of Good and Evil; it was by this route that Satan made his last, successful entrance into the garden, and turned the innocence of Adam and Eve into guilt (Book 9. 69–75, and see Book 4. 218–30). The river was thus at the very frontier of good and evil, the place of division between a good Occident and the evil Orient, east of Eden, where the guilty pair were to be banished.

The known world of antiquity, according to De Quincey, was 'cis-Tigridian'; the unknown was 'trans-Tigridian', and it harboured horrid enemies (10: 177; J2: 238). But according to Pliny, tigers could not cross water;[5] and it may come to seem plausible, when in later chapters we come across the hydrophobic dog and the drowning Sphinx, that another reason why the Tigris became De Quincey's ultimate barrier against the East was that it was the river that the tigers of southern and eastern Asia could not cross, and that confined them safely to a far East. And just as crucial, perhaps, to the attribution of this function to the Tigris, was the fact that, in reality, tigers are very good swimmers. As a result, they were to be found all over De Quincey's universe: as we shall see, there were tigers in Manchester, there were some just up the road from his childhood home at Greenhay, and they were even to be found in his own house and garden.

II

The tiger, whoever or whatever it represents, is required to bear the true, the substantial guilt of having killed Elizabeth. But it may be possible, with great tentativeness and circumspection, to trace to the tiger the sexual guilt, too, which became attached to Elizabeth's death. I have already suggested that Elizabeth's deathbed scene is in some ways reminiscent of Freud's account of the primal fantasy, not least in that it involves the sense of guilt as a pollution consequent upon an intrusion. There is an extraordinary moment in De Quincey's autobiographical writings, where he is about to be present at the reunion of a father and son who had been long separated. He is apprehensive that his own presence will lay 'a freezing restraint' upon the occasion; 'such cases of unintentional intrusion,' he continues,

> are at times inevitable; but, even to the least sensitive, they are always distressing; most of all they are so to the intruder, who in fact feels himself in the odd position of a criminal without a crime. He is in the situation of one who might have happened to be chased by a Bengal tiger (or, say that the tiger were a sherriff's-officer) into the very centre of the Eleusinian mysteries. . . . In such a case, under whatever compulsion, the man has violated a holy seclusion. He has seen that which he ought not to have seen; and he is viewed with horror by the privileged spectators. (1: 212)

To intrude upon the sexual mysteries at Eleusis was to 'violate' them; and what seems to be going on here is the guilty recollection or fantasy of some such intrusion or violation. Yet in this case it seems that the intrusion was – like failing to prevent Elizabeth's death – no crime at all. In both cases De Quincey was powerless to act otherwise; and the guilt for this imagined intrusion can therefore be passed elsewhere, to chance – the intruder just 'happened to be chased'! – and to a tiger, just as the guilt for her death can be.

This story of intrusion can be read as related to the account of a terrible fear that preoccupied De Quincey in the year after his sister's death: he had begun to buy a serial history of navigation, to be completed in an indeterminate number of parts, and he came to believe he was obliged to buy every one. In trepidation, he asked a bookseller how many volumes in all there were likely to be, and he was jokingly told to expect about 15,000. The joke was lost on De Quincey: he imagined that he would be pursued by the Stationers' Company to pay for every last volume. He computed each volume he failed to pay for as the occasion of a separate crime. He imagined a procession of carts dumping all 15,000 volumes on the front lawn of the house. 'Then,' he continues, 'the impossibility of even asking the servants to cover with sheets, or counterpanes, or table-cloths, such a mountainous . . . record of my past offences lying in so conspicuous a situation! Men would know my guilt merely, they would see it.' This fear of being exposed to public shame is the same fear as De Quincey experienced in the Whispering Gallery (1985 134–5).

He finds an analogy for his own situation in the *Arabian Nights*, in a story he had read with Elizabeth, in which a young man 'stumbles', as it were by accident, into the special preserve of an old magician. 'He finds a beautiful lady imprisoned, to whom . . . he recommends himself as a suitor;' when the old magician returns, he manages to escape, but in his haste he leaves behind some evidence of his presence. The next day the magician confronts the boy with this evidence; the boy denies the crime, and blames it on some other young man, but the magician does not believe him. The anxiety caused in De Quincey by this event and this oriental tale was increased, or so he suggests, by the fact that, with Elizabeth dead, he had no one to tell of his own 'inner experience of the shadowy panic of the young Bagdat intruder upon the privacy of magicians', or of his discovery that he had been 'contemplated in types a thousand years before on the banks of the Tigris. It was horror and grief that prompted that thought', he concludes (1985 135).

Here De Quincey himself becomes, after Elizabeth's death, a type of the Tigridian, perhaps ambiguously *cis-* or *trans-*, but certainly in the Miltonic region of oriental guilt in relation to a crime which involves an object which should be concealed with sheets, counter-panes, table-cloths, and an intrusion, insisted on as accidental, into the 'privacy of magicians'. The scenery of this crime is reminiscent equally of Elizabeth's bedroom or of a mother's bedroom: the covered body or the body that should be covered, the room entered that should not have been entered. The door of Elizabeth's room was finally locked, as De Quincey conceives, to conceal the 'dishonours' of a body whose skull had been dissected, and laid 'in ruins', by 'a body of medical men': death by hydrocephalus seems invariably to have been followed by dissection, in the decades around 1800, at least where the patients had been attended in their illness by a physician (1985 108; Rees 18: article on 'Hydrocephalus').

The illicit sight, real or imagined, of this scene of dissection may have been a part of, a version of, the story of the sexual crime De Quincey imagines he has committed; and, as so often, a version of that first story of guilt is matched by another which seems to offer to repair the first. We have already seen that the account of the visit to Elizabeth's bedroom is shadowed by an account of De Quincey's unauthorised departure from his school at Manchester, where he kissed, instead of his sister's corpse, the 'sweet Madonna countenance' of the woman in the portrait. On that occasion, he had arranged for a groom to carry downstairs 'a trunk of immense weight; for, besides my clothes, it contained nearly all my library'. The most difficult part of this task involved getting the trunk along 'a gallery, which passed the headmaster's chamber-door'. Inevitably, the groom slipped and dropped the trunk; inevitably it bumped downstairs to crash against the headmaster's door; inevitably both De Quincey and the groom were convulsed in giggles; amazingly, the headmaster slept through it all. Unlike the Whispering Gallery, this gallery could keep a secret. With immense relief, De Quincey was able to see his trunk 'placed on a wheelbarrow, and on its road to the carrier's', just as if he was sending back the very same load of guilt which, in his imagination, had been dumped on the lawn at Greenhay by the carriers employed by the Stationers' Company (3: 298–9).[6]

In a later rewriting of his memories of reading the *Arabian Nights*, the story he recalls becomes the story of Aladdin, which involves a wicked, child-murdering magician in Africa who hears the footsteps of 'an innocent child . . . on the banks of the Tigris' (1: 128–9).[7] This brief narrative, of the sound of footfalls or hoofs awakening expectation, announcing a crisis, or disclosing a guilty fear, occurs many times in De Quincey's writings. There may be a point of comparison with the primal fantasy, for, as Otto Rank pointed out to Freud, accidental noises are 'an indispensible [*sic*] part of the phantasy of listening, and they reproduce either the sounds which betray parental intercourse, or those by which the listening child fears to betray itself' (XIV: 269). We have already seen how important 'the phantasy of listening' was in the account of the visit to Elizabeth's bedroom – how somehow Thomas managed to enter the room unheard; how he was frightened by a footfall (real or 'fancied') on the stairs; how – in the shadow narrative in the *Opium-Eater*, his eventual departure from his Manchester room is precipitated by 'a sudden step upon the stairs'. One form of the persecution mania suffered by Charles Lloyd, according to De Quincey, was that he thought that he heard 'as if on some distant road . . . a dull trampling sound, and that he knew it, by a misgiving, to be the sound of some man, or party of men, continually advancing slowly, continually threatening, or continually accusing him'. A not dissimilar story of Wordsworth, on the other hand, putting his ear to the ground to listen for the sound of distant wheels, seems to represent him as one who overhears the guilty movements of others. In the 'Autobiography', De Quincey describes 'the listening for hours to the sound from horses' hoofs upon distant roads', when Thomas was waiting at Greenhay for the return his father who was 'coming home to die amongst his family'. In 'The English Mail-Coach' he claims somehow to have heard, through the terrific noise made by the coach-and-six, the 'sullen sound, as of some motion on the distant road', of the approaching reedy gig; and then again, altogether more disturbingly, 'the far-off sound of a wheel. . . . A whisper it was . . . secretly announcing a ruin' (2: 394; 1970 160; 1: 57; 13: 311–13).

The visit to the Whispering Gallery, and the story of the trunk, both involve the fantasy of overhearing and of being overheard, and it is a fear we will meet again, in passages which for other reasons too will seem to recall the circumstances, excitements and terrors of primal fantasy. The ability of the magician in the story of Aladdin to hear the pulse, a continent away, of 'one solitary infant's feet', and to isolate it from all the other sounds transmitted along the surface of the globe, seems to be another narrative of the fear that one's guilt will be publicly exposed. Now, however, that guilt is urgently disavowed, in what seems to be an attempt to repair the damage inflicted by the earlier story of an intrusion 'upon the privacy of magicians'. This new story is terrifying enough, in De Quincey's retelling, and it leaves him still in the ambiguous territory of the Tigridians; but it leaves him 'innocent', still on the right side of the river.

In the version of the tale of Aladdin which was current in collections of the *Arabian Nights* entertainments when De Quincey was a child, and before the appearance of scholarly translations by the orientalists E. W. Lane and Richard Burton, Aladdin is still a child when his father Mustafa dies; and in the place of the father there appears from Africa a mysterious figure who introduces himself to Aladdin as his uncle, presses money on his mother, and offers to take over where Mustafa had left off in equipping Aladdin to earn a living. Later, he tries to kill the boy (Forster 346–52). It may have been this intrusive avuncular figure as much as anything else which made the tale of Aladdin of such importance to De Quincey. In the revised and expanded version of the *Opium-Eater* there is an incident which it is possible to read as an attempt perhaps to pass the guilt of an intrusion on to De Quincey's maternal uncle, Thomas Penson (both of whose names were borne by Thomas), or else to identify this uncle as the chief spectator on his guilt: in either case, it involves identifying that uncle as a tiger, and seems again to suggest that the scenery of Elizabeth's bedroom can be thought of as a primal scenery. The incident is uncannily reminiscent of Lindsay's fantasy of Palmyra, which stands as the epigraph of my second chapter: a notion of the sisterly; a fantasy of ruins, of a beautiful female corpse, of oriental intruders. Between his escape from Manchester Grammar School and his walk through Wales, De Quincey attempted to contact his elder sister Mary, at the house called the Priory now occupied by his mother. He sent her a note asking her to meet him 'under the shadows of the little ruins in the Priory garden', the ruins of what remained of the original monastic establishment. He waited there for her, but instead

> in glided amongst the ruins – not my fair sister, but my bronzed Bengal uncle!
> A Bengal tiger would not more have startled me. Now, to a dead certainty, I said, here comes a fatal barrier to the prosecution of my scheme. I was mistaken. Between my mother and my uncle there existed the very deepest affection. . . . But in many features no characters could stand off from each other in more lively repulsion.   (3: 316)

I do not pretend to understand what is going on in this narrative of a secret meeting with an older sister, in ruins, prevented or interrupted by the surprise appearance of a tiger. But it seems to involve the notion of the uncle at once as an intruder and a barrier – a barrier which, to a '*dead* certainty', is '*fatal*'. The intrusion and the barrier are ambiguously, or equally, between Thomas and his sister, and between Thomas and his mother; and then, as far as his mother is concerned, the narrative is negated. Suddenly his mother and uncle (themselves brother and sister) seem to be hovering on the verge of replicating the guilty relationship between De Quincey and his sister, but just as suddenly we are told that they stand, after all, a long way apart, and are repelled by each other. The narrative seems to work just as well if the tiger is the bringer of death or the bringer of love, dividing Thomas from his sister, or alienating the affections of his mother; it seems to condense the stories of the death of Elizabeth and of the sexual pollution attached to that death, while still permitting them to be seen as different stories which may even involve different female victims, the different sisters of different brothers.

III

De Quincey, or so it seems to me, makes two kinds of move to pass on to others the specific guilt of causing the death of Elizabeth or of her various surrogates. One involves affixing it (as it must so often have been fixed in the bourgeois home) to a nurse or to a female servant – conveniently enough, the opposite of Thomas, not masculine and bourgeois, but feminine and plebeian, and capable of being imaged as a 'tigress'. In his account of Elizabeth's death, De Quincey records among his first remembrances 'a remarkable dream of terrific grandeur about a favourite nurse' (1: 32). The dream came back, he claimed, twelve years after Elizabeth's death, except that the 'favourite nurse' was now his unloved 'elder nurse', 'dilated to colossal proportions'. She was standing

> as upon some Grecian stage with her uplifted hand, and, like the superb Medea towering amonst her children in the nursery at Corinth, smote me senseless to the ground. Again I am in the chamber with my sister's corpse.   (1: 49–50)

Medea figures in De Quincey's list of the 'tigresses' of Greek tragedy (4: 73), and is of course the female child-murderer *par excellence*.

As we have seen, Elizabeth's hydrocephalus was produced, according to De Quincey, by the fact that she was 'permitted to drink tea at the house of a labouring man, the father of a favourite female servant',[8] and that at sunset 'she returned, in the company of this servant, through meadows reeking with exhalations after a fervent day. From that day she sickened.' Whether the tea had indeed been soaked up into her brain, along with the dew, is not clear, but probably De Quincey thought it had, for he certainly believed diet was a factor in the death of Kate Wordsworth, which occurred when her baby-sitter Sarah Green allowed her to eat carrots, an act, apparently, of 'criminal negligence'. The death of his sister Jane, too, seems to have been caused by 'a female servant' who had 'treated her harshly, if not brutally', some three or four days before her death, so that De Quincey could never bear to look in the face of 'the person charged with this cruelty'. There is a similar story concerning the negligent inattentiveness of the nurse of a girl who nearly drowned; and we shall come across a related incident concerning Barbara Lewthwaite, a young woman employed by De Quincey as a nurse (13: 147; 1: 33–4; 3: 435–6).

The second attempt to pass on the guilt for the death of Elizabeth involves affixing it to his elder brother William. In terms of the association of sun and Sunday with Elizabeth's death, William has the advantage of being a son, like Thomas was; but in relation to William, Thomas attempts to represent himself not as a son at all, but as a daughter. Until Thomas was eight, William was away at school, and so, records De Quincey gratefully, 'my infant feelings were moulded by the gentlest of sisters, and not by horrid, pugilistic brothers'. And according to the 'Autobiography', although when William charged him with effeminacy he 'denied it *in toto*', as a rule when taunted with his 'girlish fears', he welcomed being identified as a girl. Thomas's identity as sister was born, or so it appears from his autobiographical writings, long before his pseudo-hydrocephalus and his resurrection as Tabitha (1: 32, 56, 61, 45; for William's pugilism, see 1: 59).

Although William was still away at school when Elizabeth died, he was an appropriate receptacle of some part of the guilt attached to Elizabeth's death for just that reason. Until the age of eight, or so he tells us, Thomas hardly knew his face, and in this, as he points out in the 'Autobiography', Thomas's knowledge of William resembled his knowledge of his father, whose health obliged him to spend his declining years in hot climates until he returned to Manchester to die. The death of his father, when Thomas was not quite eight, is described in the 'Autobiography' as another tropical, if not as an oriental death, and perhaps because both his father and William were strangers to Thomas, this association with the tropics seems to pass to William after his father's death, as if William had come to occupy the place of the father. And so it no doubt seemed. After the sentence describing 'the closing hour' of his father's life, the next begins 'My brother was a stranger . . . '. William arrived home from school, and stayed home, as soon as his father died, so that if Thomas's Bengal uncle represented an intrusion, and a 'fatal barrier' between Thomas and his mother, so too did the pugilistic and tropical William (1: 58).

The history of the attempt to place William in the place of the tiger is one in which the geopolitical strategies we examined at the beginning of this book are exploited, and tested, to an extreme degree. It involves the production of William as the oriental, near-eastern other of De Quincey; the making safe of the division between them, by representing them as united against a true, far-eastern other; and then a reversal of these two others, so that Thomas unites instead with what he and William had jointly opposed, and William is projected out, as it were, beyond the Tigris, where the real monsters lurk. In the first place, then – I am following here the narrative order of the third chapter of the 'Autobiography' – William is identified as a native of the Near, rather than the Far East. Accordingly, he writes a tragic oriental drama, to be performed in the nursery; there is probably a memory here of a play the 17-year-old Thomas had himself attempted to write, an 'Arabian Drama' called 'Yermak the Rebel' (1928 154, 181). The title of William's play was at first 'Sultan Selim', but 'he soon changed the title to "Sultan Amurath", considering *that* a much fiercer name, more bewhiskered and beturbaned'. All the children were obliged to participate in this drama, and their role was to be massacred by William, who himself played the part of the beturbaned sultan. By the end of the first act, no one was left alive but the sultan himself, so that a new generation had to be created, only to be massacred again, and so on through all the remaining acts. This is not the last family massacre that William or his surrogates will participate in; nor is it the last time we will see a special significance being attached by De Quincey to the turban: that to be 'beturbaned' is somehow to be particularly terrifying (1: 67–8).

No sooner has William appeared in the identity of a near-eastern sultan, than he becomes the hostile ally of Thomas, in a long series of daily or twice-daily battles against the boys employed at a local cotton factory, which stood by a bridge over the River Medlock – De Quincey mistakenly remembers it as the Irwell – which the two brothers were obliged to cross on their journeys to and from their Manchester school. The word 'factory', we are told in a footnote, was the technical term in the 1790s for a class of building that would now be called a 'mill', and the note may help us understand one of the meanings that De Quincey may have attributed to this war with the factory boys. It is described at first as a class war, between 'aristocrats' – the name for those who, in the decades around 1800, were the opponents of a reform of the oligarchical system of government in Britain – and Jacobins. But when the factory is described, as 'South-eastern Asia' is in the *Opium-Eater*, as the *'officina gentium'*, the factory where the nations or races or peoples of the world are produced, the war becomes transfigured into a large-scale geopolitical conflict between the united forces of Frankistan – Christendom and the Sultan – on the one hand, and a 'swarm' of 'Goths and Vandals' and other more easterly opponents on the other. The war, which is fought with 'stones, fragments of slate, . . . brickbats', is also described as a struggle of the Israelites versus the Ammonites or the Philistines, of the party of humanity against 'tiger-cats and wolves', and of the Romans against the Carthaginians – William goes into battle with the cry *'Delenda est Carthago'*. In De Quincey's writings that cry is repeated at least as often as Cato repeated it in the Roman senate, but for our present purposes, one particular instance of repetition stands out. *'Delenda est Carthago'*, he intones yet again, when calling on the British to destroy the 'guilty town' of Canton; the town (as we have seen) of 'factories' and swarming myriads: the wars between the De Quinceys and the factory boys may also have been anticipations (or repetitions) of the Opium Wars (1: 68–83; U2: 23–4).

At one point in these hostilities Thomas is captured by the factory boys, and delivered over to the custody of a group of girls, who caress him and protect him, and this is the signal for William and the factory children to change places: as they become more human, William becomes more bestial. The account of the war is now broken off, to make room for a history of the local hostilities

between the two brothers. Each has invented an imaginary kingdom. Thomas's, called Gombroon, or Gombroonia, is deliberately
imagined as underdeveloped and impoverished, in an unsuccessful
attempt to escape the aggressive intentions of William's kingdom,
which is large, expansionist and apparently invincible. The terrors
inspired in Thomas by the daily battles with the factory boys were,
he says, 'as nothing', compared with the 'figurative' conflict that
developed between these two kingdoms; and with William thus
established as more terrifying than the stone-throwing Jacobin
tiger-cats, the name of his own kingdom is unveiled: Tigrosylvania
(1: 87–93).

This figurative conflict is made still more anguishing when
William claims to have discovered that the Gombroonians had tails.
So great is Thomas's shame at this revelation, which he seems
powerless to deny, that he identifies himself and his subjects as
helpless outcasts, on a par with pariahs, Jews, gipsies, lepers, the
Pelasgi, and the Pyrenean Cagots. He and they are all polluted by
'some dreadful taint of guilt, real or imputed', of which the
humiliating Gombroonian tail becomes a symbol (1: 98–101).[9] From
this terrible apprehension of guilt and shame, Thomas was released
when the King of Tigrosylvania was sent off to London to be
apprenticed to the painter de Loutherbourg. Thomas never saw him
again; he died before he was 16, of typhus fever. He describes
William's death – for which he feels anything but grief – as a
'redemption' for him (1: 115), apparently because it enabled him to
pass the guilt for the death of Elizabeth on to the unresisting corpse
of his brother, now finally and securely identified as from the Far
East, as a tiger:

> No longer was the factory a Carthage for me: if any obdurate old
> Cato there were who found his amusement in denouncing it with a
> daily 'Delenda est Carthago', take notice (I said silently to myself),
> that I acknowledge no such tiger for a friend of mine.   (1: 115)

The identification of William as a tiger, an enemy more terrifying
than the factory boys, has the effect of opening the space he vacated,
as Thomas's hostile ally, to be filled by the factory boys themselves.
When first introduced, these boys were described as Jacobins, but at
the same time it was acknowledged that 'they detested everything
French, and answered with brotherly signals to the cry of "Church
and King", or "King and Constitution"' (1: 70; my emphasis). After
the departure of the working class, in the image of the factory boys,
from this fraternal and compatriotic identity, and its migration
through a whole range of alien and inhuman identities – Goths,
Vandals, Carthaginians, Ammonites, Philistines, tiger-cats and

wolves – it will return in my next chapter, by courtesy of the death and demonisation of William, to this original fraternal position, in all that concerns the relations of Britain with its intractable eastern Empire. The requirements of making safe the psyche and the nation are the same. The working class is again available to serve the 'aristocrats' in a war against an orientalised representation of the working class itself, the horrid enemies across the Tigris.

Before we leave the geopolitics of William's identification as tiger, I want to suggest a possible additional source of that identification. In the nursery at Greenhay there was a book by Thomas Percival, the literary physician who treated Elizabeth; first published as *Moral Tales and Reflections* in 1775, it was later issued in the probably no less awesome title of *A Father's Instructions*. Among the fables contained in this book, though De Quincey does not refer to it, was one called 'Beauty and Deformity', in which a boy goes to Manchester to see a collection of wild beasts, which are described by Percival in terms thoroughly derivative of Buffon or Goldsmith. The boy is particularly struck by the juxtaposition of a camel, which, with 'the two bunches on its back' is 'one of the ugliest beasts in the collection', and the tiger, which, in addition to 'the symmetry of his limbs', has an expression of apparently 'placid sweetness' (Blake may have read this book). The keeper warns the boy not to judge by appearances: the tiger 'is fierce and savage beyond description', and, as if speaking of a problem child, he continues, 'I can neither terrify him by correction, nor tame him by indulgence'. The camel, on the other hand, from 'the sandy deserts of Arabia', is 'in the highest degree docile, affectionate, and useful'; all of which goes to show that 'mere external beauty is of little estimation; and deformity, when associated with amiable dispositions, does not preclude our respect and admiration'. The use of such a story as this to De Quincey is probably clear enough. In the spirit of the 'this/that/the other' strategy we examined in the first chapter, it can offer the role of camel to the deformed and amiable Elizabeth, in a move which, by representing her as Arabian, can acknowledge her strangeness, but also her familiarity when contrasted with the tiger, the terrifying other which threatens both Europe and the Near East (1: 130; T. Percival 1788, 269–71).

IV

To conclude this chapter, two tales of mystery and imagination. 'The Fatal Marksman' is a translation by De Quincey of Johann August Apel's ghost story *Der Freischütz*, which became the basis of the opera by Weber: no less than three translations of it appeared in Britain in the 1820s and 1830s.[10] Of De Quincey's translations and borrowings Hillis Miller has written (27n.) that his choice of what to translate seems often to be guided by 'the configurations of his own inner world', and so it will often seem in this book. The particular appeal of 'Der Freischütz' to him will become clear if I offer a brief summary; and though he was an advocate of great freedom in translation, he found everything in what follows – including the characters' names – ready made, and he made no significant change in Apel's original. [11] William, a young bailiff's clerk, is in love with Catherine (De Quincey sometimes calls her Kate), the daughter of a huntsman. Her father, however, has decided that she must marry another huntsman called Robert, or, failing him, *any* huntsman – for his own office is hereditary, and he wishes the family to preserve it, together with the farm that goes with it. In order therefore to supplant Robert and to obtain her father's consent to their marriage, William agrees to become a huntsman himself – he is already an excellent shot – and to take the necessary examination in marksmanship. Soon after making this decision, however, he finds that a spell has been cast upon his gun, and he becomes incapable of hitting anything. In desperation – for if he fails the examination he loses his bride – he determines to have recourse to magic: to sit at midnight, at a crossroads, within a circle of human skulls and cross-bones, and to cast what are known as 'devil's balls', which always hit their mark.[12]

He receives a series of warnings not to dabble in the black art. On one occasion he dreams that Kate, 'pale as death', faints away as he fires the 'probationary shot' of his examination. Another time an uncle visits him and detains him past midnight – to William he seems an 'intruder', and the occasion is reminiscent of that occasion in the *Opium-Eater* when De Quincey, expecting to meet his sister, is intruded upon by his uncle. On a third occasion a picture falls from the wall of Kate's cottage, and wounds her in the head: her 'death-pale countenance', and 'the blood upon her temples', make her look just as she had in William's dream. Finally, however, and with all due ceremony, he manages to make his 'devil's balls'; and is just preparing to go home when he is accosted by the devil, who explains the terms of the bargain between them: of the sixty-three balls William has moulded, 'sixty go true, and three go askew'. The next day William takes his examination in shooting; if he is successful, it will also be his wedding day. He takes aim at the appointed mark – a white dove – and fires. Behind him he hears a cry: Kate, in her bridal dress, has fallen, her forehead 'shattered' by a bullet. Her parents die of grief, and William ends his days in a madhouse (12: 286–313).

I pass without comment to the first of 'the immortal Williams murders', as De Quincey describes them in 'On Murder considered as one of the Fine Arts'. These murders took place in 1811, though De Quincey misremembers the date as 1812, the year when Kate Wordsworth died; he wrote his account of them in 1854. There were two sets of Williams murders, in each of which almost an entire household was murdered by one John Williams. They took place 'in a most chaotic quarter of eastern or nautical London', a quarter of 'mixed hats and turbans', where 'every third man at least might be set down as a foreigner. Lascars, Chinese, Moors, Negroes, were met at every step.' Williams himself, who had been 'a seaman on board of various Indiamen', is described by De Quincey as partaking of this general East-End and oriental colouring; his hair, 'sandy' according to contemporary accounts, becomes 'bright yellow', probably, De Quincey suggests, stained with the same dyestuff used in the Punjab for painting horses;[13] and though 'his face wore at all times a bloodless ghastly pallor', this is taken by De Quincey as to be all of a piece with his 'natural tiger character'. His 'tiger's heart', however, was otherwise 'masked by the most insinuating and snaky refinement'. This combination of tiger and snake was probably, by the mid-nineteenth century, and especially after 1857, a conventional sign in the representation of Hindus. The behaviour of the three brahmins in quest of the moonstone is described by Wilkie Collins as alternating between 'tigerish quickness' and a politeness which is 'snaky' (13: 74–8; Collins 106).

Williams's first set of murders took place on a Sunday: much is made of this, though at no point does De Quincey remind us that Elizabeth too died on a Sunday. His victims were the family of a man called Marr. Marr himself may have sailed in the same Indiaman as Williams to Calcutta; his 'sweet, lovely young wife', whom Williams may have desired, was thought to have been the occasion of the quarrel between them. The murderer slipped unobserved into the Marrs' shop a few minutes after midnight on Sunday morning, when the 'servant girl, a grown-up young woman', had slipped out in search of some oysters for the family supper. Once inside, he locked the door, and began the massacre of the family: Mr and Mrs Marr, their eight-month old baby whose sex is never determined, and a living-in, 13-year old apprentice boy (13: 80–2).

The carnage itself is described by De Quincey only after it has happpened, though in technicolour and in detail. While it is happening, the narrative positions us, and itself, outside the door, in the place of the returning servant girl, whose real name was Margaret but who – perhaps, as Plumtree points out, to distinguish her from De Quincey's wife Margaret – is renamed Mary. This young woman has already been unobtrusively but firmly blamed, in

De Quincey's usual manner, for failing to communicate to Mr Marr her suspicions about 'the indistinct image of a stranger' she had seen earlier outside the shop, and for failing, therefore, to prevent the ensuing murders. The characteristic position of the young female servant in De Quincey's narratives of the deaths of girls and young women seems to coalesce here with the position he occupies himself in the narrative of Elizabeth's death. Now we are invited by De Quincey to 'attach ourselves' to Mary 'in vision', and to see through her eyes what happens when she returns to the shop and knocks at the door (13: 85–7).

Instead of the bustling sound of a family, she hears on the other side of the door the creakings and footsteps of a single person quietly descending the stairs and moving along the passage to the door: these are the first of many such 'accidental noises' in the account of the Williams murders which may remind us of Rank's remarks on 'the phantasy of listening'. There follows a famous sequence of extraordinary power, in which 'he, the solitary murderer, is on one side the door; Mary is on the other side'; he working out how to entice her in, she becoming increasingly on her guard and apprehensive (13: 88). The parallel, in this context of footfalls and locked doors, between a curious De Quincey outside, with the medical men and their tools of dissection inside, and this pairing, with Mary outside and the 'butcher' inside, with his 'ship-carpenter's mallet' and 'carving-knife', is only too clear; and it forewarns us of what will eventually be found when the alarm is raised, the murderer makes his escape, and the house is entered. All four of those inside have been struck on the head with the mallet, and then had their throats cut; but De Quincey concentrates particularly on the death of the infant. In the cradle, the bedclothes were 'in a state of indescribable confusion', and

> the hood of the cradle had been smashed to pieces. It became evident that the wretch had found himself doubly embarrassed – first, by the arched hood at the head of the cradle, which, accordingly, he had beat into a ruin with his mallet, and, secondly, by the gathering of the blankets and pillows about the baby's head. The free play of his blows had thus been baffled. And he had therefore finished the scene by applying his razor to the throat of the little innocent; after which, with no apparent purpose, as though he had become confused with the spectacle of his own atrocities, he had busied himself in piling the clothes elaborately over the child's corpse. . . . No one incident . . . throughout the whole tissue of atrocities, so much envenomed the popular fury against the unknown ruffian as this useless butchery of the infant.
>
> (13: 93–4)

The involute that took shape earlier, and was clearly related to De Quincey's guilty fantasy of his sister's bedroom, is evidently repeated here. There is an 'intrusion', a locked door, a listening at it, and a foot on the stairs; there is something covered by a pile of bedclothes; and there is something, the 'hood' of a cradle, which stands in for a child's head. That head is left 'a ruin', and is discovered to be so, when the door is finally unlocked. There is a tiger and fortuitously enough, his name is Williams. [14]

5

Hydrophobia: Out in the Midday Sun

The Affghans, as they rushed furiously on, cut right and left with surprising force, and swords as sharp as razors, not only at armed and active soldiers and sipahees, but at the wounded as they lay, at their own terrified animals, at every object which crossed their path. A wild *fusillade* was opened upon them by the troops on the slopes of the citadel, and, in the midst of a scene of indescribable confusion, the native soldiers, gathering in threes and fours around each furious Affghan, shot and hunted them down like mad dogs, until the destruction of the whole party was completed.

Henry Havelock, *Narrative of the War in Affghanistan in 1838–9*, 2: 83.

Just as I was going to sleep, there sounded in the night air, a scream, as of a dying woman close at hand, which chilled the marrow in my bones. It was repeated, mingled with cries and barks, which swept past the club-house. It turned out to be only a pack of jackals running over the Esplanade in the moonlight.

W.H. Russell, *My Diary in India, in the Year 1858–9*, 1: 109.

I

In an essay on Hazlitt published late in 1845, De Quincey attempts to illustrate his belief that Hazlitt's jacobinal dislike of social distinction was more than 'merely political', it was 'morbidly anti-social', an aspect of his general loathing of the human race. Unintentionally, no doubt, the anecdote De Quincey tells seems better calculated to make that point about himself, not Hazlitt. In Pall Mall the Duke of Cumberland was acknowledging with a royal bow each passer-by who, as was customary when a member of the royal family walked by, removed his hat as a mark of dutiful respect. When he arrived at Cockspur Street, however, the Duke was similarly greeted, in the sight of Hazlitt, by a 'negro' crossing-sweeper. This placed the duke in a right royal dilemma. Should he bow? – surely his royal highness could not condescend so far! Should he ignore him? – a royal duke should surely make a better return for a demonstration of loyalty, even when made by the lowest of his subjects. Eventually he hit upon a solution which won the admiration of De Quincey, and of every bystander except Hazlitt himself: he gave him half a crown. Hazlitt was outraged: the crossing-sweeper was a fellow-subject with the Duke, capable of paying taxes or committing treason; he was 'a specimen . . . of the *homo sapiens* described by Linnaeus'; he was, Hazlitt insisted, 'entitled to a bow'.

Hazlitt's error, as far as De Quincey is concerned – and it is clear that he expects his readers to agree with him on this point – was in believing that the crossing-sweeper, whom he describes as 'a paralytic nigger', was beyond all doubt a member of the human race. De Quincey is not at all sure that he was 'human at all': 'law', he acknowledges, 'conceived him to be a man, however poor a one, though medicine, in an under-tone, muttered sometimes a demur to that opinion'. He pretends to leave the question open, whether the sweeper was 'man or beast', but when, a few lines later, the black becomes 'a grub, and such a very doubtful grub', he seems to have found a means of giving formal expression to his doubts, and of resolving them at the same time. The black was not human (11: 346–50).

This was written in 1845, after the formal abolition of slavery in the British Empire, and when the ensuing racist backlash against the emancipated slaves was already well established. De Quincey, however, was certainly old enough to remember one of the slogans of the abolition movement, placed in the mouth of a black slave represented as abject, incapable of helping himself, and entirely unthreatening to whites. 'Am I not a man and a brother?' this supplicant was made to inquire, or rather to plead.[1] For De Quincey the question must have made only a crooked sort of sense. According to the logic imputed to the slave, if slaves were men – which unless they were women was hardly to be denied – then they were also brothers, and worthy to be treated with brotherly love. According to the logic that governs De Quincey's perception of brothers, however, to be a brother was not necessarily to be a man at all: brothers like William, or like Cain with whom the murderer Williams is compared, could be tigers, just as well as men. Or they could be dogs: Williams was described also as a 'bloodhound', an 'accursed hound', and a 'wolfish dog'. Tiger or dog, it came to much the same thing for De Quincey: the names of both animals were frequently employed as a word of abuse of particular power against 'orientals'; and according to De Quincey, 'the lion and the tiger are the merest curs in nature' (13: 74, 84, 93, 113; 9: 162).

Though the late De Quincey describes the mutinous sepoys of 1857 as 'dogs' and as 'hounds', his general practice, in line with western European tradition, was to reserve those terms for the abuse of Muslims and Jews.[2] Moors and Arabs are 'heathen dogs', 'infidel dogs', 'misbelieving hounds' (7: 268; 11: 400, 432). But the caninisation of the Jews who appear in his writings is a rather more complex affair. De Quincey quite clearly participates in a generalised anti-Semitism which enables him, for example, to use the word 'Jew' as a term of abuse, or (as we saw in Chapter 1) to refer to the 'Jewish taint', and to describe it as a 'leprosy'. But perhaps because of his own self-fictionalisation as outcast, as leper, as Wandering Jew, and perhaps also because of the geopolitical position of the Holy Land as a buffer-state against a further East, he could write passionately in defence of the humanity of Jews, and as we shall see he even wrote a novella which offers itself as a lesson on the general dangers of anti-Semitism, and on the particularly German brutality of assessing Jews at toll-gates as 'swine' (10: 384; 12: 275). These contradictory attitudes are especially evident in De Quincey's various discussions of the Jewish historian Josephus, for whom De Quincey nourished an extraordinary hatred. He believed that Josephus had betrayed the Jews to the armies of Vespasian and his son Titus, and for this crime De Quincey repeatedly reviles him by the word 'Jew'. He thus manages to suggest at one and the same time that if it is reprehensible to be a bad Jew, in the matter of one's political loyalties, it is also reprehensible to be a Jew at all.

The worst crime of Josephus, however, was that he had joined in the celebrations of the overthrow of his 'motherland'. And 'there is many an intelligent little girl, not more than seven years old', writes De Quincey, who 'would indignantly refuse to give the sanction of so much as a momentary gaze upon a spectacle abominable in all Jewish eyes', 'the pollution of triumph'. This young girl has turned up from nowhere, and has intruded on a scene of pollution – even by refusing to do so – quite as mysteriously as the Bengal tiger turned up in the middle of the mysteries of Eleusis. But her introduction enables the text to turn once again to the image of Judaea, weeping under the palm-tree, which had become a part of the complex involute of the death of Elizabeth; the coin stamped with that image had in fact been issued in celebration of the Roman victory in the Jewish war. The girl is now transmuted into Judaea: for even if, writes De Quincey,

> she could descend to an emotion so humiliating as curiosity, she would feel a silent reproach fretting her heart so often as she beheld upon a Roman medal that symbolic memorial of her desolated

home – so beautiful and so pathetic – *Judaea figured as a woman veiled, weeping under her palm-tree*: Rachel weeping for her children.

(7: 248)

I want to postpone to a later chapter the discussion of what may now seem the rather familiar scenery of this version of the coin – the child's 'curiosity' at the 'pollution' of the 'motherland'; the 'desolated home'; the sudden translation of the seven-year-old into a weeping mother. For the moment, what concerns me is the connection about to be made between this young girl, who is obviously, whatever else she is, a figure for Elizabeth, and the hysterical description of Josephus, in the very next sentence, as 'this hound – hound of hounds, and very dog of very dog' (7: 248). The dog here takes the same place beside the weeping Judaea, as the tiger does in the Brocken-spectre essay. And in 'The Household Wreck', another Jew betrays another young female victim: the narrator has bribed Manasseh, 'a Jew from Portugal', to help his innocent wife Agnes escape from prison. He turns out, however, to be 'a murderous villain', a 'hound', a 'dog', who attempts to murder her instead (12: 222–5).

II

The scene of Thomas's last memory of William, on the very day of his brother's departure for London, was the garden at Greenhay, on (as is so often the case with De Quincey's memories) a glorious June morning; the dews, like those which killed Elizabeth, 'had not entirely exhaled'. As we have already seen, a brook ran along the side of the garden, and made a boundary between the garden and the countryside beyond. William, De Quincey tells us, had once considered jumping this brook, as Remus had jumped 'the infant walls of Rome', but he soon thought better of it; perhaps he remembered that Remus's act of derision had been rewarded by death at the hands of Romulus, his brother. The garden gates were built on a little bridge spanning this brook, so that, if the gates were closed, the garden could not be entered. On this particular morning, the gates were indeed closed, and the Quincey children, in apparent safety, were playing on the lawn – all but one of them surrounding the charismatic William, with Thomas, the pariah, standing apart and watching the others (1: 116–17).

In 1843, when De Quincey was reading and reviewing *Ceylon and its Capabilities*, by J.W. Bennett, he would have come across an anecdote about another June day in Ceylon. 'On 12th of June 1827, whilst we were at dinner with Mr Tranchell and his family, a rabid pariar dog, which had been chased from a neighbouring village, through the sacred grounds of the Moorish mosque adjoining Mr Tranchell's estate, ran into the room'. Mr Tranchell, believing he had discovered a cure for hydrophobia, was entirely unconcerned, but Bennett himself was unwilling to put the cure to the test, and was about to shoot the dog, he tells us, when there was a sudden shower of rain. 'The moment the animal felt its deadly influence, it was seized with convulsions, and expired upon the spot' (Bennett 108).[3] This tall story – rabid dogs are not themselves hydrophobic, though often believed to be – may be one of the sources of what happens next in this account of June at Greenhay, which was composed in the early 1850s. Suddenly, the peace of the garden is disturbed by the sound 'as of some great mob', indicating 'hostile and headlong pursuit'; a minute later a mad dog appears – like the dog in Ceylon it has been chased from a neighbouring village – and pauses at the garden gates. Unable to enter the garden by the normal route, he lingers on the bank of the brook as if to jump. Briefly, Thomas and the dog seems to recognise each other as kindred souls: the boy looked 'searchingly' into the dog's eyes, and the dog 'looked most earnestly at myself, and the group beyond me'.[4]

But whatever sense of mutual recognition and identity there may briefly have been, between pariah dog and pariah boy, it is immediately intruded upon by William, who, unlike Thomas, 'did not in the least suspect the real danger', and who invites the mad dog to attempt the leap. Apparently exhausted and hydrophobic, the dog refuses to be tempted. Finally, the immense crowd of pursuers appears – working-class, apparently, dressed for the stable, and armed with pitchforks.[5] The dog is driven off and eventually killed. Once again, the relation between the working class and some threat closer to Thomas has been turned inside out. The mob beyond the water is on Thomas's side after all; the threat is driven away, as the Jacobins, like the sepoys in Havelock's account of the storming of Ghuznee, take on the task of killing the mad dog, and take up in the process an intermediate and a protective position between it and Thomas.

'Freedom won and death escaped' is Thomas's entirely ungrieving comment on the events of a day which has seen the departure of William for London, the death of the mad dog, and the successful shifting of the identity of mad dog from Thomas to William. For there is no doubt that his narrative is inviting us to see the departure and death of the dog as a figurative version of what Thomas wishes for William, and of what did indeed happen to him when he died, in London, of typhus fever. According to Benjamin Rush, the American physician who corresponded with Thomas Percival, an occasional accompaniment of typhus fever (which as we have seen was taken to be an oriental fever) was hydrophobia. The dog had bitten two cavalry horses at a nearby barracks, of whom 'one died in a state of furious hydrophobia some two months later, but the other (though the more seriously wounded of the two) manifested no symptoms whatever of constitutional derangement'. It may be that here again Thomas is identifying with Elizabeth in her hydro-cephalus, and claiming to participate in her suffering; as if, like the two horses, they had both been bitten by the mad dog, by William, though Thomas had recovered from the bite, just as in the person of Tabitha he also recovered from what he suspected to be hydro-cephalus. Again according to Dr Rush, typhus fever was often 'the remote cause' of hydrocephalus, and one symptom of hydrocephalus was hydrophobia (1: 117–19; Rush 2: 210–3).

William may also be figured in the story, told in 'Suspiria', of the pet dog who bit another young girl, also a relation of the De Quinceys, in the head. The dog had the kind of name associated by De Quincey with the 'beturbaned' ferocity of the tragic hero Sultan Amurath: he was called Turk. When De Quincey was still a young boy he had been given a female kitten, more or less at the same time as the whole family was given the thoroughly masculine Turk as a present from their Leicestershire relations. The dog had 'bitten off' the cheek of his young cousin Emma, which miraculously, however, 'healed without a scar'. This escapade did not, apparently, make him a dangerous or an unsuitable gift, because the family at Greenhay needed, for security's sake, a dog with 'a moderate degree of fierceness'. As a guard-dog, Turk proved his credentials straight away: when he met Thomas's 'poor kitten', he 'laid her dead on the spot', or as De Quincey puts it a couple of pages later, 'he had killed the object of my love' (1985 121–5).[6]

De Quincey hated dogs – with the exception of course of 'noble English bull-dogs' – and he acknowledged that his fear of them was a fear of contracting hydrophobia. Even in the nursery at Greenhay, he would have learned from one of the tales that Thomas Percival seems to have written for the purpose of terrifying his children that 'there was a general alarm concerning mad dogs in Manchester'; in this story, a mild-mannered spaniel called Sylvia, who must have been consorting with one of those rabid Mancunians, expires peacefully on the kitchen floor, watched by the grieving children of the family. In 1818, when he was editing the *Westmorland Gazette*, De Quincey was bitten by a dog, and was convinced he was contracting the disease. But he seems to have found a remedy: among the 'plethora of . . . reports of dog attacks' and of stories about rabies with which he filled the newspaper, there is one which claims that a whole kennel of hounds had been successfully treated for rabies by the administration of opium (W 28th November 1818).[7] As will readily be imagined, the killing of dogs was a more congenial topic to De Quincey than saving their lives. The favoured method appears to be to stone them to death: brickbats and pieces of paving-stone were the weapons used in the war against the Jacobins; and where William is imaged as a mad dog, it is appropriate that he should be driven off, as an outcast, and stoned by the missiles of the Jacobins (J2: 76; T. Percival 1788 170–1; Caseby 155; 7: 339; L232).

'What', asks De Quincey, in the first sentence of his review of William Mure's *Journal of a Tour in Greece*, 'are the nuisances special to Greece which repel tourists from that country? They are three – robbers, fleas, and dogs'. He deals with the robbers and fleas at great speed; it is the dogs he wants to talk about, and he devotes much of the essay to them, so that a topic which occupied a brief and playful chapter in Mure's two-volume book comes to take over nearly half of De Quincey's essay. In a fanciful expansion of a single incident of Mure's journal, De Quincey claims that whenever a stranger approaches a peasant's door,

> out bounds upon him by huge careering leaps a horrid infuriated ruffian of a dog – oftentimes a huge *moloss*, big as an English cow, active as a leopard, fierce as a hyena, but more powerful by much, and quite as little disposed to hear reason.

These huge dogs, it seems, are scattered all over western Asia, whether Turkish or Persian, and all over central Asia as well. They are basically an oriental phenomenon, and the fact that they are encountered everywhere in Greece is a reminder that in 1842 Greece had only recently become independent of the Ottoman Empire. De Quincey believes that the best weapon of defence against Greek dogs is a Greek paving-stone, a *chermadion*, and he cites a legend of Hercules as authority for this recommendation. But a *chermadion* is not always to hand, and so he spends six jovial pages on the stoning of dogs, in which the shape, size and quality of suitable stones is discussed. (7: 331–49).

The topic of stoning dogs with paving stones, in particular, turns out to give De Quincey an opportunity to get back at William for suggesting that the Gombronians had tails. It appears that when De Quincey was living in the Lake District, the dogs of the region were in the habit of standing in his path and preventing him from proceeding on his way. He used to argue his right of passage, or so he tells us, on two grounds: that he was a good Latinist, 'whereas all the world knows what sort of Latin is found among dogs'; and that, unlike dogs, blacks and brothers, he partook 'of a common nature with the king', and therefore had a better right to use the king's

highway than any 'low-bred quadruped with a tail, like you', Now
Latin is not Greek; but it is still worth recalling that William's
claim that Gombronians had tails grew out of a lesson on
Monboddo's discussion of the Greek aorist tense. Thomas took
some interest in the topic, but as for William, 'aorist indeed! Primus
or Secundus, what mattered it? *Paving-stones* were something,
brickbats were something, but an old superannuated tense!' (7: 340; 1:
95, my emphasis) The volumes of Monboddo lay around their
tutor's room for weeks, and it was in them William discovered
Monboddo's speculation that the human race originally had tails –
just as, William added, the Gombronians still have. The cluster –
dog/bad at classical language/tail/paving stone – seems to confirm
the identification of William as dog, and to return the insult to the
King of Tigrosylvania.

If dogs cannot be stoned, they can be drowned, and this may
indeed be the worst possible death for the rabid dog who is believed
to be hydrophobic. In *The Stranger's Grave*, Mr Stanley rescues a
little boy called William from drowning, following a skating
accident – William is the younger brother of a character called
Elizabeth, who is in love with Stanley. In the process, however,
Stanley's dog is drowned. This seems to be a good, a conscientious
way of saving brother William (who was 'an excellent skater'), while
killing him at the same time. When Stanley realises that his dog is
missing, he collapses with grief, and is diagnosed as suffering from
hydrocephalus(1823 45–59; 1: 64).

III

All these narratives of dogs, whether mad or simply undisciplined,
can be seen as attempts to kill William in effigy, or to orientalise him,
and sometimes both. In the remainder of this chapter I want to
discuss several more such attempts, whether successful or not, to kill
characters who can be read as surrogates of William, who are often
orientalised villains, and who in most cases seem to threaten violence
to a young child, usually a girl. They are all narratives, I take it,
which seek to do two things: to identify William as the true
aggressor of Elizabeth, the active agent of the death which Thomas
failed to prevent; and to stage a reparative drama, in which – if things
work out – the surrogate of William will be killed and Elizabeth will
be saved or resurrected. I shall begin with the famous incident in the
Opium-Eater, when De Quincey's Grasmere cottage is visited by an
itinerant Malay, whom he takes to be (like the murderer Williams) a
seaman. The description of this incident concentrates on the tableau
formed by Barbara Lewthwaite, the Malay, a 'tiger-cat', beturbaned

like the Sultan Amurath, and a 'little child from a neighbouring cottage' (a little boy, but not at first identified as such) who is gazing up at the Malay and clinging to Ms Lewthwaite for protection. As an act of friendship, De Quincey gives the Malay a present of a large quantity of opium, divided into three pieces, which he consumes as one mouthful. It was very much more than a lethal dose, but to De Quincey's relief he hears, in the days following the incident, no report of a Malay or other beturbaned man being found dead on the roadside (3: 402–6).

If the Malay had died, the responsibility would apparently have been his own, not De Quincey's, for the Malay bolted all three pieces at one mouthful. And yet the total quantity of the gift was, so De Quincey tells us, enough to kill – according to which edition of the *Opium-Eater* you read – three or (later) six dragoons and their horses, so that even if the Malay had eaten only one piece, he might well (according to De Quincey's computation) have killed himself (1985: 57; 3: 405). If we pause to do the arithmetic, in short, the incident seems to be inviting us to see that by this gift De Quincey may indeed been intending to stone the Malay to death, so as to afford the child the protection which it sought but could not expect from Barbara Lewthwaite, and which young Thomas had been unable to give his sister. And the issue is raised again in a story that De Quincey sets up, in a note to the late revision of the *Opium-Eater*, as a parallel to or repetition of the incident, and which seems to function, yet again, as a reparative version of an earlier narrative which had ended unsatisfactorily.

This note begins by reminding us of that 'impressive picture' of Barbara 'in her girlhood, with the turbaned Malay and the little cottage child', and with De Quincey as spectator. In the new tableau Barbara appears as the nurse of Margaret, De Quincey's eldest daughter, nearly two years old, who is playing the part of the cottage child; the part of the Malay is played (improbably I know) by a caged finch, which had been given to Margaret as a pet, and is now mysteriously sick. Margaret is convinced her bird needs some 'yoddunum' to restore its health; and so De Quincey puts 'a little diluted laudanum near to the bird' – whether inside or outside the cage is not clear. Next morning, watched by Barbara, Margaret and De Quincey, 'the bird rose on its perch, struggled for an instant, seemed to be expanding its wings, made one aspiring movement upwards, in doing so fell back, and in another moment was dead'. The death by opium De Quincey had tried but failed to inflict on the Malay has been successfully inflicted on the finch: the little girl is safe. That the Malayan 'tiger-cat' could be successfully impersonated by a sick caged bird seems as I say improbable; but if the Malay was to be impersonated by an animal at all, as William constantly is, it clearly had to be one that De Quincey could square up to with a measure of confidence in the likely outcome of their struggle (3: 460–3).

The suspicion that the incident with the bird is the representation of a successful murder in effigy of the Malay, and so of William, is increased in the speculations that follow the Malay's departure, on just how much opium it does take to kill a man. De Quincey offers his own experience in evidence, comparing (as we saw in Chapter 1) his own ingestions of opium with the experiments of, among others, the Brighton doctor who inoculated himself with hydrophobia. The hydrophobic dog at Greenhay, we recall, bit two cavalry horses, and managed to kill just one of them. There is a linkage, I am suggesting, between these various texts, constituted by the Malay and the lethal gift of opium, the gift of bird or dog, and the desire to procure the death of a dog or tiger-cat in order to prevent those animals from inflicting death on a child. De Quincey gives a lethal dose of opium to the bird and to the Malay, enough to kill not one but three, not three but six cavalry horses, as if to prevent a repetition of the deaths inflicted by the rabid dog and by Turk, the canine surrogates of William (3: 405–6).

The incident with the Malay can also be read, and certainly should also be read, in just the opposite direction to the reading I have offered. The argument of this book is not simply that De Quincey expresses and intensifies the fears that govern his perceptions of his private life by representing the objects of his fear as oriental – as tigers, as sultans, Turkish or Asian dogs. My argument is also – and this will become clearer when we examine his accounts of events in imperial history – that he expresses and rationalises his fears of the Orient by treating the history and politics of India, China and elsewhere as a series of narratives which seem to repeat those of his mythologised personal history. The Malay is to be killed because he is a surrogate of William; William is to be killed because he is a surrogate Malay.

IV

John Williams committed a second set of murders, twelve days after the first: fortuitously, the victims of this outing included a Mr and Mrs Williamson, a 70-year-old, 'patriarchal' tavern-keeper and his wife; a housemaid was also murdered. Two occupants of the house escaped, 'a young journeyman' who lodged with the family, and 'a little grand-daughter', who was in fact 14, but whom De Quincey describes as 'about nine years old', the same age, there is perhaps by now no need to point out, as Elizabeth at her death. Her name, though De Quincey does not say so, was Catherine, or Kitty (James and Critchley 64). The two survivors owed their safety to the fact that they were in bed, on the first floor, when Williams entered the premises: those who died were on the ground floor and in the basement. 'The reader' is invited by De Quincey to view the incident from the position of the young journeyman, who may be placed, by the description of Williamson as 'patriarchal', in the position of the surrogate son of him and Mrs Williamson. The house door is suddenly shut and locked with 'a crash, proclaiming some hand of hideous violence'. Alerted by the sound, the journeyman opens his own bedroom door and listens; and then, driven by 'the fascination of killing', he creeps stealthily downstairs. He does this only after the wife, husband and housemaid have all been killed. From the bottom of the stairs, he observes the murderer through a half-open door, 'hanging over the body of Mrs Williamson', and searching her pockets.

The journeyman is thus put in a position where only he can act to prevent the death of the young girl at the hands of Williams. At first he finds himself 'paralysed' by fear, and so 'evidently fascinated' by the events he was witnessing that he had walked 'right towards the lion's mouth'. This second episode, however, is reparative of the first, and seems to make everything come out right. The journeyman returns upstairs, and, at every moment expecting to hear Williams – the words are clearly reminiscent of 'The English Mail-Coach' – 'come racing upstairs at a long jubilant gallop, and with a tiger roar', he knots some sheets together, suspends them from his window, slides to the ground, and raises the alarm. He has saved the child from 'ruin' by saving himself; though powerless to resist the lion/tiger, he has 'overreached' him. This interpretation of the journeyman's actions is entirely De Quincey's: as James and Critchley point out, the evidence he gave at the inquest suggests that 'in his desperate anxiety to get out . . . alive he had apparently given [Kitty] no thought'. Williams managed to escape, but was soon arrested. He was found hanged in his cell, and (though De Quincey does not say so) he was buried at a crossroads, and a stake driven through his heart (12: 97–118; Burke 263; Plumtree in Snyder 156; James and Critchley 82–4, 148–63).

The reparation of the first Williams murder, where the child dies, by the second, where the child is saved, may itself repeat a pair of stories De Quincey had inserted in the *Westmorland Gazette* in the brief period of his editorship in 1818 and 1819. One of these is the report of a lion hunt in India, in which, confronted by a lioness, a man stands 'panic struck, unable to discharge his piece, or to run away. She had him thrown down and got him completely under her, and his turban in her mouth'. The story can be read as a reversal of the narrative suggested by Tipu's clockwork toy – this time it is an Indian, even Tipu himself, and not a British soldier, who is powerless beneath the wild cat.[8] But whatever reparative work of that kind the *Gazette* story may do, it is also evidently a repetition of the dream in which De Quincey finds himself 'impotent', lying down before a lion; and from this point of view we can read the second of these *Gazette* stories as reparative of the first. It is a story which De Quincey borrowed from a German newspaper, and it describes how a seven-year-old boy saves his sister from a mad dog 'by wrapping a coat round his arm as bait' (Caseby 161, 156).

V

By far the most successful representation of the death of William, a death which appears to secure the resurrection of Elizabeth on the very terms that De Quincey had demanded – that she should not be *'changed'* – occurs in the fictionalised history 'The Spanish Military Nun'. The story permits, at least, such a reading of the extraordinary events it describes. Catalina De Erauso was placed by her father, a hidalgo of northern Spain, in a convent in the town of San Sebastian, a few miles along the coast from Fontarrabia, the setting for the death of Emily in *The Stranger's Grave*. Catalina – De Quincey insists on calling her Kate – escapes from the convent and, assuming the dress of a man and the vocation of a soldier, soon finds herself in South America, under the command of her own generous and protective brother, a dashing cavalry officer. Kate manages to identify him, but he does not identify her, either as a woman, or as the sister he has not seen since she was three. One night, however, and without recognising who her opponent is, Kate finds herself involved in a duel with her brother, and kills him. She has now no choice but to become a deserter, and the only possible means of escape is across the Andes, towards the eastern side of the continent.

The hardships of the journey over the mountains, undertaken in a spirit of the deepest 'penitential sorrow' for having murdered 'the one sole creature that loved her upon the whole wide earth', form a consciously mystical centrepiece to De Quincey's otherwise arch and jocular narrative, and one which reworks the account of Elizabeth's death and funeral. The summits of the mountains are described as 'the upper chambers of the Cordilleras', and are reminiscent, therefore, of the 'upper chamber' inhabited by Tabitha, and the 'upper chamber' of the lover of the Daughter of Lebanon (see above, p. 47). The ascent and descent of the mountains are represented as a matter of climbing up and down a 'staircase'. Kate, and some other deserters she is travelling with, see a 'strange spectacle' in those 'upper chambers', the spectacle of a corpse: a man is apparently sitting on a rock; when approached and tapped on the shoulder, he sprawls face upwards in the snow and reveals by his 'ghastly', 'frightful' features that he has frozen to death. At the very sight of him, her two companions perish, and Kate is left alone with the corpse, and 'alone with her own afflicted conscience'.

But as if the frozen mountaineer, whom she has *not* killed, replaces in the narrative the brother whom she had indeed 'dismissed from life', Kate suddenly wonders if she has not been 'executing judgment upon herself', 'running from a wrath that was doubtful, . . . flying in panic – and behold! there was no man that pursued'. She prays, and the narrative explodes into an apostrophe which takes us immediately back to the deaths of Jane and Elizabeth, deaths now transfigured into the occasions of resurrection which previously, unlike the annual deaths of flowers, they had failed to be:

> Oh! verdure of human fields, cottages of men and women (that now suddenly, in the eyes of Kate, seemed all brothers and sisters), cottages with children around them at play . . . oh! spring and summer, blossoms and flowers, to which, as to *his* symbols, God has given the gorgeous privilege of rehearsing for ever upon earth his most mysterious perfection – Life, and the resurrections of Life – is it indeed true that poor Kate must never see you more?

In answer to this question, and as if in answer to her prayer, Kate realises that she has crossed the Andes, and after passing through 'a mass of rock, split as into a gateway', and figured as the 'gates of paradise', she finds that she is 'descending insensibly the mighty staircase'. 'As the dove to her dovecot from the swooping hawk – as the Christian pinnace to the shelter of Christian batteries from the bloody Mahometan corsair – so flew . . . the poor exhausted Kate from the vengeance of pursuing frost' (13: 188–203).

Kate survives, and is resurrected without even going to the trouble of dying first. She enters paradise, not by rising to heaven but by descending the staircase from the upper chambers of the Andes, towards the imagined pastoral world where all are brothers and sisters, and where the dead are rescued from an oriental death at the hands of 'bloody Mahometans', or are resurrected as flowers are, unchanged, as material and not as spiritual bodies, and on this earth. The confusion of Kate's sex seems to allow her to stand for Elizabeth *rediviva* in Thomas, just as Tabitha did; and by representing as an accident the killing of an elder brother whom she had no reason to wish dead, and by recasting the sight of Elizabeth's body as the sight of a dead man, the narrative offers De Quincey the chance to imagine himself as liberated from all guilty thoughts towards Elizabeth and William, and with the advantage that, instead of Elizabeth dying in that upper chamber, William dies. A better outcome could not be imagined.

If narrative could always repair our psychic wounds simply by telling the story of our sufferings in the way we would like them to be told, we would hardly need to tell them, or never the same one twice. But we cannot be sure what story it is that we 'want' told, and if we could be, narrative could never tell it 'simply', for the parts of agent, victim, spectator, for example, that are constituted by narrative, are continually being auditioned for by a host of unemployed actors, and no one can be sure of holding on to a part, or to the same part, even for the length of a single sentence. 'The Spanish Military Nun' can be read as a reparation of De Quincey's guilt, and it can be read, just as easily, as a repetition of the experiences imagined to have caused it. Like Fanny of the Bath road, Kate De Erauso – did De Quincey read it as eSauro? – is related to a crocodile; her father is described, in the space of very few pages, as an 'old', a 'noble', a 'sublime' crocodile, a crocodile 'still weeping forth his sorrows', a crocodile with an 'abominable mouth', and (twice) a plain 'crocodile' (13: 161–87). If the brief thought 'crocodile' meant that the most terrible oriental and Egyptian chimeras were forever attached to the image of Fanny, what price the occidental purity of Catalina?

Worse still, the happy thought of renaming Catalina after De Quincey's object of obsession, Kate Wordsworth, has the insidious effect of exposing Kate to the very tiger she is intended to escape from and destroy, or – worse still – of converting her into it. Catalina's 'original name' is translated as 'pussy', De Quincey tells us; but having translated this in turn into 'kitty', and 'kitty' into 'Kate', he quickly finds his heroine infected with tigridiasis. Within a page she is a 'future tigress', and the cub of a tigress, with 'tropic blood' in her veins. Twenty pages later 'the tiger that slept in Catalina wakened at once', and she is soon 'a little wild cat' (13: 163–88). In narratives whose central character assumes the clothes and outward identity of the opposite sex, a rule of transposition is established by which the sexes of the protagonists can be reversed. If according to this rule we play Kate's tigerish identity through 'The Spanish Military Nun', it becomes the stale tale of a younger brother, a tiger, who killed (but could not help it) his loving, generous elder sister, and who stumbled across her corpse in an 'upper chamber'.[9]

6

The King's Evil: The House of De Quincey

> One sphinx, in particular, made a great impression on me; they say all sphinxes are male, but the features of a really sweet, pretty girl, could not be mistaken; and though her nose, part of her mouth, and chin were gone, yet one hardly missed them, what remained was so pretty and elegant. One pitied the poor thing being tacked to such an uncouth body as that of a sphinx. . . .
>
> W.W.Ramsay, in Lindsay, *Letters on Egypt, Edom, and the Holy Land*, 104n.

> I feel that a stranger either does not see the Sphinx at all, or he sees it as a nightmare. When we first passed it, I saw it only as a strange looking rock; . . . Now I was half-afraid of it. The full serene gaze of its round face, rendered ugly by the loss of the nose, which was a very handsome feature of the old Egyptian face; – this full gaze, and the stony calm of its attitude almost turn one to stone.
>
> Harriet Martineau, *Eastern Life, Present and Past*, 254.

There is no narrative that speaks more clearly of the hospitality of narrative to the endless permutation of actors than the story of Oedipus. And no story seems to have fascinated De Quincey more than the Theban myth of the house of Laius, and especially of the events dramatised in the *Seven Against Thebes*, the *Oedipus Tyrannus* and the *Antigone*, which are repeatedly returned to and rehearsed in his writings. The myth provided, in the first place, the opportunity for De Quincey to nurture his hatred for William, in the story of the 'preternatural malice' that divided two brothers. A 'defrauded' younger brother, Polynices, becomes a pariah, expelled from his native city, when his right to the throne is usurped by his elder brother, 'the scoundrel Eteocles'. The 'malice' between these 'two fierce rival sons' is so intense that when both are killed, and 'the corpses of both . . . were burned together on the same funeral pyre (as by one tradition they were), the flames from each parted asunder, and refused to mingle'. So deep an impression does this story of the funeral make on De Quincey, that he repeats it on three different occasions in his writings. In addition, the myth of the house of Laius provides him with the image of a younger sister who makes a favourite of Polynices, who gives up her lover and her marriage for his sake, and who secures a grave for him at the certain price of her own. 'This female love was so intense that it survived the death of its object', and thus reciprocated De Quincey's undying love for Elizabeth. And Antigone herself became the object of a new nympholepsis, when her part was played on the Edinburgh stage by Helen Faucit: 'Is it Hebe? Is it Aurora?' De Quincey represents himself as asking, when she first steps out upon the stage (4: 120; 6: 139, 146; 10: 365, 382).

The love of Antigone for her pariah brother is a repetition, of course, of her no less devoted love for her father, who is still more a 'pariah' than Polynices, because 'he was a murderer, he was a parricide, he was persistently incestuous'. This triplet of accusations seems to have appealed to De Quincey – elsewhere he announces that the king was connected 'with acts incestuous, murderous, parricidal', and Edward Stanley, who left his girlfriend to drown, slept with his niece, and drove his father to an early grave, also denounces himself as 'an incestuous person, a murderer, and a parricide' (1985 130n.; 1823 68). Antigone too was willing to make herself 'a houseless pariah, lest the poor pariah king, thy outcast father, should want a hand to lead him in his darkness'. And in a story in which, as De Quincey points out, sons are brothers and daughters are sisters, Antigone's love for her father is a sisterly, as well as a filial love. The place of Oedipus, no less than that of Polynices, offers a place of identification for Thomas – and in both places he can luxuriate in the limitless love of his sister, in the role of co-pariah and co-wanderer, Ann-tigone (10: 365; 6: 149).

There is another place in the story, alongside the role of Eteocles, where William can be accommodated. According to Pausanias, quoted in the *Encyclopédie* (15: article entitled 'Sphinx'), some believed that the Sphinx was an illegitimate daughter of Laius, so that Oedipus was her brother. And the bestial nature of the Sphinx, who combined the head, face and breasts of a woman with the wings of a bird, the claws of a lion, and the body of a dog, means that her femininity is no obstacle to regarding her, in turn, as the brother of Oedipus. For 'the woman of Greek tragedy', according to De Quincey, in a passage already alluded to, is 'not woman as she differed from man, but woman as she resembled man'; 'Medea or Clytemnestra, or a vindictive Hecuba', is 'the mere tigress of the tragic tiger', a replica of masculine violence in female form. That De Quincey had seen the Sphinx in the light of a brother to Oedipus seems likely from a sentence in the last paragraph of his essay on the

Sphinx: 'both of these enemies were pariah mysteries, and may have faced each other again with blazing malice in some pariah world' – where the 'blazing malice' seems to be a repetition – or a foreshadowing – of the 'malice so intense' that led the pyres of Eteocles and Polynices to blaze separately. And finally, according to De Quincey, when the Sphinx found her riddle answered, she flung herself into the sea and drowned. According to all other authorities I have looked up, she flung herself from a rock and was dashed to pieces on the ground. That a death by drowning should apparently have been invented for the Sphinx by De Quincey suggests that she belongs, for him, with the other ferocious beasts – tigers and mad dogs – who threaten death but who cannot cross water (4: 73; 6: 150–1, 145, 150).

But in a story in which the relations of each member of the family are so insistently doubled, there are no easy limits to be put to the identifications the story permits and produces between the house of Laius and the house of De Quincey. It was impossible simply to choose, among these proliferating connections, relations, and cast-lists, those that favoured a certain view of things, for it was impossible to be sure what view of things was favourite. Thus, among the identifications thrown up by the story, or rather by De Quincey's version of it, is one between Antigone and the Sphinx, and therefore between the Sphinx and Elizabeth. When the Sphinx drowns in De Quincey's version, 'the billows closed over her head'; when Antigone dies – and in other versions of the story, she killed herself, like the Sphinx, and also on dry land – she 'trod alone the yawning billows of the grave', as the face of Ann was lost to Thomas in what appeared to be a 'billowy ocean', a sea 'paved with innumerable faces' (10: 365; 3: 441).

It is possible also to see in the Sphinx the shadowy figure of Mrs Quincey, Thomas's mother. There is a passage in the *Opium-Eater* where De Quincey describes once more his dream of 'languishing impotence' when confronted by an 'all-conquering lion' (3: 316). Whatever else it might represent, the lion in this version of the dream is quite clearly a figure for his mother, who has just 'unmasked' the 'whole artillery of her displeasure' on Thomas for absconding from school. De Quincey writes of 'the chilling aspects of her high-toned character', of her readiness to assume that any action requiring to be explained in many words must be a bad action; whereas he, 'predisposed to subtleties of all sorts and degrees,'

had naturally become acquainted with cases that could not unrobe their apparellings down to that degree of simplicity. If in this world there is one misery having no relief, it is the pressure on the

heart from the *Incommunicable*. And if another Sphinx should arise
to propose another enigma to man – saying, 'What burden is that
which is only insupportable by human fortitude? I should answer
at once – *It is the burden of the Incommunicable*.   (3: 315)

The connections are evident enough here, if their significance is not:
there is a lion who reduces the man to impotence, a mother who
reduces him to silence, and mediating between them a Sphinx, both
lion and woman, who poses a riddle which can be answered,
promptly enough, only by a word which denies the possibility of
answers. The language of this passage – of unmasking, of disrobing,
of chilling looks – composes an involute which we will come across
again in each of the next two chapters, in each case in connection
with the maternal character.

As we have seen, among the many characters in the story who
share with Oedipus the identity of 'pariah' are Antigone and the
Sphinx. Antigone shares that identity by sharing with her father/
brother 'the hardships and perils of the road' – she becomes, like
Ann, or like Thomas in Wales, a pedestrian pariah, a variety of
pariah status that De Quincey compares and contrasts, in the
Opium-Eater and elsewhere, with the pariah status of sufferers from
leprosy and scrofula (3: 342; H8 1852 337; 1: 106). She also
participates of course in the more general evil the king has
unwittingly brought on the family, an evil which is more than an
individual guilt, is a kind of hereditary sin, the closest the pagan
mind could approach to the Judaic and Christian notion of a sin
which is diffused like 'a scrofula', like the King's Evil, 'through the
infinite family of man' (6: 142). According to Dr Percival, the
majority of children who contracted hydrocephalus were 'strumous',
that is to say, were sufferers from scrofula (Rees 18: article on
'Hydrocephalus'). If Elizabeth before her death was one of these; or if
De Quincey, reading up at a later date the literature on hydrocephalus, came to imagine she had been, then the story of the house of
Laius seems to be a way of voicing an account of Elizabeth's death as
the destruction, at once necessary and unforgivable, of an individual
– whether Oedipus or Polynices, Antigone or the Sphinx – whose
infection had tainted the whole family.

7

Diplopia: Two Girls for Every Boy

I find it difficult sometimes to perceive any difference between a Copt and a Muslim Egyptian, beyond a certain downcast and sullen expression of countenance which generally marks the former; and the Muslims themselves are often deceived when they see a Copt in a white turban.

E.W. Lane, *Manners and Customs of the Modern Egyptians*, 535.

The disease . . . was invariably attended with delirium. This person assured me, that he had the horror to see his own child dragged to the door by eight or ten cats, whom he with difficulty scared away; and affirmed it as his belief, that more people were killed by dogs and cats, or died from hunger, than under the disease itself. None would approach an infected house, and no patient would even assist another.

Alexander Burnes, *Travels into Bokhara*, 2: 125.

Were it not for the self-denying ordinance, the point of which will emerge later, which permits me to select my epigraphs only from works contemporary with De Quincey, this chapter would have been introduced with these lines from the last page of *Othello*:

> *Oth.* . . . And say besides, that in Aleppo once,
> Where a malignant and a turban'd Turk
> Beat a Venetian, and traduc'd the state,
> I took by the throat the circumcised dog,
> And smote him thus.   [*Stabs himself.*
> *Lod.* O bloody period!
> *Gra.*   All that's spoke is marr'd.
> *Oth.* I kiss'd thee ere I kill'd thee, no way but this,
> Killing myself, to die upon a kiss.
>   [*Falls on the bed, and dies.*
> *Cas.* This did I fear, but thought he had no weapon;
> For he was great of heart.
>   (*Othello*, V, ii, 353–62).

'I kiss'd thee ere I kill'd thee' – the sentence might have been written for De Quincey, to enable him to articulate the two stories of the guilt he bore for the death and violation of a girl or woman who, as we shall see, could appear to him in the guise of Desdemona as well as of Antigone. And the lines in Othello's previous speech speak just as clearly of the issue that is beginning to complicate my account of De Quincey's myth of childhood – the issue of identity and its instability. It is as an adopted Venetian, one who has 'done the state some service', that Othello evokes this oriental other, this enemy and traducer of Venice, the 'turban'd Turk'. But where the story he has been telling – arguably a story of self-justification – seems about to end, and to end with the dispatch of that 'circumcised dog', it suddenly goes on for one word too long, and goes entirely out of control. 'I smote him *thus*. [*Stabs himself*.' Suddenly, and without ceasing to be the Venetian, Othello is the Turk as well: the word 'thus' collapses the distinction between the European self and the oriental other, in a moment of self-destructive verbal anarchy which 'marrs' all that Othello had said before. For Lodovico and Gratiano, it is almost as if the suicide is an afterthought, produced by that afterword: had the 'period', the full stop, come just one word earlier, Othello might have survived into Act VI. The racial distinction that here collapses has been fragile throughout the play; but this speech, and the rejoinders of Lodovico and Gratiano, suggest that any distinction language makes it may also break, of its very nature, or as an effect of the very imperfect control we have over what we say. 'All that's spoke is marr'd' – Gratiano's comment on the Othello's speech takes the form of a gnomic, semi-proverbial utterance about the nature of speech itself; and it is all the more appropriate to the argument of this chapter that the comment is made at a moment of sexual violence and of racial confusion.[1]

I

In a paper of 1919, Freud discusses a fantasy which he believes is especially common among female patients and especially interesting when encountered in them, and which he sums up in the sentence 'a child is being beaten'. The linguistic form of that sentence, which he represents as the form in which it finds expression in analysis, is crucial to the character of the fantasy: the passive verb, the unspecified agent, the indeterminate sex of the victim. In analysis, the fantasy turns out to have three separate phases, all condensed into a single narrative by that question-begging syntax, and all accompanied by feelings of considerable pleasure. In the first phase, the victim is someone other than the person producing the fantasy, and the sentence 'a child is being beaten' can be represented by another in the form 'my father is beating the child *whom I hate*'. In the second phase, the agent remains the same but the victim has changed, and the wording runs '*I am being beaten by my father*'. In the third phase, the agent has changed – it may be left indeterminate, or it may be a representative of the father such as a teacher, but it is never the father himself. The child has become plural – the place of the victim is now usually occupied (in girls' fantasies) by a group of unknown boys. If the person producing the fantasy can be located, it is now in the place of the spectator (XVII: 185–6). The meanings of the fantasy in its various phases, the desire, the fear, the guilt that find expression in it, are not what concerns me, although the sibling rivalry it speaks of seems to speak only too volubly to the case of De Quincey. I have referred to Freud's paper to make a point not about psychoanalysis but about the indeterminacy and instability of narrative itself.

Throughout this book we have been watching the developments and mutations of two related stories, or two clusters of stories, concerning the death of Elizabeth. The first is the story of a murder, and the second of a violation: in the first, De Quincey feels guilty for having failed to prevent his sister being killed; in the second he feels no less guilty, it seems, for having kissed her when she was dead. On various occasions it has seemed that the same guilt, for the same sin of omission or commission, is finding expression in two different stories, and sometimes those two stories seem to have been condensed into a single scene, but never so thoroughly as to conceal the work of condensation itself. The loose ends of one story or the other have not allowed that single scene to generate what we call a seamless narrative.

In the 'The Spanish Military Nun' and in De Quincey's various rehearsals of the Oedipus myth, we began to notice that those narratives of De Quincey's guilt were a good deal less stable than my first accounts of them suggested: the parts of agent, victim, spectator, were beginning to circulate among different actors, so that what at first appeared to be a story of reparation could turn out merely to be repeating the story it was trying to repair. If it is of the very nature of narratives that they are as unstable as the tales of Kate and Oedipus turned out to be, we had better make an attempt to understand how that instability functions in relation to the original two stories about guilt and the death of Elizabeth. These stories too will turn out to be capable of generating, out of an originally rather non-committal syntactical matrix, a series of variants in which the agents, victims and spectators may change, and apparently unitary identities will split apart. What we cannot do, however, is to assign these variants to the various phases of De Quincey's psychic development; we have no grounds on which to do so, and have no alternative therefore but to treat each narrative as coexisting simultaneously with all its variant forms.

The first story, expressed in a single sentence, goes like this: '*son fails to prevent son (sun) murdering sister*'. There are two other versions of the story, however, which seem to propose two different kinds of reparation. One would be '*son rescues sister from murderous son*'; the other would be '*son murders sister and is murdered by son*' (or by mob acting as friends of son – we will meet the Jacobin infantry again soon, wreaking more mob vengeance on Thomas's behalf). Reparative versions of a story may seem logically posterior to the versions they repair, but this is no reason to treat them as later in order of invention, or as anything other than coexistent with those versions.

The second main story, the story of the kiss of death, can be summed up in one of its versions as: (a) '*brother secretly violates dead sister*'; and this version seems to be *shadowed* by two others – I put it like that partly because the relation between them and version (a) is obscure to me, and partly because, so far at least, they themselves have seemed hardly more than shadows, murky and hard to make out. One of these shadow versions seems to go: (b) '*brother secretly sees/hears dead sister violated*'; this version may be reparative of version (a) – 'I didn't really kiss her, I just saw . . . ' – or vice versa, (a) may repair (b) – 'I didn't really see, I just kissed'. The other shadow version is much more familiar, in that it is the same story as is told by the primal fantasy: (c) '*son secretly sees mother violated*'. In another variant of (a), a new character appears as the agent of violation; the son and the brother enter here in pairs, to produce sentences such as (d) '*brother sees sister violated by brother*'; '*brother sees mother violated by brother*'. If we assign priority to version (a) – '*brother secretly violates dead sister*' – we can talk of the son and brother splitting into pairs in version (d); but we can equally give priority to (d), and talk of them condensing into a unity in (a). In our analysis of De Quincey's narratives we will see both things happening: characters dividing in two, characters melting into one.

Most of us, I take it, attempt to repair what De Quincey called the afflictions of childhood with fantasy narratives of various kinds; and for most of us, most of the time, the attempt no doubt produces a provisional kind of stability. Such fantasy narratives do not always work, however, and one reason for this is to be found in the nature of narrative itself. When we lay De Quincey's stories out as I have done, as simple transactions between agents, victims and spectators, some of the problems involved in the attempt to use one narrative to repair another begin to emerge. Some of the reparative stories seem to entail a splitting of the agent in two. The son splits into a bad and a good son, a bad and a good brother; and though names and distinguishing characteristics can be affixed to each – William and Thomas, elder and younger, boy and not-really-boy – the distinctions between them may seem to be less stable than what makes them seem the same, so that the narratives in which they appear may generate a diplopia, a double vision: the younger brother may become bad, the elder brother good. Equally, in some narratives the positioning, or the moral character, of an individual agent or victim in a particular version of the story becomes ambiguous, as if two different characters have been uneasily condensed into one.

Sometimes we can see this ambiguity being produced at the level of syntax, as in this sentence from the second Williams murder: 'The reader must suppose him at this point watching the murderer whilst hanging over the body of Mrs Williamson, and whilst renewing his search for certain important keys' (13: 104 – the 'him' is, unambiguously, the young journeyman, whom I proposed as the surrogate son of Mrs Williamson). This is a sentence which seems to join the two stories of guilt: there is a murderer, and there is a violator who is observed by a spectator. It is clearly important that these three roles should be very carefully distributed between the available actors: the murderer and the violator must be the same person, the spectator must be someone else. But the syntax seems unwilling to allow the story to be as clear-cut as might be wished by a narrator innocent of all evil thoughts towards the victim. Just who is 'hanging over the body of Mrs Williamson'?

The relations of identity and difference between good and bad sons and brothers are not the only instances of such narrative instability. In a more or less similar way, the stories in which the mother and the sister are made objects of violation may also repeat each other, and propose a relation of identity between the two females or their surrogates; and this may result in the attribution of an ambiguous moral character – innocent/guilty – to either, for both may be fantasised as complicit in scenes which can also be interpreted as violations. What is more, images whose function seems to be to identify the narrative position or moral character of one character may suddenly start circulating among others, until we can never be sure who's who. The turban, the dog, the creak on the stairs, are only some of the images which have hitherto seemed to define difference, but which in this chapter will come to suggest identity. And all this narrative instability is encouraged, of course, by what seem to be unacknowledged desires and repulsions, which can find expression in all these substitutions and transfigurations. The result is that William, Elizabeth, the mother and Thomas himself can all become alternatively and simultaneously objects of love and objects of hate.

The reparative narratives invented by De Quincey may have done their job quite well, quite often; often, however, they may have been experienced not as reparative but as merely repetitive; and often the slippages between one character and another may have been experienced as producing a narrative chaos which generated its own new forms of anxiety. It is when and why the stories seem not to work that I want to consider in this chapter and the next, and I shall take as my text an incident from one of De Quincey's translations from the German, 'The Incognito, or Count Fitz-Hum', from a short story by Friedrich Laun. There is a moment in this story where the Count, unable to disperse a crowd of vocal petitioners by any other means,

> resorted to a *ruse*. He sent round a servant from the back door to mingle with the crowd, and proclaim that a mad dog was ranging about the streets, and had already bit many other dogs and several men. This answered: the cry of 'mad dog' was set up; the mob flew asunder from their cohesion. . . . Farewell now to all faith in man or dog; for all might be among the bitten, and consequently all might in turn be among the biters.   (12: 428)

Hitherto the cast of characters we have considered have mostly either been aggressors or victims, the biters or the bitten. From now on we will continually have reason to suspect that those who are biters must have been bitten, and that those who are bitten must therefore be biters. And as De Quincey's translation points out, this seepage of each identity into the other is best understood as an effect of language. It is not the presence of a real mad dog among the crowd that gives rise to their suspicions, their loss of 'all faith in man or dog'; the real problem is the dog's absence. The mad dog is present only in language, only as it is summoned up by the performative cry 'mad dog'; and it is the fact that the cry, the sign, has no referent which causes everyone to look round so anxiously to find one, and to find it everywhere, in everybody.

II

In a previous chapter I represented the second Williams murder as a successful story of reparation: brother saves sister from murderous brother, who dies. But the narrative tells itself in another way too. On several occasions I have pointed out that Thomas is disturbed in Elizabeth's bedroom when, through the closed door, he hears 'a foot (or I fancied so) on the stairs. I was alarmed. . . . Hastily therefore, I kissed the lips that I should kiss no more, and slunk, like a guilty thing, with stealthy steps from the room'. The parenthesis here, '(or I fancied so)', suggests clearly enough that the foot on the stairs may be a projection of his own guilt as well as of his own fear – and that, therefore, he has cast himself in two places, inside the room, listening for sounds outside, and outside, listening in, and that the 'foot on the stairs' is as much his own as are the 'stealthy steps' with which he slinks guiltily away.

In the first of the Williams murders, Mary, as the spectator, is placed outside the house, listening to the 'creaking sound' made 'on the stairs' by the murderer, and 'the dreadfall footfalls' in the passage. In the second, the journeyman, as spectator, is inside the house, and, hearing the door slam, descends the 'old, decaying stairs, that at times creaked under his feet'. The journeyman is now positioned exactly as the murderer was in the first murder story, and though the creaker on the stairs is now spectator, not agent, a connection has been made between them which the narrator now busily attempts to dissolve. In what is his last act as the spectator of the story, before he becomes the agent of saving the little girl, the journeyman notices something

which eventually became more immediately important than many stronger circumstances of incrimination: this was that the shoes of the murderer, apparently new, and bought probably with poor Marr's money, creaked as he walked, harshly and frequently

It is the murderer, this sentence tries to insist, that is the creaker: so firmly is his creaking attached to the identity of murderer, that it was his creaking that identified him as murderer, to the satisfaction of the police. He creaks harshly, as a murderer would; his creaking ties him to the story of the Marrs, where he was the creaker, not the journeyman. These creaking shoes seem to put everyone back in their proper identities, until the journeyman, upstairs again, hears 'the sullen stealthy step of the murderer creeping up through the darkness . . . the step which he had heard was on the staircase'. No murderous creaking now; just the creeping foot on the stair, and the 'stealthy steps', the very image of Thomas inside (and outside) the bedroom of his sister (13: 88, 101–11).

The difficulty of distinguishing brother from brother, Thomas from William or Williams, is as much an issue in the last of the three stories that conclude De Quincey's essay on murder.[2] This is the story of the McKeans, two brothers, who in May 1826 went to a remote country inn near Manchester, with the intention of stealing the savings of a benefit club which were entrusted to the safe keeping of the landlord. There were four residents at the inn: the landlord, his wife, a boy in his early teens, and a young servant-woman – Masson, the editor of the *Collected Writings*, names her as Elizabeth Bates, though De Quincey does not give her name. The brothers drugged the landlord by slipping some laudanum into his punch; and then the elder of them asked the servant-girl to show him up to the room which the brothers were to share that night with the young boy. The younger McKean positioned himself at the bottom of the stairs, 'so as to be sure of intercepting any fugitive from the bedroom above'. Once in the bedroom, the elder McKean approached the girl and 'threw his arms around her neck with a gesture as though he meant to kiss her'; but instead he cut her throat, and she sank to the floor. The boy saw all this from his bed, and managed to rush downstairs – past the younger brother grappling with the landlady – and out of the inn. The brothers, unable to find him, and uncertain whether he had succeeded in raising the alarm, abandoned their attempt at robbery. The landlady, 'though mangled' by the violent embraces of the younger brother, recovered, and the landlord slept through it all. The brothers were caught, convicted and executed.

This is a story which offers an embarrassment of positions to De Quincey. Who is the killer, who the kisser, who the embracer? – are they the same or different? – how clearly can we differentiate between the brother upstairs and the brother downstairs? Thomas can find himself in the elder brother, upstairs, who seemed about to kiss Elizabeth, but killed her instead, and the effect of such an identification might either to be to distinguish kisser from killer (to kill is *not* to kiss) or to identify them (to kiss *is* to kill), and so to identify the surrogates of William and Thomas. But Thomas can find himself also in his usual place as the younger brother, who kills no one, but who is seen to be committing an act of violence which may seem indistinguishable from a sexual act. By analogy with the story of the escape from school – and the analogy is very clear – he can occupy both these positions simultaneously. The younger McKean had positioned himself at the foot of the stairs 'to intercept any fugitive from the bedroom above'; when Thomas was himself a fugitive from his upper chamber at Manchester he 'stood waiting at the foot of the last flight', while the groom above him had attempted to carry down the load of books which is a load of guilt. Finally, De Quincey may find himself also in the role of spectator, the wakeful boy, who watched the apparent kissing, actual killing of Elizabeth, who saw the 'life-and-death' conflict at the foot of the stairs, and like the journeyman is suddenly translated from spectator to rescuer, for much is made of the fact that the boy, again like the journeyman, by rescuing himself, rescues others.

If the position of the spectator/rescuer is the most comforting of the three, it is so only because the other two positions can evidently accommodate De Quincey no less appropriately; this is a story in which he may be everywhere. He can also find himself, for example, in the laudanum-soaked landlord, too stoned to prevent Elizabeth's death. But as Laplanche and Pontalis have pointed out, there may be 'multiple entries' in a story such as this, and the subject may find itself not only in the grammatical subjects and objects of the verbs, but even in the verbs themselves. There is a place for De Quincey on either side of the antithesis 'flee'/'intercept', into which the story is continually being resolved: the younger brother positioned to 'intercept' fugitives at the foot of the flight of stairs; the retreat of Elizabeth Bates 'intercepted' by the elder McKean; the landlady 'intercepted' by the younger; the failure of the elder, again, to 'arrest the boy's flight'; the attempts of both brothers, when fugitives, to 'evade being intercepted'; their fear of 'intercepting enemies'. He can find himself equally in the verb 'watch', which belongs at all times to the narrator, and at one time or another, in active or passive form, to the younger brother watching at the foot of the stairs, the boy watching in the bed, the elder brother watching to see if the boy is asleep; the two brothers watching out for possible captors; possible captors looking out for the brothers, and so on (Laplanche and Pontalis 22–3).

The ubiquitousness of the positions that De Quincey can find himself occupying may relate to his suggestion that the brothers were treated harshly by being executed for their crime. A modern, more enlightened court would have discovered, he insists, some extenuating circumstances: 'whilst a murder more or less was not to repel them from their object, very evidently they were anxious to economise the bloodshed as much as possible. Immeasurable, therefore, was the interval which divided them from the monster Williams'. In an essay on Judas Iscariot, in whom he recognises a fellow pariah, a fellow Wandering Jew, a fellow exponent of the kiss of death, De Quincey insists that Judas's crimes amounted to no more than 'spiritual blindness' and 'presumption'; but in the first, 'he went no farther than . . . his brethren', and 'he outran his brethren' only in the second. Williams is described, however, in terms that refuse to acknowledge any common identity, any brotherhood, between him and De Quincey: the 'monster', the 'tiger', the 'accursed hound' is guilty as hell, and is, those words insist, *other than Thomas* (13: 118–24; 8: 181).

This differentiation, however, is no more secure than all the rest, and Thomas seems repeatedly to merge with the surrogates of bad brother William. If we go back to the story of the dog Turk who wounds the head of Emma and kills the kitten, the strangest thing about it is that whereas the mad dog at Greenhay was killed, Turk was forgiven. He was, apparently, so melancholy, and so oppressed, because so kennelled and chained, that he could not help doing what he did. In making this defence, De Quincey quotes a snatch of Virgil, on 'the rage of lions repining at [literally, 'refusing'] their chains'. Now De Quincey frequently describes his addiction to (Turkish) opium in terms such as 'the yoke of opium', 'the bondage of opium', from which he seeks 'liberation'. In the 'Original Preface' of 1822 to the *Opium-Eater* he speaks of opium addiction as 'the accursed chain which fettered me', and in the long attack on Coleridge with which the final version of *Opium-Eater* begins, he describes Coleridge's unsuccessful attempts to break his own addiction as a refusing of 'the fierce over-mastering curb-chain, yet for ever submitting to receive it in the mouth'; and he quotes that very snatch of Virgil, on the anger of lions that refuse to accept their bondage. The whole point of this version of the preface is to insist that, contrary to what Coleridge had claimed, there was no 'distinction, separating my case as an opium-eater from his own': the lines of Virgil apply as much to Thomas as to Turk or Coleridge (3: 419–21, 211, 230, 225). The logic of identification in this intertextual knot seems to run something like this: Turk is a mad dog, so Turk is William; but a Turk is an opium-eater, so Turk is Thomas; so what Turk does must be forgiven.

III

If Thomas is continually finding himself in the position of William, he is also continually finding William in the place of Elizabeth, with the apparently disastrous result that any story of a killing in effigy of William is in danger of becoming a story about killing Elizabeth. I can make the point by referring to another dog, the one belonging to Edward Stanley in *The Stranger's Grave*. So far I have represented the drowning of this animal as a double event in which William is both saved and killed. And so it might remain, except that the story obviously anticipates the story later in the novel in which a young woman is saved and another young woman is left to drown; and except too that the dog in question is not called Turk but Flora, or flower. As a result, the incident of the drowning dog may be read as involving a series of substitutions which takes us all the way from William to Elizabeth in one of her floral incarnations: William is dog, dog is drowned, dog is female, female is drowned, Elizabeth is drowned, Elizabeth is William.[3]

Furthermore, in his account of the stone-throwing wars he and William waged against the factory boys of Manchester, De Quincey recounts an incident when, having been taken prisoner, he is passed over to a group of factory *girls* for safe keeping. These girls treat Thomas as 'a privileged pet' – they kiss him, caress him, call him twice (affectionately) a 'little dog', and 'rescue' him from the dangers of war. The story may be read as a reparative version of the story of Turk, and of Thomas's reluctance to kiss the dead Elizabeth; it makes kissing safe for boys and girls alike; but it makes Thomas, like William, like Elizabeth, a dog, and so able to participate in a series of three-way substitutions, displacements, condensations, which make it impossible to distinguish the good from the bad, Thomas from William, the good sister from her terrifying other (1: 78–85).

A more straightforward example of a death in effigy of William as also a death in effigy of Elizabeth is the story of Barbara Lewthwaite and the bird, which formed a kind of coda, or reparative repetition, of the story of the visiting Malay. It was the identifying attributes of the Malay – his turban, his tigerish character, the threat he represented to the child – which allowed us to see him as a surrogate of William; and it was the staging of the stories of the Malay and of the bird – in both the various actors were disposed in similar positions – which allowed us to read in the death of the bird the death of William-as-Malay. But in the preamble to the account of the bird's death, so much is made of roses, of June, of death, and of little girls that we can hardly avoid reading the bird's death as a repetition of Elizabeth's as well (3: 460–3). And it may be that all the stories which involve a beturbaned victim, or even a beturbaned aggressor, may be stories which evoke Elizabeth as readily as William in his roles as Sultan and Malay.

We have already uncovered a covert story, whose key word is 'ruin', in which the violation of Elizabeth seems to involve the dissection of her skull, customary in all cases of hydrocephalus. This may be – we cannot know – what is screened by the story of the guilty kiss, a betrayal like Judas's which leads to a girl's death, and which (as a violation of her innocence) 'ruins' and 'dishonours' her (the Daughter of Lebanon, a transfiguration of the prostitute Ann, was 'a poor ruined flower', 3: 452). In 'Suspiria', De Quincey claims that in later life he saw 'a similar case' of dissection to Elizabeth's: 'I surveyed the corpse (it was that of a beautiful boy, eighteen years old, who had died of the same complaint) one hour *after* the surgeons had laid the skull in ruins; but the dishonours of this scrutiny were hidden by bandages, and had not disturbed the repose of countenance'. The beautiful boy was De Quincey's son William, who died in 1834 (1985 108, and see P1: 304–5).[4]

The turban, as bandage for the dissected skull, will appear again soon; and if we think back to the association between ferocity and turbans exploited by William as Sultan Amurath, and if we remember that, in early nineteenth-century Britain, the turban was far more often an article of female attire than of male, we will discover a crucial image in the process of figuration by which is projected on to Elizabeth the identity attributed also to her elder brother, the identity of something irredeemably other, feared, and hated. In this identity, she is the subject of a new narrative (and now imperative) syntax: not simply 'sister dies' or 'sister is saved' but 'sister must die'. The *Westmorland Gazette* story, of the lioness standing over the beturbaned man (see above, p.78), can suggest something of the relentless interchangeability of William and Elizabeth in De Quincey's imagination. The turban belongs to both, the character of wild beast belongs to William, but femaleness belongs to Elizabeth: so who is doing what to whom?

In this light, the apparently accidental death of the bird, the apparently unwanted by-product of what seems to have been represented, however covertly, as a deliberate attempt to kill the Malay, begins to look like a happy accident. We saw how, in 'The Spanish Military Nun', the roles of sister and brother each seemed able to be occupied by persons of either sex, and that this resulted, in part, from the representation of Kate as tiger-cub and as tigress. Kate, like Fanny of the Bath Road, was descended from a crocodile. Of the troop of oriental and heraldic horrors that were inseparable from the thought of Fanny, De Quincey writes:

> as the cubs of tigers or leopards, when domesticated, have been observed to suffer a sudden development of their latent ferocity, ... so I have remarked that the caprices, the gay arabesques, and the lively floral luxuriations of dreams, betray a shocking tendency to pass into finer maniacal splendours.   (13: 291)

Fanny, we recall, was just such a 'floral luxuriation', a rose in June, and so Fanny, the logic of this seems to suggest, was herself analogous to a tiger-cub, waiting to grow up and turn ferocious. She was always, like the rose in June, an image of her own impending death; now, as tiger-cub, she is about to become a murderer. She is not simply inseparable from the terrifying animals of the Orient; like William, she *is* one of them, and must be killed. At the end of 'The Spanish Military Nun', Kate Erauso is missing presumed drowned, in a passage of carefully engineered mystery (13: 236−7, 250). There is more than one way to kill a cat, or a kitten, or a sphinx, half-woman, half-cat; but in the absence of a dog like Turk to do the job for him, drowning is probably De Quincey's favourite method.

IV

Even where Elizabeth or her surrogates are not apparently entangled with William and his, they may take on an alarming ambiguity of moral character, whether because De Quincey has passed to them the guilt of his own imagined violation of his sister, or because (but it may come to the same thing) they are imperfectly disentangled from the idea of the apparently violated but perhaps complaisant mother. This moral ambiguity is demonstrated with almost programmatic clarity in a posthumous fragment of 'Suspiria' entitled 'Who is this Woman that becknoneth and warneth me from the Place where she is, and in whose Eyes is Woeful Remembrance? I guess who she is'.

This vision can be read as in part a reworking of 'Strange fits of passion': De Quincey dreams himself travelling towards the cottage of a woman who is 'like a rose in June'. The fragment implicitly associates the premonition of Lucy's death with the landscape of the lakes and with the death of Elizabeth, caused, it will be remembered, by the exhalation of dew. The narrative of the vision begins:

> It is a sweet morning in June, and the fragrance of the roses is wafted towards me as I move – for I am walking in a lawny meadow, still wet with dew – and a wavering mist lies over the distance. Suddenly it seems to lift, and out of a dewy dimness emerges a cottage, embowered with roses and clustering clematis.
> (J1: 16–17)

A halo hangs over the cottage, like the *aureola*, the glory, that surrounded the 'ample brow' of Elizabeth, and a figure emerges from the cottage door – a figure whose sex is not disclosed until after the dream has faded. The figure seems to combine in its ambiguous gestures the two characters of Elizabeth from the two stories of De Quincey's guilt. First it beckons to De Quincey 'with waving arm and tearful uplifted face', then, frowning, it waves him away. He ignores the warning, and continues to advance, but the vision fades 'and all that remains to me is the look on the.face of her that beckoned and warned me away'. The ambiguity of the woman's gestures is repeated in the character of the cottage itself: one image speaks of the 'Spirit of peace, dove-like dawn that slept upon the cottage', and so associates it with Dove Cottage, first Wordsworth's residence, then De Quincey's; another speaks of 'the raven over the infected house', the figure in which the thought of Desdemona's supposed infidelity appears to Othello's memory. The cottage may be the House of De Quincey, at once a haven of mildness and peace, and a lazar-house, infected by infidelity or the fear of it (J1: 17–18).

He represents the woman as someone who has died, who is 'now in the spiritual world, abstracted from flesh'. Her 'searching glance', and 'the look of reproach' in 'the sweet sunny eyes in the sweet sunny morning of June' challenge him to remember things passed thousands of years ago; and they offer him a glimpse of 'glory in despair, as of that gorgeous vegetation that hid the sterilities of the grave in the tropics of that summer long ago; of that heavenly beauty which slept side by side within my sister's coffin in the month of June.' This woman had for years, he writes, appeared to him in dreams – 'oftentimes, after eight years had passed, she appeared in summer dawn at a window', as if recreating every eight years the scene of the eight-year-old Elizabeth's death (J1: 17–18). She even appears in the last of De Quincey's essays on China, probably written at about the same time as this 'Suspiria' fragment:

> Suppose, for instance, that China peremptorily declined all com-mercial intercourse with Britain, undeniably, it was said, she had the right to do so. But, if she once renounced this right . . . China wilfully divested herself of all that original right to withdraw from commercial intercourse. She might say *Go*, or she might say, *Come*; but she could not first say, *Come*; and then, revoking this invitation, capriciously say, *Go*.   (U2: 28–9)

This association with China, one of the most demonised countries in De Quincey's imaginary geopolitics, helps give some colour to the ambiguity of 'this monitory Hebe'. Her face was 'the sweetest face . . . that I had ever seen'; it was also 'terrific', 'awful', terrified itself and striking terror in him (J1: 19). And then – as with the discontinuity of a dream, and the grammar of a hurried draft – he writes:

> Thus, on any of those heavenly sunny mornings, that now are buried in an endless grave, did I, transported by no human means, enter the cottage, and descend to that breakfast-room, my earliest salute was to her, that ever, as the look of pictures do, with her eyes pursued me round the room, and oftentimes with a subtle checking of grief, as if great sorrow had been or would be hers.
> (J1: 19–20)

Though De Quincey 'enters' the cottage, he also 'descends', apparently habitually, to the 'breakfast-room', where, regularly, the woman in the vision is the first person he kisses, and where her eyes pursue him round the room with an apparently habitual anxiety. The relation-ship here envisaged may be between, ambiguously, mother and son, sister and brother, wife and husband. The passage recalls two others in particular: the incestuous morning kisses of Edward and Emily, and the breakfast-time memory of the wronged child-bride Agnes, the victim of perjury in 'The Household Wreck', on her last morning in the house soon to be infected with typhus fever.[5]

In this mysteriously waving woman, as if in an Ophelia, the innocent Sarah and the guilty Emily are cohabiting. She is, accordingly, uncertain of salvation; she was:

> but as if she had been . . . chosen to have been the aurora of a heavenly clime; and then suddenly she was one of whom, for some thousand years, Paradise had received no report; then, again, as if she entered the gates of Paradise not less innocent; and, again, as if she could not enter; and some blame – but I knew not what blame – was mine.   (J1: 20)

The anguish that adheres to her may finally be represented as the ambiguous suffering of one who is either the unwilling victim of a violation, or the reluctant or repentant participant in an act of mutual guilt: 'she looked as though . . . she sought to travel back to her early joy – yet no longer a joy that is sublime in innocency, but a joy from which sprung abysses of memories polluted into anguish' (J1: 21). [6]

No less alarming is the double vision of Agnes, wife of the first-person narrator of 'The Household Wreck'. When Agnes fails to return from the shopping trip which has led to her arrest, her husband waits for her on the high-road that stretches away to the city. What he sees there is described in terms which could hardly have been better chosen if the expressed intention of the passage were to illustrate the instability of identity in narrative, the slippages by which narrative functions and moral characteristics melt into each other:

> from occasional combinations of colour, modified by light and shade, and of course powerfully assisted by the creative state of the eye under this nervous apprehensiveness, I continued to shape into images of Agnes forms without end, that upon nearer approach presented the most grotesque contrasts to her impressive appearance . . . one deception melted away only to be succeeded by another.   (12: 177)

Whatever else it is, this ambiguity of appearance is an expression of the ambiguity of her husband's unwelcome, and, we are assured by the narrative, unfounded suspicions of her moral character. She has been accused of petty theft by a shopkeeper, name of Barratt, who had been importuning her for immoral purposes, and who, not unlike the mad dog at Greenhay, is finally killed by the righteous violence of a furious mob. Her husband cannot suppress the 'horrid thought' that Agnes may herself be responsible for her own 'pollution'; was she 'open to temptations of this nature?', he wonders, even before he hears of the attempts at seduction and imagines the case to be a simple matter of petty theft (12: 210–2, 216, 232).

Moreover, according to her husband's narrative, Agnes's own appearance is more than partly responsible for the alleged ambiguity of her character. For 'when you saw only her superb figure', and 'the measured dignity of her step, you might for a moment have fancied her some imperial Medea of the Athenian stage' – Medea, the tigress, the murderer of children, with whom a hated childhood nurse is compared in the narrative of the death of Elizabeth:

> But catch one glance from her angelic countenance, and then, combining the face and the person, you would have dismissed all such fancies, and have pronounced her a Pandora and an Eve, expressly accomplished and held forth by Nature as an exemplary model or ideal pattern for the future female sex.   (12: 165–6)

The suggestion that the ambiguity of Agnes's appearance will be resolved when we realise that she is not really like Medea at all, and that when her face and figure are seen together she is really like Pandora and Eve (of all women), has the effect of accentuating that ambiguity of her character. Officially, she has been framed by a conspiracy between the seducer and an evil nursery maid; unofficially, she is open to be seduced, like Eve; like Pandora, her very function is to bring down evil upon men. Agnes is an innocent wife, proof against all attempts to seduce her; she is a childlike mother; she is a seducer, her body a box of diseases, of the oriental fevers with which she infects her husband and her child; she is a tigress, murderer of children.

V

The woman as child-murderer is the subject of Tieck's complex Gothic narrative 'Liebeszauber', 'The Love-Charm', which De Quincey translated in 1825 with very little deviation or elaboration. Roderick and Emilius, close friends, are distinguished from each other rather as, in the 'Autobiography', the extrovert William is distinguished from the melancholic and lonely Thomas. Emilius is in love with a beautiful young woman to whom he has never spoken: he sees her only in the illuminated window opposite his own, as she teaches a young girl whom she has adopted to read, to sew, to knit. Though Emilius does not know it, his secret, unspoken love is reciprocated (12: 434–41).

One evening Roderick goes to a masked ball, dressed as a beturbaned Turk – though, as a precaution, he leaves in Emilius's room his Turkish dagger, for 'it is a bad habit,' he says, 'carrying about toys of cold steel: one can never tell what ill use may be made of them'. When Roderick has left, and on the off-chance that his unknown beloved will also be there, Emilius too decides to go to the ball. On his way there, as he pauses and rests within the doorway of a church, he sees what he believes at first is a fellow-masker, dressed in a scarlet bodice embroidered with gold, who has chosen to wear an especially tasteless mask. He soon realises, however, that it is 'an old woman of the utmost hideousness'. He overhears her plotting some appalling but unnamed piece of witchery with two mysterious men in cloaks, of whom we hear nothing more. As if to reassure himself that there is good as well as evil in the world, he turns to gaze at a sculpture of Mary and the infant Jesus which adorns the doorway of the church, and he reflects that the unseen love of God for his children is perfectly represented in the image of the mild and blessed Virgin embracing the child she loves.

When Emilius arrives at the ball, he looks round for his unknown mistress as much in fear as in hope, 'for the belief that her beloved face might perchance be lying hid beneath some odious mask was what he could not possibly bring himself to'. Disappointed or relieved at failing to find her, he leaves early, and has just finished composing some verses in his room when his beloved appears, in négligé, in the opposite window. She is lovelier than ever, he decides, with her hair loose, and her bosom uncovered – and yet she looks 'pale, frozen up . . . like a marble statue'. She is accompanied by the old woman in the scarlet bodice, and together they cut the child's throat. Emilius faints away (12: 440–51).

The rest of the story takes place on Emilius's wedding day, in the summer of the following year. We learn that he has only recently recovered from a 'violent nervous fever' which induced in him an entire forgetfulness: he has now remembered most, but not all, of his past. Virtually his first act, on recovering his senses, was to propose to a beautiful woman he sees sitting by the side of the road. There is a mystery too in this woman's past: a few years ago, it appears, she had taken 'a lovely little orphan child into her house, to educate her'; when the girl was seven years old, she was 'lost, during a walk through the town; and . . . nobody could ever find what became of her'. Since that time the woman has been enveloped in 'an air of silent melancholy' (12: 451–9).

As the evening falls, the bride – whose name, as De Quincey points out in a note, we never learn – withdraws to change into her ball-dress. '"She does not know", said Emilius to Roderick . . . "that I can pass from the next room into hers through a secret door; I will surprise her while she is dressing"'. He too withdraws, and in his absence Roderick and the other guests decide to mask themselves, and to proceed in a grotesquely jovial procession to the bridal chamber. Roderick himself chooses as his costume a dress with a scarlet bodice and gold embroidery, which his tailor recently purchased from 'an old crone'; as for his mask, it 'would melt even Medusa to a grin'. The maskers dance through the house in a wild train, upstairs, along the gallery, into one of the bedrooms. Suddenly, with a shriek, the bride rushes out from her bedroom, in négligé again, 'in a short white frock . . . with her lovely bosom all uncovered'. She is followed by Emilius, who, with the Turkish dagger that Roderick had long ago entrusted to his safe keeping, stabs her in the bosom and cuts her throat. An ugly old woman, one of the bride's attendants, grapples with Emilius; together they fall over the railing of the gallery and both are fatally injured. It emerges that Roderick, in the red bodice, had burst into the bride's room, where Emilius was 'playing with the dagger'. The sight of the red bodice had rekindled Emilius's memory of the crime. The old woman, before she dies, confesses everything (12: 459–63, 466).

It is the multiple image of femininity in this story that seems to demand most attention. Femininity is here a dangerous puzzle, a maze of mirrors with no centre, a face disguised by an unending series of masks. The destructive instability of the feminine can be settled, stabilised, only by being destroyed, but even in death it continues to destroy. The beauty of the young woman appears at first as the form of maternal virtue, but is then almost immediately revealed as the mask of maternal vice: we are early told that she felt herself capable of making any sacrifice to obtain Emilius's love, and she murders the child either, as the story's title suggests, as part of a witchcraft ritual, intended to charm Emilius into loving her, or perhaps (more prosaically) because the child is a bastard who must be got rid of if she is to represent herself as eligible for marriage. In short, the ambiguity of the young woman – object of pure delight, object of an illicit (because voyeuristic) desire for which her own beauty is to blame – is represented in the contrasted figures of the other two female characters: lovely, innocent childhood, hideous old age. She remains out of focus, nameless, explains De Quincey in a long note, so that 'there may be no distinct object for our disgust to fasten on'; her deep melancholy, he suggests, invites us to pity rather than to loathe her (12: 441, 466).

The men in the story are less sinister than the women, but are still sinister enough. The critical event that seems to precipitate what follows is the passing of the Turkish dagger from the beturbaned Roderick to Emilius, who, as he thereby takes on the phallic power of his friend, takes on, it seems, something he can neither use properly – it is a 'toy', something he 'plays' with – nor control. He takes on also a guilt which is indeterminately sexual and homicidal, or rather, perhaps, he takes on a sexual guilt which is redeemed by also being homicidal: for to kill a child-murdering woman is no doubt to be understood as an act of justifiable revenge. The double vision by which the ferocious character of William-the-Turk is taken on by a surrogate of Thomas is by now familiar enough. We should notice, however, how the vestiges of guilt cling to the William character; there is the ghost of a narrative which seems to be attempting to return to Roderick some of the guilt which, with the dagger, he had passed to Emilius. It is Roderick who (innocently enough, it seems) gives Emilius the murder weapon. Before he goes to the masked ball he borrows Emilius's cloak, in order (he explains) to cover his infidel Turkish dress while he listens to the music in a nearby church (12: 440); and it is outside this church that Emilius later hears the old woman conspiring with the two cloaked men. Roderick also suggests to a friend that Emilius should 'apply to an old woman, and make use of sympathetic cures' for his melancholy (12: 447); and, finally, it is the sight of Roderick, in the red bodice and the Medusa-like mask, in the same room as his half-naked wife, that recalls to Emilius's memory the scene of the forgotten murder – or, we might reflect, of a scene still more thoroughly forgotten.

More even than in the character of Emilius, De Quincey can surely be found in the act of looking at, of spying upon, of overhearing. As much as in the Turkish dagger, the guilt that circulates in this story seems to be found in the act of spying upon – from the opposite window, through the secret door – a woman who is half naked, and who is a mother, or who appears in the place of a mother. Until the very end of the story, this act is associated with Emilius, but in the last paragraph it moves across to belong with Roderick, when he bursts into the bride's room, to find her 'almost dressed', and Emilius 'playing with the dagger'. The guilt associated with spying upon the woman's nakedness can be returned to her only by making what she does, what she is *seen* to do, the occasion of the worst imaginable crime that De Quincey can imagine, the murder of a young girl. On both the occasions when she is discovered in a state of undress, her guilt is also discovered; De Quincey's diplopia sees to it that, as her body is exposed, so is her crime. The nameless bride in 'The Love-Charm' was the first of many women in De Quincey's writings to be exposed in that double sense.

8

The Plague of Cairo: and the Death of a Theory

Softly he stroked the child, who lay outstretched
With face to earth; and, as the boy turned round
His battered head, a groan the Sailor fetched
As if he saw – there and upon that ground –
Strange repetition of the deadly wound
He had himself inflicted. Through his brain
At once the griding iron passage found;
Deluge of tender thoughts then rushed amain,
Nor could his sunken eyes the starting tear restrain.
William Wordsworth, 'Guilt and Sorrow' 487–95.

On reaching the ruins I descended into the newly opened trench, and found the workmen. . . . They had uncovered the upper part of a figure, the remainder of which was still buried in the earth. . . . It was in admirable preservation. The expression was calm, yet majestic, and the outline of the features showed a freedom and knowledge of art, scarcely to be looked for in works of so remote a period. The cap had three horns, and, unlike that of the human-headed bulls hitherto found in Assyria, was rounded and without ornament at the top.

I was not surprised that the Arabs had been amazed and terrified at this apparition. It required no stretch of imagination to conjure up the most strange fancies. This gigantic head, blanched with age, thus rising from the bowels of the earth, might well have belonged to one of those fearful beings which are described in the traditions of the country as appearing to mortals, slowly ascending from the regions below.
Austen Henry Layard, *Nineveh and its Remains*, 1: 65–6.

I

In all De Quincey's writings, there is no more disturbing instance of double vision than his description of the nebula in Orion, in the essay 'System of the Heavens As Revealed by Lord Rosse's Telescopes' (8:

2 *The Discovery of the Gigantic Head*, from A.H. Layard, *Nineveh and its Remains*
(1849)

7–34). The description is of the nebula as it appears in a drawing
made by Sir John Herschel, illustrated in a book by De Quincey's
friend John Pringle Nichol, Professor of Astronomy at the University of Glasgow. The drawing shows the nebula as a gas or fluid
form, punctuated with a very few stars: as Nichol explains, the

nebula was not 'resolved' – not discovered to be composed of stars – until it had been examined by the huge telescope of Lord Rosse at Parsonstown in Ireland. Thereafter it was generally accepted that that the whole nebula consisted of stars, most of them too minute to be discerned individually, though nowadays the nebula is not thought to be stellar (Nichol 50–6; Herschel 610; Schaffer 139).

The essay begins with a playful discussion of the question of the age of the earth, a discussion which enables the oblique utterance of an ambiguity which, as we have already seen, is at the centre of De Quincey's myth of his childhood, and of its own central event: the experience, whatever it amounted to, in the bedroom of Elizabeth at Greenhay. The earth is described both as 'mother' earth, and as the 'sister' of the other planets; and these different ways of describing it are part of a series of verbal substitutions by which ambiguities of identity and character are rehearsed, under cover of an arch acknowledgement of the impropriety of inquiring too closely into a woman's age. The mother – as mature woman – and the sister – as little girl – are condensed into one, in such phrases as 'our dear little mother', or 'our mother Tellus is . . . a lovely little thing.' They are separated out again, by the question, 'Is she a child . . . or is she an adult', a question which has implications for the moral character of the earth as well as its age. De Quincey visualises 'her' successively as a 'spirited', 'sportive', but 'innocent girl' of 'the playful period of twelve or thirteen', as 'a fine noble young woman, . . . well able to take her own part, in case that . . . she should come across one of those vulgar fussy Comets disposed to be rude and take improper liberties', and as an old woman, 'decaying' or 'decayed'. These questions in turn are pushed aside as meaningless by the argument, for example, that even if we could compute the earth's age exactly, we would still have no way of deciding whether 'she' was young or old. But though these questions of age and moral character are thus tidied away to make room for the main business of the essay, the description of the Orion Nebula, they are destined to return, in all their untidiness, as that description proceeds (8: 8–12).[1]

Until he had seen Herschel's map of the Orion Nebula, De Quincey tells us, the most sublime object he had ever seen was the sculpture of the head of Memnon in the British Museum. This colossal bust, then generally referred to as the 'Younger Memnon', now as Rameses II, was brought to London from Egypt in 1818 (Figure 3). The sublime grandeur of Memnon's expression, and the silence of what seems his 'saintly trance', are symbolic, De Quincey suggests, of the divine peace, of eternity, and of diffusive love. The no less sublime image of the nebula in Orion, the 'dreadful cartoon' which De Quincey describes as the pendant of the Memnon (Figure 4), is in every way its opposite: it is 'frightful' in its magnitude and its

3 Rameses II (the 'Younger Memnon').

depth; the silence which emanates from it is also the silence of eternity, but it comes 'from the frost and from the eternities of death' (8: 17)

The invocation of Memnon returns us immediately to the bedroom of the dead Elizabeth, and to the 'experience' there, which De Quincey had first described in 'Suspiria', written a year before 'System of the Heavens'. As he stood looking at Elizabeth's body, he heard 'a solemn', 'mournful', 'Memnonian' wind. In the reworking and annotating of this passage in the 'Autobiography', he mistakenly identifies the Younger Memnon with another colossal statue at Egyptian Thebes – the 'vocal', the 'melodious' Memnon' – which emitted at sunrise, as the sun warmed the air within 'certain cavities in the bust', 'a solemn and dirge-like series of intonations'.[2] The passage in 'Suspiria' continues by rehearsing the terms which would come to be applied to the bust in the British Museum: the sound of the wind is 'saintly'; it is 'in this world the one sole *audible* symbol of eternity'. And this mournful sound precipitated in De Quincey an appropriately Memnonian trance, in which he hears something, and sees something. What he hears is another oriental wind, 'some Sarsar wind of death', associated with 'frost, gathering frost'. A *çarçar* is the Arabic name for a cold wind, and here it seems to stand in the same relation to the saintly sound of the 'Memnonian' wind as the deathlike silence emanating from the Orion Nebula stood in relation to the saintly silence of the head of the Younger Memnon (Lindsay 79–85, M. Russell, 213–21; 1985 105–6; 1: 41–2).

What he sees is a 'vault' which 'seemed to open in the zenith of the far blue sky, a shaft which seemed to run up for ever . . . to pursue the throne of God', a throne that 'fled away continually'. In the version in 'Suspiria', an apostrophe follows, omitted from the later 'Autobiography', and beginning 'Oh flight of the solitary child to the solitary God – flight from the ruined corpse to the throne that could not be ruined!' The trance is then broken, and there follow the kiss, the footfall, and the hurried exit (1985 105–7). It is, I begin to think, to this trance that we should look, more than to the kiss that followed, if we want to understand the meanings that De Quincey's writings ascribe to the bedroom scene. And it is what De Quincey saw, or believes or imagines or even forgot he saw, in this trance, that is rediscovered in the terrifying image of the Orion Nebula.

The recent observations of nebulae by Lord Rosse were described by Nichol as the acts of an instrument of remarkable 'space-penetrating power'. He had recounted, with what is best described as mounting excitement, how the frigid nebula, confronted with an 18-inch mirror, a 10-foot telescope, even a 3-foot mirror, had obstinately chosen to remain an unresolved and shapeless mist,

Finally, however, it had surrendered to Lord Rosse's new instrument, 'a tube', as Nichol described it, rather breathlessly – for these are the last phrases of a sentence 225 words long – 'whose vast eye is SIX FEET in DIAMETER!' At last we can contemplate the nebula 'in its unveiled magnificence' (Nichol 51–5, 6).[3] De Quincey's account, though less preoccupied with instrument size than Nichol's, takes on a tone no less lubricious and violent. The process of resolving the nebula has been an act of penetration, of intrusion and violation by an instrument of extraordinary power. The nebula in Orion had 'resisted all approaches from the most potent of former telescopes'; finally, it has been 'forced' to show itself, it has been 'unmasked'. The new observations of the nebula constitute an 'exposure', and one no less appalling, De Quincey assures us, than the 'exposure' in *Paradise Lost* of 'Milton's "incestuous mother", with her fleshless son and with the warrior angel, his father' (8: 14–18). The 'incestuous mother' in question, of course, who also appears to De Quincey in the last opium dream described in the *Opium-Eater* (3: 446), is Sin, the daughter as well as the lover of Satan. But in 'System of the Heavens', the nebula is apparently an image both of the mother herself and of a scene in which mother, son and father all participate, and the incest may equally as well be between the mother and Death, her son by Satan.

The nebular hypothesis, which had been 'made' in the 1830s and fathered on Laplace and William Herschel, has been summarised by Simon Schaffer in an excellent essay on John Pringle Nichol, the most influential of its expositors (Schaffer 134–5). 'In its simpler versions,' writes Schaffer,

> the nebular hypothesis was taken as giving an astronomically proper account of the origin of the Solar System through the action of natural law upon a condensing and rotating gaseous nebula of gravitating matter. It was claimed that as this cloud contracted, rings of matter would be precipitated into space at regular intervals. Each ring would then make a planet. The central condensed clouds produced the Sun.   (Schaffer 132)

In short, the hypothesis represented nebulae as the places of original 'cosmogony', where gas or fluid condensed into solid stars and planets. It may be that most primal scene of all, therefore, that De Quincey is figuring in the form of the original act of incest described in *Paradise Lost*.

The elaborate description he offers, 'of the Nebula in Orion, as forced to show out by Lord Rosse', needs to be quoted at length; it will avoid confusion if I explain that he is describing the drawing by

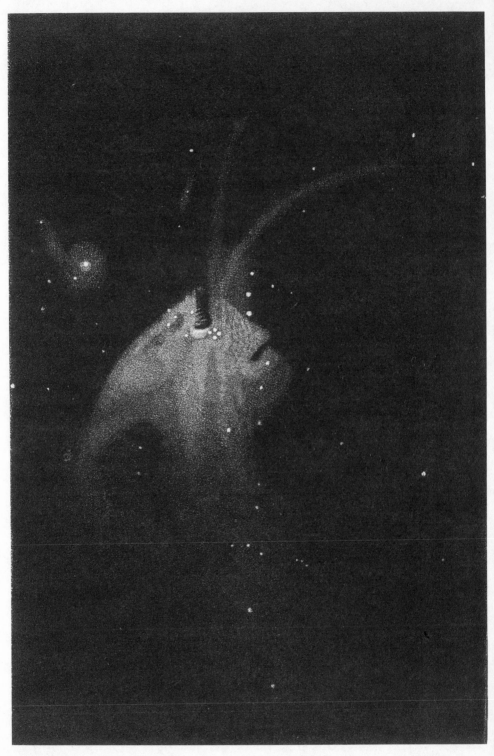

4 The Nebula in Orion, from J.P. Nichol, *Thoughts on . . . the System of the World* (1846).

Sir John Herschel, and refers to the later observations by Rosse only at the end of the paragraph.

> You see a head thrown back, and raising its face (or eyes, if eyes it had) in the very anguish of hatred to some unknown heavens. What *should* be its skull wears what *might* be an Assyrian tiara, only ending behind in a floating train. This head rests upon a beautifully developed neck and throat.... The mouth ... is amply developed. Brutalities unspeakable sit upon the upper lip, which is confluent with a snout; for separate nostrils there are none. Were it not for this one defect of nostrils, and even in spite of this defect ... one is reminded by the phantom's attitude of a passage, ever memorable, in Milton: that passage, I mean, where Death first becomes aware, soon after the original trespass, of his own future empire over man. The 'meagre shadow' even smiles ... [De Quincey quotes, as illustrating 'the attitude of the phantom in Orion', *Paradise Lost* Book 10: 267–8, 272–81]. But the lower lip, which is drawn inwards with the curve of a marine shell – oh, what a convolute of cruelty and revenge is *there*! Cruelty! – to whom? Revenge! – for what? Pause not to ask; but look upwards to other mysteries. In the very region of his temples, driving itself downwards into his cruel brain, and breaking the continuity of his diadem, is a horrid chasm, a ravine, a shaft, that many centuries would not traverse; and it is serrated on its posterior wall with a harrow that is partly hidden. From the anterior wall of this chasm rise, in vertical directions, two processes: one perpendicular and rigid as a horn, the other streaming forward before some portentous breath ... one is inclined to regard them as the plumes of a sultan. Dressed he is, therefore, as well as armed. And finally comes Lord Rosse, that glorifies him with the jewellery of stars: he is now a vision 'to dream of, not to tell': he is ready for the worship of those that are tormented in sleep: and the stages of his solemn uncovering by astronomy, first by Sir W. Herschel, secondly by his son, and finally by Lord Rosse, is like the reversing of some heavenly doom, like the raising one after another of the seals that had been sealed by the Angel in the Revelation.   (8: 18–21)

This description owes something to Nichol, who had referred to the nebula as possessed of a horn, a mouth, and of branching arms; and a later description by Sir John Herschel in turn owes something to De Quincey's – the 'brightest portion' of the nebula, he writes, 'offers a resemblance to the head and yawning jaws of some monstrous animal, with a sort of proboscis running out from the snout'. But however well established the practice of seeing in nebulae the shapes of humans and animals may have become, De Quincey's description was recognised, by Nichol among others, as unusually elaborate, excessive, over the top. For De Quincey appears to have seen some very particular shape indeed in the nebula, which seems to take on the characteristics, at one time or another, of the various characters from the myth of De Quincey's childhood. For example, we can discover William in the general ferocity and bellicosity of the head, but also in the fact that it is now the head of Death, the son of Sin, rather than of Sin herself. In particular, of course, the description of the excrescences that protrude from the head like 'the plumes of a Sultan' – like the plumes that would decorate the turban of a Sultan – is reminiscent of William in his role as the fierce beturbaned mass-murderer Sultan Amurath in the nursery at Greenhay. There is also a layer of mythological meaning which may be relevant here. Memnon was the son of Eos, or Aurora, who though married to Tithonus had a taste for carrying off young men of notable beauty, among them Orion. Thus Aurora, who elsewhere is a figure for Elizabeth (see above, p.35), can stand in relation to Memnon indifferentiably as mother or sister, but in the youthful Orion we can discover the younger of those two characters in De Quincey's personal mythology, William and the Bengal uncle, who appear as intruders upon his relationship with the female members of his family (8: 19n.; Nichol 51–6; Herschel 609; L360).

But as soon as we imagine those plumes as ornaments of a turban, then the nebula, in spite of his biological sex, can become a surrogate of Elizabeth as well, and more particularly of the 'ruined corpse', lying on her bed: – the head thrown back in a hatred that is also 'anguished'; her neck and throat 'beautiful'; her skull no skull, but what '*should*' be one, wearing what '*might*' be 'an Assyrian tiara' – a '*tiara* of light' had seemed to crown the 'ample brow' of Elizabeth.[4] And 'breaking the continuity' of that tiara, that 'diadem', 'driving itself downwards into his cruel brain', is the 'horrid chasm' which becomes, in turn, a 'ravine', a 'shaft', the same shaft, apparently, as appeared in the Memnonian trance of 'Suspiria'; the same 'abysses of memories polluted into anguish' in 'Who is this Woman'; even the same 'chasms and sunless abysses' into which De Quincey 'seemed every night to descend' in his opium dreams (3: 435). What De Quincey saw, of thought he saw, or imagined himself as seeing, in that bedroom trance, this passage suggests, was the dissected head of Elizabeth, her turban of bandages failing to hide her wound.

The 'serrated harrow' may be a memory of the instrument used in the operation, and I do not point that out as a mere matter of curiosity. When De Quincey suffered his first hydrocephalus scare (and recovered from it in the identity if 'Tabitha') the surgeon attending him had used 'an awful word' – had 'talked of trepanning'. When the enraged 'mob' takes its revenge on Barratt, the attempted seducer of Agnes in 'The Household Wreck', he manages before he dies to give a list of those whom he had trepanned, and had failed to 'trepan . . . into the sacrifice of their honour' (1: 159; 12: 233). To 'trepan' means both to 'entrap', and 'to operate upon with a trepan', 'a trepan' was a saw, a serrated blade, used in dissections of the skull, and this is not the last time we will come across what may be a play upon these two meanings. The association in the novella between trepanning and the 'sacrifice' of honour by a willingness to be seduced may suggest a link between the ruining of Elizabeth's body and its pollution, the imagined ruining of her reputation.

It is this image, this portrait head, which De Quincey proposes as the pendant of the colossal bust of the Younger Memnon; as the extreme of the sublime of terror, as the bust is an extreme of the religious sublime. Both images, of course, are represented as oriental – the Memnon as Egyptian, the nebula as Assyrian, and as a sultan – and both are in that sense images of what is other to De Quincey, who appears in this essay in the character of an amateur of western science and philosophy. The two images, I suggest, have entered the essay as a linked pair, in the same way as the Memnonian and the 'Sarsar' winds were paired in 'Suspiria', and together they are participating in another example of a 'this/that/the other' strategy. The comparison of the two heads involves an attempt to make safe, to domesticate the image of Memnon, by simultaneously invoking and opposing to it the appalling image of the nebula, represented as absolutely other. There is something, I am therefore suggesting, that is represented for De Quincey by the bust, which is utterly terrifying, and which can be made safe only by acknowledging the terror it inspires, and by simultaneously projecting it outside the domestic space, and into the outer space inhabited by the nebula.

To understand what the nature of this terror might be, we need to return yet again to the bedroom. In 'Suspiria', Thomas hears the Memnonian wind at a very specific moment in the narrative. He has entered the room; has looked for his sister's bed; has seen the tropical sun shining through the window. He then turns to look at the body, rehearsing, as he does so, the questions he hopes will be answered by his inspection of it. Had the features 'suffered any change'?

> The forehead, indeed, the serene and noble forehead, *that* might be the same; but the frozen eyelids, the darkness that seemed to steal from beneath them, the marble lips, the stiffening hands, laid palm to palm . . . could these be mistaken for life? Had it been so,

wherefore did I not spring to those heavenly lips with tears and
never-ending kisses? but so it was *not*. I stood checked for a
moment; awe, not fear, fell upon me; and, whilst I stood, a solemn
wind began to blow.   (1985 105)

He hears the Memnonian wind at exactly the point when, having
steeled himself to expect to see a change everywhere except in
Elizabeth's forehead, he turns to look at her, and finds that he cannot
kiss her. When De Quincey examined the bust of the Younger
Memnon in the British Museum, he would have noticed two things
about it in particular, neither of which he mentions. Just below its
right shoulder there is a deep hole, supposed to have been made by
the French of the Napoleonic survey, who had apparently attempted
to divide the bust into pieces for greater ease of transportation (James
9–10); it may have been this hole that led De Quincey to believe that
the Younger Memnon was the 'melodious' statue which produced
music from 'certain cavities in the bust' (1: 41n.). Secondly, a large
section of the apparently beturbaned head, from the right temple to
the crown,. is missing. It is by virtue of the wound in her own
forehead, itself never directly spoken of by De Quincey, that
Elizabeth can be refigured as the Orion Nebula, ugly, brutal,
vengeful. But the chasm in the head of the Orion Nebula has its
counterpart in the stone head of Memnon, so that by virtue of the
same wound as makes her an object of terror, Elizabeth can bring to
mind the statue of Memnon, can be figured as Memnon, and can be
imagined as taking on the peaceful, loving and saintly character of
the statue. The bust of Memnon becomes reminiscent of another of
Elizabeth's surrogates, the *Mater Suspiriorum* in the prose fantasy
'Levana and Our Ladies of Sorrow', a woman 'humble to abject-
ness', the visitor of the Pariah, the Jew, the slave and the prisoner.
She wears 'a dilapidated turban' (like bandages coming loose?) –
literally, a turban whose stones are crumbling or missing (13:
366–7).

Through all this, however, the nebula in Orion, ambiguously a
surrogate of William and of Elizabeth, can be a surrogate of the
mother too. One of Orion's mythological attributes is the lion's
skin, which, together with the language of unmasking, exposing,
and the terrifying aspect of the nebula, may relate the nebula to the
involute connecting the mother, lion and Sphinx that we discovered
in Chapter 6. The last lines of the description of the nebula revert to
the notion of the exposure of an evil mother first suggested in the
quotation from Milton, when the nebula, masculine though he has
become, is finally described as 'a vision "to dream of, not to tell"' –
the phrase is borrowed from Coleridge's 'Christabel', and refers to

the evil 'lady Geraldine' who is threatening in the poem to usurp the place of Christabel's dead mother.[5] The 'vision' in question is the sight of Geraldine half naked, as, watched by Christabel, she undresses for bed. Once again the nebula is subjected to an 'uncovering' at the hands of astronomy, and once again the sight is terrifying. And once again, the exposure of the body of the woman involves the exposure of a crime for which she is held responsible. In this essay there is a double exposure, of the nebula itself, and of the theory of its composition, and both were figured by De Quincey in the form of a woman's body. 'Dr Nichol,' he wrote in a letter of 1846 to his daughter Margaret, 'has destroyed – utterly without mercy cut the lovely throat of – the *Nebular Hypothesis*' (P1: 336).

In fact, though Nichol accepted that the Orion Nebula had been resolved, his faith in the existence of 'truly nebular fluid' and in the correctness of the nebular hypothesis remained unshaken. Nor does De Quincey himself appear to have regarded the hypothesis as entirely disposed of by Rosse's observations. And in his way of looking at things, the fact that Nichol 'cut the throat' of the hypothesis may be a guarantee of the depth of his attachment to it: in one of his autobiographical sketches De Quincey claims that it is a mark of a man 'desperately in love' – 'in love, that is to say, to a terrific excess' – that he would 'dally . . . with the thoughts of cutting his own throat, or even (as the case might be) the throat of her whom he loved above all the world' (Schaffer 141–2; 8: 30; 1: 174).

II

At this point I want to introduce a third portrait into the gallery, 'the horrifying decapitated head of Medusa', as it was described by Freud in his short paper of 1922, 'Medusa's Head'. According to Freud, 'to decapitate = to castrate', and

> the terror of the Medusa is thus a terror of castration that is linked to the sight of something. Numerous analyses have made us familiar with the occasion for this: it occurs when a boy, who has hitherto been unwilling to believe the threat of castration, catches sight of the female genitals, probably those of an adult, surrounded by hair, and essentially those of his mother.
>
> (XVIII: 273)

One place where this catching sight of may be imagined as having occurred is in the fantasised primal scene. It was (so he came to believe) in observing his parents' intercourse that the 'Wolf Man' was brought face to face, so to speak, with 'the reality of castration . . . for now he saw with his own eyes the wound of which his Nanya [his nurse] had spoken'. What is staged in the primal fantasy, and in the discovery of the 'reality' of castration, is also the discovery of sexual difference, understood as a difference between those who have managed to keep the penis, and those who have only a wound where the penis once was, and now display, like the Medusa's head, 'the terrifying genitals of the mother' (XVII: 45–6; XVIII: 274)

The head of the Medusa thus belongs with the Younger Memnon and the Orion Nebula, by virtue of the wound which it both represents and displays. The juxtaposition of the three suggests that the confusion of identity generated by the bedroom scene, the confusion between mother and sister, so elaborately recapitulated at the beginning of 'System of the Heavens' in the discussion of the earth's age, may be a confusion also between the two different wounds by which each may be imagined as identified. In the myth of De Quincey's childhood, the narrative of the primal fantasy – the narrative which every child must put inside its head if it is to come to know its sexual origins and its sexual destiny – may have become overprinted and confused with the narrative of a different wounding. The 'vault', the 'shaft' which De Quincey describes as appearing to him in the trance before the kiss may thus be understood as the wound in Elizabeth's head or as the vagina of the mother; the serrated wound in the skull of the nebula becomes also a *vagina dentata*; and the image of the bandaged Elizabeth, whose appearance repels De Quincey from kissing her, is now inseparable from the image of a woman 'who is unapproachable and repels all sexual desires', because, like Athene with her aegis, she displays 'the terrifying genitals of the mother'. These identifications seem to confirm and to make sense of De Quincey's own remark, in 'System of the Heavens', that the 'exposure' of Milton's ' "incestuous mother" ' would have been 'essentially the same exposure' as the unmasking of the nebula, with its dreadful head wound.

There are other moments too, in De Quincey's writings, where his text seems to point to a similar identification of wound and wound. In the dream essay 'The Daughter of Lebanon', for example, discussed in Chapter 3, it seems to be pointed to, literally, by the evangelist who has taken it upon himself to restore the 'ruined' daughter of Lebanon to her father's house. As the reformed prostitute lay on her deathbed, suffering from the feverish symptoms which attend hydrocephalus, the evangelist 'raised his pastoral staff, and, pointing it to her temples, rebuked the clouds, and bade that no more should they trouble her vision'. A page later 'he raised his pastoral staff' once more, and pointed it to the sky, which parted to reveal an 'infinite chasm'. There follows a scene which is both a love-making and a death, in which, 'in rapture', the Daughter of Lebanon

> soared upwards from her couch; immediately in weakness she fell back; and, being caught by the evangelist, she flung her arms around his neck; whilst he breathed into her ear his final whisper, 'Wilt thou now suffer that God should give by seeming to refuse?' – 'Oh yes – yes – yes',was the fervent answer from the Daughter of Lebanon.

and those are her last words, before she falls back dead (3: 454–5).

We have already glanced at the moment in 'The English Mail-Coach' which describes 'the far-off sound of a wheel' as 'a whisper . . . secretly announcing a ruin that, being foreseen, was not the less inevitable; that, being known, was not therefore healed'. The 'ruin' here is again a wound, foreseen (and therefore seen in the imagination), and apparently impossible to heal. It is a ruin that will occur unless De Quincey can 'seize the reins from the grasp of the slumbering coachman', whose hand, however, 'was viced between his upper and lower thigh'. The wound that will be suffered by the girl in the reedy gig seems at this point in the narrative to be fantasised as an irreparable sexual wounding – as something that can be prevented only if De Quincey can take control of what is clamped between the coachman's thighs, and this, he tells us, was 'impossible'. The story of the mail-coach and the fragile gig can thus perhaps be read as the story of a doomed attempt to prevent the act or the event which produces sexual difference or the knowledge of it, and which produces therefore the image of woman as monster. In the subsequent dream fugue, however, the danger that threatens the girl in the reedy gig – or the generalised girl that takes her place in the narrative – is envisaged as a danger to her head and to her arm. De Quincey imagines her sinking into a quicksand.[6] He watches until, first, 'only the fair young head and the diadem of white roses around it were still visible to the pitying heavens; and, last of all, was visible one white marble arm' (13: 312–3; 321)

We have met this disembodied arm earlier in 'The English Mail-Coach', in the story De Quincey discovered in Humboldt, of the Indian girl who struggled with a crocodile and lost 'the lower portion of her left arm'. The story is, literally, of a disarming, of a dismemberment – of a wounding by which the girl may become the very monster that she is trying to escape. In the story of Fanny, 'the granddaughter of a crocodile', which may have developed from Humboldt's anecdote, the severed arm and hand themselves take on an independent existence as the place and indicator of the 'unutterable horrors of monstrous and demoniac natures' that the beautiful

Fanny evokes. The vision of those 'wild semi-legendary animals –
griffins, dragons, basilisks, sphinxes' appeared to De Quincey in the
form of a 'towering armorial shield', with

> as a surmounting crest, one fair female hand, with the fore-finger
> pointing, in sweet, sorrowful admonition, upwards to heaven,
> and having power . . . to awaken the pathos that kills in the very
> bosom of the horrors that madden the grief that gnaws at the
> heart, together with the monstrous creations of darkness that
> shock the belief, and make dizzy the reason of man.   (13: 290n.)[7]

The severed arm here seems to function as an image in which are
condensed the wounded head and the wounded genitals: it is at once
the 'crest', and it is what becomes disembodied when we are
'disarmed'.

In the dream fugue which concludes 'The English Mail-Coach',
these terrifying images of monstrous creations no longer take the
form of griffins or basilisks: they are to be found in the ruined
woman herself, in the form of a female child who returns from the
dead as woman. The fugue opens with the image of 'woman
bursting her sepulchral bonds' – a vision described as 'too fearful for
shuddering humanity on the brink of almighty abysses! – vision that
didst start back, that didst reel away, like a shrivelling scroll'. The
story which follows, of the child disappearing beneath the quicksand, is answered a few pages later by another image of resurrection,
the child now 'grown up to woman's height' and rising like a martyr
in her bloody and crimson robes: 'clinging to the horns of the altar,
voiceless she stood – sinking, rising, raving, despairing; and
behind . . . dimly was seen . . . the shadow of that dreadful being
who should have baptised her with the baptism of death'. These
resurrections, it seems, repair nothing: the girl who died *should have*
stayed dead; risen from the grave, a mature and terrifying woman,
her dismemberment, her irreparable wound, simultaneously
announces her as female and questions the manhood of De Quincey.
No wonder then that the resurrection envisaged for sisters that die,
in this text as in 'The Daughter of Lebanon', is absolutely not a
coming back to life. At the end of the dream fugue God is asked to
'snatch' the girl in the reedy gig – now De Quincey's 'sister
unknown' – from 'ruin'; from the ruin of the collision, of course,
between mail-coach and gig, but perhaps also from the ruin of
castration, and from the loss of innocence it entails; and when God
promises her eternal life, he is also promising her (to the relief of
those who have not died) eternal death (13: 318–9, 325–7)

But the argument of Freud's brief essay on the Medusa's head is
more complex than I have so far pointed out. If the boy child can be

imagined as shrivelling or shrinking in fear from the sight of what is symbolised in the head of the Medusa, that sight also makes him 'stiff with terror, turns him to stone'; at the very moment that he discovers the possibility of losing the penis he becomes aware that he is still in possession of it, 'and the stiffening reassures him of the fact' (XVIII: 273). The vision of the disembodied arm as 'surmounting crest' may thus be recounted as much in triumph as in fear, and it is certainly triumph which predominates in what may be a more elaborate, and a much more disturbing, instance of the identification of wound and wound, in the chapter of the 'Autobiography' which deals with De Quincey's childhood reading. He has offered to give an example, from among the books he read when a child, of the special ability he claims to have had for 'evoking the spiritual echo' which may be 'lurking' in the 'recesses' of a word or sentence (1: 124). The first such case of what he calls this 'colossal sublimity' is from Phaedrus, who wrote fables in the manner of Aesop; and the language of De Quincey's account of it is so charged as to need quoting verbatim. Phaedrus was a slave, and 'naturally', therefore, he

> towered into enthusiasm when he had occasion to mention that . . . the Athenians had raised a mighty statue to one who belonged to the same class in a social sense as himself . . . and rose above that class by . . . intellectual power. . . . These were the two lines in which that glory of the sublime, so stirring to my childish sense, seemed to burn as in some mighty pharos: –

> > "Aesopo statuam ingentem posuere Attici;
> > Servumque collocârunt eternâ in basi":

> *A colossal statue did the Athenians raise to Aesop; and a poor pariah slave they planted upon an everlasting pedestal.* I have not scrupled to introduce the word *pariah*, because in that way only could I decipher to the reader by what particular avenue it was that the sublimity which I fancy in the passage reached my heart. This sublimity originated in the awful chasm, in the abyss that no eye could bridge, between the pollution of slavery – the being a man, yet without right or lawful power belonging to a man – between this unutterable degradation and the starry altitude of the slave at that moment when, upon the unveiling of his everlasting statue, all the armies of the earth might be conceived as presenting arms to the emancipated man, the cymbals and kettle-drums of kings as drowning the whispers of his ignominy, and the harps of all his sisters that wept over slavery yet joining in one choral gratulation of the regenerated slave. I assign the elements of what I did in

> reality feel at that time, which to the reader may seem extravagant, and by no means of what it was reasonable to feel.   (1: 125–6)

Crucial to what I take to be the submerged argument of this passage is the connection between the fact that a slave, when emancipated, is made a 'man', and has the right to bear arms, and the notion that the boy child too becomes a man when he recognises himself as potent, as 'armed', in contradistinction to the class of castrated females. De Quincey, it will be recalled, felt 'disarmed', experienced a 'languishing impotence' in the lion dream, in which he imagined himself as failing to rescue a fellow-creature from death; in the story of the lion hunt from the *Westmorland Gazette*, the beturbaned man attacked by the lioness was 'unable to discharge his piece' before the beast had 'him thrown down and got him completely under her' (see p.78). The ceremony of the 'arming' of the slave and pariah in this passage can be read as a narrative which tries to repair the lion dream and the defeat by the lioness, and which, like the cymbals and kettle-drums that accompany the ceremony, attempts to drown 'the whispers of his ignominy'. De Quincey himself vicariously 'towers' with the slave Phaedrus, as they both contemplate the recognition of a fellow-pariah as, truly, a 'man', the recognition made visible by the 'colossal statue' that is 'raised' to his memory. But this colossus, this tower, this 'pharos' or lighthouse makes him a man only by contrast with the opposing images of the 'awful chasm' and the unbridgeable 'abyss', in which the 'sublimity' De Quincey speaks of, evidently a thoroughly phallic grandeur, is said to have originated. In the context of the language of pollution, of pariahs, of whispers of shame – the language in which his guilty memories of the bedroom scene find expression – this abyss seems to function ambiguously once again as the wound caused by dissection and by castration, imagined in relation and contrast to its triumphant opposite, the erect penis. The passage seems to echo the juxtaposition, in the image of the Orion Nebula, of the 'rigid' and 'perpendicular' horn and the deep wound, as if both passages are figurings of a scene of sexual difference and its discovery.

The couplet by Phaedrus, De Quincey writes, would be 'emasculated' if its opening were less 'all-pompous'; certainly it is the occasion for an urgent assertion of masculinity on the part of De Quincey. The couplet gave him, he claims, his 'first grand and jubilant sense' of the 'immeasurableness of the moral sublime', and of the sublime evoked, as it frequently is from Burke onwards, as a power almost undisguisedly phallic.[8] The statue raised to Aesop is another and a different pendant to the statue of the Younger Memnon; and the exaltation and celebration of Elizabeth's saintly virtues that was enabled by associating her with that statue has turned out to be rather an exaltation of the phallic power of Thomas, fantasised in the most brutal form. A more unambiguous example of the aggression that must always have been involved in the Victorian desire to 'put women on a pedestal' could hardly, or so I hope, be imagined; it is not hard to sympathise with the expression of embarrassment, almost of apology, with which the passage ends (1: 125–7).

This aggression against Elizabeth and her surrogates, and the desire to perform an act of sexual violence against them, is still more explicit in another story of an emancipated slave in the reign of the emperor Commodus, derived from Herodian, and included in the 'Introduction' to De Quincey's sequence of essays on the Caesars. The slave in question, a man of 'noble qualities, and of magnificent person', had liberated himself, and had devoted his life to avenging himself on the inhabitants of the place of his slavery, somewhere in Transylvania. Outlawed by an imperial edict, he and his men resolved to make their way separately and secretly to the emperor's palace at Rome, where they intended to 'penetrate' into 'the inmost recesses of his . . . consecrated bed-chamber – and there to lodge a dagger in his heart'. Commodus was delivered at the last minute from 'the uplifted daggers' of his would-be murderers; but though the attempt failed, De Quincey declares himself unable to find words to express his admiration for the 'energetic hardihood' of the slave. He delights in the manificent irony whereby Commodus, busy with imperial politics, and 'watching some potent rebel of the Orient at a distance of two thousand leagues, . . . overlooks the dagger which is within three stealthy steps, and one tiger's leap, of his own heart'. The slave – a tiger from Transylvania – is apparently a type of William, the King of Tigrosylvania; but the fantasy is of the slave, of the pariah, of Thomas, taking on the identity, the arms, and the potency of his brother, and himself doing that violent and dirty deed, in the 'recesses' of a bedroom, which William the tiger had done (6: 238–40).

III

Throughout this chapter we seem to have been dealing with a 'this/that/the other' strategy, in which the oriental or orientalised images of Memnon and the Orion Nebula are so organised as to enable distinctions to be made, and a line of defence to be marked out, between different aspects of the common meanings attached to them both. One such meaning is the Orient itself: Egypt, or rather ancient Egypt, the terrain of western scientific archaeology, as against the melodramatic image of the plumed sultan, Amurath or Tipu, or as against Assyria, a land more hostile, more remote than Egypt, and whose capital Nineveh had only just been (mistakenly) located in 1846 (the year of the original publication of 'System of the Heavens') on the eastern side – the *other* side – of the Tigris. Another such meaning may be Death, imagined (as so often) as an alien, an oriental event: the opposition of the Younger Memnon and the nebula may be read as a new version of the opposition in 'Suspiria' between the two winds, Memnonian and *çarçar*, both winds of death, but one ancient Egyptian, the other modern Arabic. And as I argued in my introduction, these orientalised images and images of the Orient may also be the location of a displaced politics of class. These phrases in the description of the nebula – 'You see a head thrown back'; 'Revenge! – for what?' – recall a similar pair of phrases in De Quincey's denunciation of the Reform Bill, 'On the Approaching Revolution in Great Britain'. The class of petty shopkeepers, he writes there, will use the opportunity of the passing of the bill to exact a terrible revenge on the aristocracy: ' . . . revenge! for what? My friend, throw your eyes back . . . ' (B30 1831 323).

The echo of that article of 1831, in the description of the nebula in Orion, suggests an archaeology whereby the exacavation of a racial fear may reveal a class fear, or vice versa – strata of anxiety which in turn conceal, or are concealed by, a sexual fear. For no less evidently, the opposition between the damaged head of Memnon (nowhere represented by De Quincey as damaged), and the wounded skull of the nebula, engenders two different images of the body of the woman. The stone lips of Memnon recall the 'marble' lips of Elizabeth's corpse, or of that corpse before Thomas came too close: they are no longer flesh, and belong, as it were, to a 'spiritual body'. The nebula in Orion is an image of the woman as irredeemably and absolutely other, threatening, inhuman, monstrous, by a wound which has literally *disfigured* her – has left its terrible mark on her face, so that the lips are the place of 'brutalities unspeakable', of 'cruelty and revenge', utterly unapproachable and repellent. This opposition recalls Harriet Martineau's account of the Sphinx which stands as the epigraph to Chapter 6: at distance, a rock; from close to, a nightmare, a veritable Medusa's head, wounded, and turning the spectator to stone. A similar opposition occurs everywhere in the texts by De Quincey we have been reading. It is used to distinguish *that* Elizabeth (seen from across the room) from the *other* Elizabeth (seen from close to); or Elizabeth from the mother; or Antigone from Medea; or the pure beauty of the foster-mother in 'The Love-Charm' from her accomplice in crime, the scarlet old woman aptly impersonated by Roderick in a mask that would 'melt even the

Medusa to a grin'; or the sweet, motherly, 'madonna countenance' of the Manchester portrait from the 'Medusa's head' attributed by De Quincey to the murderer Williams – displaced on to him, it might seem, as, bending over the body of a young mother, he was secretly observed by the petrified young journeyman.

But wherever the opposition appears, and however it functions, it is intrinsically unstable. The distinction between the bust of Memnon and the nebula can be compared, up to a point, with the distinction made by Bakhtin, between the 'classical body' and the 'grotesque body'. The first is a bourgeois ideal, the representation of the body as perfect, smooth, unyielding, and – especially – as sealed, impermeable, *homo clausus*, in Norbert Elias's exact phrase. The second is a phenomenon of popular life (or constructed as such in the bourgeois imagination), an image of the body as fleshy, obese, and *open*, its multiple orifices at once the source of its multiple pleasures and of the disgust it causes in the bourgeois. The distinction is almost perfectly replicated by the contrast between the stoniness of Memnon, whose lips are sealed, and the nebulousness of the nebula, multiply fissured, infinitely permeable and penetrable (especially by Lord Rosse's 'instrument'), its mouth cracked open, its orifices disfigured from pathways of pleasure into holes of horror. The crucial point where the distinction falls short of Bakhtin's, however, is the very point which made the statue of Memnon a fit emblem for the female body in general, and for the body of Elizabeth in particular: the missing section of the head, including the right temple. If we add that missing fragment to De Quincey's text, the opposition of statue and nebula, classical and grotesque becomes a distinction without a difference, which conjures two bodies, both wounded, both open, out of the *same* body. What makes the body of the woman safe, or at least serves to control her – her supposed castration – is precisely what makes it terrifying. It is the impossibility of making the distinction which produces the continual need – and the continual failure – to do so (Bakhtin 18–30, Elias 249–63).

We are dealing with one of the classical stereotypes of femininity, as that which is transcendent and/or most abject: femininity as in the heavens or in the deepest abysm, or femininity as simultaneously heavenly *and* abysmal – it does not matter which, so long as the dualism is somewhere preserved. And in so far as so many of De Quincey's stories seem to gravitate towards this most predictable and banal of images of woman, the sequence of what I have described so far might be seen, once again, in another light. For it is one of the attested responses to the problem of sexual difference that the woman, either fetishised as perfect or slandered as base, has to be endlessly punished for what the boy thinks he has discovered in her. In this case, the whole narrative of Elizabeth's bedroom, the death and then the gradually revealed fact of her mutilation, would be, not origin, but a second-order narrative, one which punished the woman for a horror of which she appears to be the victim but is believed to be the source. Thus a story which appears to lament the death of a sister would instead – or in addition – serve the purpose of punishing her or women in general for the fact of their sex. The story, indeed, *is* the punishment, for the punishment is in the endless retelling of a tale which is never just the recollection of a trauma, but is also the merciless and apparently somehow pleasurable repetition of a fantasy in the most fundamental sense of the term. For it is a central property of fantasy that an event can serve a (psychic) purpose as narrative even if it refers to a moment which concretely happened in the past. This might also help to explain why De Quincey has such problems, in spite of all the versions he constructs of the story, of disposing of his guilt; the guilt resides in the story itself, and the more its versions are multiplied, the more guilt they are required to repair.

De Quincey is explicit in 'System of the Heavens', as he is elsewhere, that he does not take the visible horrors of his psychic life to be objective: what he sees in the map of the Orion Nebula is a projection of himself. To make the point, he advances a quasi-Kantian epistemology:

> In reality, the depths and the heights which are in man, the depths by which he searches, the heights by which he aspires, are but projected and made objective externally in the three dimensions of space which are outside of him. He trembles at the abyss into which his bodily eyes look down, or look up; not knowing that abyss to be, not always consciously suspecting it to be, but by an instinct written in his prophetic heart feeling it to be, boding it to be, fearing it to be, and sometimes hoping it to be, the mirror of a mightier abyss that will one day be expanded in himself.   (8: 15)

The 'abyss' here seems to offer itself as an analogue of the chasm, shaft or vault that De Quincey sees in the 'cruel brain' of the nebula, and has a visionary sight of, in his Memnonian trance, in Elizabeth's bedroom. But as the passage suggest, the emotions attaching to that abyss are the subjective accretions of the image; and the image itself is not so much objective as *objectified* – cast out, *as if* absolutely other, *as if* no part of exactly what it *is* a part of, the psychic imaginings of De Quincey himself.[9] I have no idea, and it seems very possible that De Quincey had none, whether he had indeed seen the wound in Elizabeth's skull, and whether, having been checked by that sight from kissing her, he later found the courage to do so. Both versions of his narrative of the scene in Elizabeth's bedroom are entirely ambiguous on the question: both include the elaborate vision of the 'vault', the 'shaft', which appeared just as he turned to look at her face; both make it clear that he did not see Elizabeth's corpse again, after it had been 'examined' by 'a body of medical men' (1: 42–3; 1985 105–8). But supposing he had, it would still be impossible to represent that moment as the true and final origin of the afflictions of De Quincey's childhood and old age. The fantasies that select or produce the narratives of his myth of childhood are so intertwined, superimposed, mutually reparative, mutually repetitive, that they must be thought of either as a single involute or not at all.

9

Homicidal Mania: Tales of Massacre and Vengeance

We hear that Gen. Nott has arrived at Ghuznee, has blown up the new bourj in the city, and has put to death nearly every man, woman, and child found there. We cannot be surprised at the men taking signal vengeance; but we fear the news is too good to be true.

Lady Florentia Sale, *A Journal of the Disasters in Affghanistan*, 415.

The old fanaticism will again be dominant. Woe to the Christian who presumes to ride on horseback in the streets of Damascus, or who is so unwise to appear rich enough to have a horse at all! The Beyroutees must discard their white turbans, if they would keep their heads safe.

John G. Kinnear, *Cairo, Petra, and Damascus*, 340.

I

De Quincey's interest in murder was not confined to the kind of domestic butchery lovingly described in the essay on the Williams and the McKean murders. He had a taste for massacres on a grand scale, whether fictional or historical, and he was fond of attempting careful and quasi-judicial discriminations of the degree of guilt, and even the degree of justification, which could be imputed to them. Broadly speaking, massacres which he regarded as unprovoked or as unjustified by military expediency he represented as entirely unforgivable. Massacres on the other hand where it could be argued that the number of deaths was less than might have been expected; or where the victims were old; or which were the culmination of hot pursuit – such massacres, in differing degrees, he was prepared to regard as much less blameable. Massacres carried out in the way of revenge for serious crimes – such as threatening the boundary that divides West from East, or belonging to a regiment other members of which are guilty of rape and murder; or being the employee of someone indirectly involved in the humiliation of a mother – these as we shall see he not only condoned but relished. At its best, revenge for De Quincey is always vastly in excess of the crime: a whole mouthful of teeth for a tooth.

There may be a relation between this interest in vengeance which is in excess of its occasion, and the continual failure of De Quincey's narratives of reparation to repair anything at all. They failed to do so because the characters which the narratives sought to exonerate, to protect, to accuse and to destroy could so seldom be kept from merging into each other. Most complicated of all, the surrogates of himself in these stories were as liable as the other characters to be translated into the wrong place and the wrong identity – like Othello who, smiting the Turk, kills himself. 'Any of us would be jealous of his own duplicate,' De Quincey claims in an essay on Landor,

> and, if I had a *doppel-ganger* who went about personating me, copying me, and pirating me, philosopher as I am I might . . . be so far carried away by jealousy as to attempt the crime of murder on his carcase; and no great matter as regards HIM. But it would be a sad thing for *me* to find myself hanged; and for what, I beseech you? for murdering a sham, that was either nobody at all, or oneself repeated once too often.   (11: 460–1)

Since a doppelganger[1] is only a spiritless copy of oneself, a mere carcase housing a borrowed soul, a nobody, to kill him is no murder; but if your duplicate *is* a nobody, what does that make you? In some manuscript jottings for a continuation of the essay on murder as a fine art, De Quincey tells the story of a murderer called Outis ('but doubtless he indulged in many aliases') who at Nottingham, circumstantially enough,

> joined vehemently and sincerely, as it seemed, in pursuit of a wretch taxed with having murdered, twelve years previously, a wife and two children at Halifax, which wretch (when all the depositions were before the magistrate) turned out to be the aforesaid Mr Outis.   (J1: 77–8)

For all I know this story may be as true as De Quincey represents it to be. But if so, this man who finds himself, in relation to the same crime of murdering a woman and children, in the positions both of the pursuer and the victim, was as providentially named as Williams himself. 'Outis' is in pursuit, it seems of his own doppelganger, his own 'nobody'; in Greek οὔτις means 'nobody', and Οὔτις was the alias assumed by Odysseus to deceive Polyphemus.

What on earth can you do if you are impersonated by nobody, and if you believe, like De Quincey, that you must kill nobody if you are to restore the uniqueness of your own identity? How can you be sure of killing the right person, or anyone at all? For a possible solution we might look to a series of stories by De Quincey in which the hero decides to avenge some appalling crime by killing *everybody*, In these narratives of universal mayhem, an innocent victim, female and beautiful, is killed, and vengeance is taken against everyone who could conceivably be connected with this crime, until only the male hero is left, secure no doubt that his identity could not now be confused with anyone else's, for nobody was left alive. Ah – but then if Nobody was indeed the one person still alive, he too must die; and he does. 'I make a wilderness, and call it a pacification', wrote De Quincey, ventriloquising the sentiments appropriate to 'the military character'; and such stories, by making a desert, may have been attempts by De Quincey to make a kind of peace with himself (1: 80).

But before we turn to these stories of general revenge, it is worth glancing back at the visit of the Malay in the *Opium-Eater*, an incident in which, I suggested, De Quincey's gift of opium was to be read as a (more or less symbolic) attempt to procure the death of the Malay so as to prevent him killing the little child. This interest in large-scale and more or less indiscriminate revenge, however, puts a large question mark against either De Quincey's motives or his choice of toxin. Malays in the eighteenth and early nineteenth century had a 'character' for violence (Marsden 242, Cordiner 1: 144); they were known by all East India hands as the most terrifying orientals of all; 'the most vindictive and ferocious of living beings', according to Sydney Smith, whose 'curiosity' had 'always been highly excited by the accounts of this singular people'. They are 'ferocious, treacherous, and revengeful', wrote Robert Percival, and their 'unparalleled barbarity' is attributed by some to 'the quantity of opium they take from infancy, in consequence of which they are in an almost perpetual state of delirium' (Smith 1: 82–3; R. Percival 171).

The connection between the opium habit attributed to Malays, and their equally notorious habit of running 'amuck', had been denied by William Marsden, the late eighteenth-century expert on Malay culture, but belief in it was still widespread. Smith, in an early manifestation of the fear of the 'yellow peril', was sure that 'one day or another, when they are more full of opium than ususal, they *will run a muck* from Cape Comorin to the Caspian' (Smith 1: 83).[2] Percival acknowledged that the Malays sometimes enjoyed lucid, opium-free intervals, but they used these, he believed, merely to plot the violent enterprises which they would then undertake in 'a state of temporary madness' induced 'by means of bang' – to 'bang' oneself, he explains, is to take opium.

When a Malay has suffered any injury or grievance, real or imaginary, and ever so slight, the most dreadful thirst of revenge appears to take possession of his whole soul. He makes a vow to destroy the object of his vengeance, together with every other person who comes in his way, till he meet death from some hand or another. To prepare himself for this dreadful exploit, he takes a large quantity of bang, then draws his poisoned kreese, and rushing headlong into the street, stabs indiscriminately every one that comes in his way; at the same time crying aloud, *amok, amok*, or kill, kill, from whence this horrid mode of revenge is termed by Europeans *running a muck*.   (R. Percival 178)

De Quincey thought that opium acted as a stimulant on the nervous system, not as a narcotic, and thus had every reason to believe that it would work on Malays as hashish did on assassins – or as the heady brew of class hatred and constitutional reform worked on the petty shopkeepers of Britain. The Malays who subsequently appeared in De Quincey's dreams, and ran 'a-muck' at him, were no doubt under the influence of the drug, or so he seems to suggest in a footnote about 'the frantic excesses committed by Malays who have taken opium'. Seen in this light, the gift of opium may be read as an attempt either to kill the Malay and to prevent his violence, or to provoke him to an indiscriminate massacre of innocents; and according to how we read it, we may recognise the Malay as a surrogate not of William only, but of a range of other characters in the *dramatis personae* of De Quincey's myth of childhood, and in particular of De Quincey himself (3: 381–7, 405 and n.)

Among De Quincey's works of fiction there are three stories of indiscriminate revenge: 'The Peasant of Portugal' of 1827 and 'The Caçadore' of 1828, both stories of the Peninsular War with almost identical plots, and 'The Avenger' of 1838. There is also the novel *Klosterheim* of 1832, in which the hero *appears* to have massacred, in secret and in disguise, whole households of people, all of whom turn out at the end of the novel to have been his allies, not his enemies, and to have survived after all. In addition to these, *The Stranger's Grave*, though not a revenge tragedy, tells an analogous kind of story: the deaths in that novel can all be seen as caused, more or less indirectly, by the hero, or to result from his own evil actions, but they may still offer him the perverse and pleasuring reassurance of having made every possible doppelganger disappear, before disappearing himself.

II

'The Peasant of Portugal: a Tale of the Peninsular War' (1827), has only recently been attributed to De Quincey by Grevel Lindop. It is the story of Juan Taxillo, who is the usual kind of romance foundling, discovered with tokens of noble paternity, but brought up as a peasant. One of these tokens is an 'exquisite' sword which Juan uses in the resistance offered by his village to 'a regiment high in favour with Napoleon'. So successful is this resistance that the officer commanding the French force gives his men permission 'to put the village to fire and sword, and pillage and massacre, at their own unlicensed will, its unfortunate inhabitants'. Accordingly, some members of the French regiment rape and then murder Juan's young wife Marguerita (as we have seen, De Quincey's wife was called Margaret). Juan swears by his noble sword to take his revenge on the 'bloodhounds' responsible – indeed, on 'every fiend incarnate of the accursed regiment whose ruffians have perpetrated this deed'. One by one, and sometimes two by two, soldiers of the regiment are found dead; they disappear even in mid-conversation with their comrades. It is discovered that Juan was 'the one unaided destroyer', and eventually a poor peasant from the neighbouring village offers to reveal to the French Juan's place of concealment. The entire regiment follows him to Juan's secret cave; they enter it; the guide disappears; and in his place, as an 'avenging spirit', appears Juan, who lights a train of gunpowder and blows everyone up, himself included. 'Death,' he explains, 'is the only blessing left to me after revenge' (1827 13, 16, 18, 20, 24).

'The Caçadore' (1828) is another recent attribution, made this time by Edmund Baxter. It involves once again a young and athletic Portuguese peasant, Velasquez, whose betrothed is once again raped and murdered, once again by a French soldier. The rape was witnessed, because interrupted, by the girl's father and uncle, who are promptly murdered along with the young woman. As the story develops, the identity of Velasquez, the would-be avenger of this crime, is increasingly superimposed upon that of its perpetrator. The Frenchman was remarkable for possessing 'enormous moustaches', 'white as the driven snow', the sign, it seems, of the superior power and maturity by which he had usurped the position Velasquez should have occupied. The night after the death of his betrothed, Velasquez's hair turns 'from black to snow-white', though in him this seems to be a sign of his attenuated power. The Frenchman wears the sign of the phallus so conspicuously and arrogantly on his face that it is no surprise when the revenge meditated against him, in the name of defending the honour of 'sisters' and 'wives', is described by Velasquez as 'cutting off this miscreant from the face of the earth'. Nor is it particularly surprising that, when the French detachment has been successfully ambushed, Velasquez himself is unable to perform the desired operation: instead he is shot, first in the face or head, so that 'his jaw was broken, and hung down', and then in the groin – 'and this time he *could not* rise' (De Quincey's emphasis). At the conclusion of the story the superimposition becomes literal: the corpse of the caçadore is discovered lying across that of the French soldier, as if in a re-enactment – and reparation – of the scene of the rape. Velasquez, it appears, after inflicting various gashes on the already lifeless body of the Frenchman, 'had died in the act of striking a blow, which he had not the strength to complete, for the point of the knife had penetrated the skin, and then had been driven no further, the hand having become powerless in death'. The scene is reminiscent of the story in the *Westmorland Gazette* of the lioness standing over the turbaned man, described on page 78 (1828 9, 13, 10, 11, 14, 15.).

The killing of the Frenchman is accomplished by a young Scots officer. As Velasquez, wounded in two places, lay writhing on the ground, 'he called to Niel Cameron not to let the officer escape; . . . Niel dashed forward; and, at last, penetrated within ten paces of the officer; – he drew a pistol, fired, and the Frenchman fell from his mule'. Cameron, who here so transparently inherits the phallus from the prematurely aged and now castrated Velasquez, is the younger and 'more ardent' of two brothers serving with the Portuguese; he is shot in his turn by the dying rapist. Everyone, therefore – aggressor, victim, intruders, would-be avenger, success-ful avenger – is dead by the end of the story; together with no less than 80 Portuguese and 150 French soldiers, all sacrificed in retribution for the brutality of one officer and for the arrogance of his immense moustaches. Only the narrator survives, though with the tell-tale mark of the sympathetic survivor, the mark of a wound where 'a ball grazed my head' (1828 14).

The narrator, indeed, is in many ways the crucial character in the story, the privileged spectator on the whole scene. He represents himself as by no means easy in his mind at being involved in an exploit 'more nearly resembling private vengeance than public warfare'. But his men insist on participating in Velasquez's revenge,[3] and he can justify his own presence at the ambush as an attempt to recall them to their duty. The need for such a justification emerges clearly as the scenery of the ambush is described: it is described as a 'defile', a 'deep ravine . . . covered with bushes and brush-wood', and seems to repeat as a crudely sexualised geography the unlocalised skyscapes and spacescapes of vaults, chasms, abysses, shafts, ravines, that we are familiar with from the bedroom scene and its analogues. It is here that 'the French column' is to be 'cut off to a man'. Equally familiar, in the context of what thus invites comparison, once again, with the scenery of the primal fantasy, is the apparent wound the narrator 'chanced' to see as, lying alongside Velasquez, he caught sight of his 'ghastly expression', an expression which still causes him 'almost to shudder' as he recalls it. Velasquez looked 'more like a corpse than a living man', except that 'the state of intense excitation in which he was had caused him to bleed at the nose, and the blood had trickled down upon his upper lip unheeded, and clung and clotted on his moustache'. Familiar too is 'the anxiety necessarily attending *lying in wait*' (De Quincey's emphasis), the alertness of the narrator's ear to 'the least noise', and the absolute silence maintained by the ambushing party (1828 12–3).

This fantasy of hearing or of being heard, transposed into a context more or less military, found its way several times more into De Quincey's writings. In a passage of his recollections of the Lake Poets which we have already glanced at, and which was omitted from the collected edition, he describes an occasion, one of several, during the Peninsular War, when he and Wordsworth, eagerly expecting news of 'some great crisis in Spain', walked up Dunmail Rise, near Grasmere, to await the carrier who brought the London newspapers. They waited on what De Quincey describes as

> that narrow field of battle on the desolate frontier of Cumberland and Westmorland, where King Dun Mail, with all his peerage, fell, more than a thousand years ago. The time had arrived, at length, that all hope for that night had left us: no sound came up through the winding valleys that stretched to the north . . . . At intervals, Wordsworth had stretched himself at length on the high road, applying his ear to the ground, so as to catch any sound of wheels that might be groaning along at a distance.   (1970 159–60)

This was written in 1839; and two years later, when writing of the passage of the British expeditionary force through Afghanistan during the invasion of that country, he responded to some very similar circumstances in Mountstuart Elphinstone's description of the Khyber Pass with an appropriately breathless excitement:

> "If a single traveller endeavour to make his way through, the noise of his horse's feet sounds up the long narrow valleys, and soon brings the Khyberees in troops from the hills and ravines: . . . ". What a picturesque circumstance is that of the unfortunate traveller's giving warning against himself by the hollow sound of his horse's hoofs echoing up the narrow corridors amongst the rocky hills!   (B49 1841 300; and see Elphinstone 1815, 357)

Some years later again, in the dream fugue that concludes 'The English Mail-Coach', and soon after the girl with her diadem of roses has been swallowed by the quicksand (see above, p.117), the figure of listening for the sound of an advancing army in a valley appears again, bearing this time the traces of Elphinstone's narrative. The 'tears and funeral bells' that announced the girl's death are now described as having been 'hushed by a shout as of many nations', and

> by a roar as of some great king's artillery, advancing rapidly along the valleys, and heard after by echoes from the mountains. 'Hush!' I said, as I bent my ear earthwards to listen – 'hush! – this is either the very anarchy of strife, or else' – and then I listened more profoundly, and whispered as I raised my head – 'or else, oh heavens! it is *victory* that is final, victory that swallows up all strife.' (13: 322)

The sound is apparently revealed, in the next section of the fugue, to be the sound of the 'secret word' arriving, 'which word was – *Waterloo and Recovered Christendom!*' But the 'final' victory is more capacious and more ambiguous than that: it is the triumph of an innocent, 'unknown sister', or of a 'raving, despairing' woman, over death; or it is the triumph of death over the sister, so that she can never return in the form of the woman; and all this in the context of what we have come to recognise as primal scenery (13: 322–7). And all these images of wartime listening, of being overheard in wartime, seem to recall the scene of ambush in 'The Caçadore', a scene which ends with one corpse stretched out across another, in a displaced enactment of the primal fantasy which emphasises above all the connection of sexuality and violence, the impossibility, even, of imagining them apart. The connection is further secured, in 'The Caçadore', by the representation of the face and head as the place where death is to be inflicted, and as the displaced site where sexual identity is to be discovered. It is a representation we have met before, and we will meet it again, several times.

III

Maximilian Wyndham, the hero of 'The Avenger', is the nephew and heir presumptive of an immensely rich English earl, and a 'marvel of manly beauty', who arrives in 1816 in a little German university town to improve his Greek. He is already a distinguished soldier, having served brilliantly with the English at Waterloo and, as his name suggests, he is himself partly English, though quite how much seems doubtful – he has a 'somewhat Moorish complexion', and there is a story that his mother was 'a gipsy of transcendent beauty'. Gipsies, of course, are in De Quincey's reckoning pariahs, and we begin here to get the sense of another contradictory identity, insider and outsider, aristocrat and outcast, English and oriental, like the English Opium-Eater. The narrator, a German professor, observes in him 'a profound sadness', such as 'might have become a Jewish prophet, when laden with inspirations of woe' – a sadness which is surrounded by a 'perplexing mystery'. Wyndham falls in love with the most beautiful young woman in the town, Margaret Lieben-heim, the daughter of a merchant, and his love is enthusiastically returned (12: 271, 237, 240–1).

The first murders are reported by a rustic girl to the entire élite of the town assembled together at a ball. She announces that her elderly uncle has been killed, along with his wife, two of his maiden sisters, and an elderly female domestic. Three weeks later two old bachelors and their two sisters are found murdered, and, once again, a young niece manages to escape death by having been fortuitously absent from the house when the killings happened. Then an elderly currier is killed, but his youthful wife is spared; she had seen and heard nothing, but it was apparent that more than one murderer had been involved. Nothing less than a 'mob' participates in the next murder, in which a single elderly man is killed and a female servant escapes; in the fifth, two aged ladies who keep a school are murdered, and two teenage sisters, pupils at the school, survive. In the forest outside the town the local jailer is found crucified.

In the mean time, two things have happened which have an important bearing on the eventual denouement. Wyndham and some fellow students have formed a vigilante group, which has been hopelessly unsuccessful in tracking down the murderers. And the aged professor/narrator, coming upon Wyndham asleep in his bedroom, has discovered in his room the miniature painting of 'a lady of sunny Oriental complexion, and features the most noble that it is possible to conceive'. She looks, he decides, like 'the favourite sultana' of Mahomet, or of Amurath, the sultan impersonated – as ferocious and beturbaned – by William in the nursery theatricals at Greenhay (12: 251). From various later indications in Wyndham's behaviour, he decides that the painting is of a dead woman, probably his mother. When Wyndham wakes up, he kisses the miniature, in a gesture reminiscent of De Quincey on his last night at Manchester Grammar School.

Finally, the house of the Liebenheims is attacked, and her father and his two sexagenarian sisters are murdered. Margaret is spared, but is found in a state of shock, and shortly afterwards gives birth to a premature son, who dies in a few hours. The scandal this excites is quickly silenced: she and Wyndham, it appears, had been secretly married eight months earlier. Margaret becomes feverish, delirious, and dies – the text speaks of crocuses, roses and resurrection. Wyndham dies too, apparently by taking poison, but he leaves the professor a full written narrative of his life, in which he acknowledges himself to be the murderer and the leader of a gang of student-assassins, apparently conceived after the pattern of the one of the various groups dedicated to murder which seem to have fascinated De Quincey: the original Syrian 'assassins', the 'thugs', or – perhaps especially – the Jewish Sicarii described by Josephus, who murdered, De Quincey tells us, on principles which were at once erroneous and divine (1966 229; 7: 150–1; and see 8: 428–9 and n.; 13: 21–2, 62–4). This gang has been helping Wyndham to conduct his blood vendetta, in revenge for the deaths of his father, his two sisters, and (especially) his mother. For their deaths he seems to hold responsible all the burghers of the unnamed university town who had been alive at the time.

Wyndham's mother was 'a Jewess . . . of exquisite beauty', who claimed descent from 'the royal houses of Judea' (12: 273); his father, though partly English, had reluctantly become a member of the French army, and had been stationed in the university town. While various French officers make sexual advances to Wyndham *mère*, a French general tricks Wyndham *père* into a minor breach of military discipline and has him imprisoned. The traduced soldier angrily denounces his accusers and persecutors, is tortured, and dies. His wife (are you still with me? – this is the Jewess, Wyndham's mother) repeats his denunciations of the magistracy, for which she is sentenced to be publicly scourged, on two separate occasions, on her naked back.

Wyndham's narrative now eagerly invites us to witness another of De Quincey's scenes of maternal 'exposure':

> The day came! I saw my mother half undressed by the base officials – I heard the prison gates expand – I heard the trumpets of the magistracy sound! She had warned me what to do. I had warned myself. Would I sacrifice a retribution sacred and comprehensive for the momentary triumph over an individual? If not, let me forbear to look out of doors; for I felt that, in the self-same moment in which I saw the dog of an executioner raise his accursed hand against my mother, swifter than the lightning would my dagger search his heart. When I heard the roar of the cruel mob, I paused; endured; forbore. I stole out by by-lanes of the city . . . I returned, and found my mother returned. She slept by starts, . . . and, when she awoke and first saw me, she blushed, as if I could think that real degradation had settled upon her. . . . She had disdained to utter a shriek when the cruel lash fell upon her fair skin.   (12: 278)

The mother dies of a fever before she could be 'forced out again to public exposure', for the second instalment of her punishment (12:

280). Wyndham's sisters die too, the elder – Berenice – after being compelled by the jailer to sleep with him, the second – Mariamne – in grief at the loss of Berenice: the story repeats here the plots of *The Stranger's Grave* and 'The Daughter of Lebanon', with their pairings of sisters ruined and sisters pure. As regards Berenice, it is a source of relief, as well as of horror to Wyndham, that 'such advantages as the monster pretended to have gained over her – sick, desolate, and latterly delirious – were, by his own confession, not obtained without violence' (12: 284). This surrogate of Elizabeth is here the subject of a fantasy that a rape has been inflicted on her when she was exhibiting some of the symptoms of Elizabeth's hydrocephalus. This fantasy is indulged under cover of a concern for her moral purity and of a justification for the extraordinary (even for Wyndham) violence of his revenge. Berenice and Mariamne were the names also of two female relations of Herod the Great: Mariamne was his wife, Berenice was at once his sister and his daughter-in-law. By Herod's orders Mariamne herself, and Berenice's husband, Herod's son, were both murdered. As we shall see, the massacre of the innocents, in which Christ was intended to die and which was also perpetrated at the command of Herod, was a favourite theme of De Quincey's. By a tortuous logic, the jailer in 'The Avenger' is crucified in exact retribution for the death and violation of Berenice, a type of Elizabeth, a massacred innocent, and so a surrogate of, and fellow-victim with, Christ himself.

With the death of his mother and sisters, Wyndham became a Wandering Jew, but eventually organised a band of fellow-Jews willing to help him exact retribution from the town; they all enrolled as students, and the gang of avengers was identical with the gang of vigilantes. Wyndham's narrative is remarkably offhand about the justifications for the other murders: 'the details of the cases,' – this is all it says – 'I need not repeat'. On our behalf, however, the professor is seen to regard the vendetta as entirely justified: the starting point of his narrative is the desire to make it clear that the murders were not 'a blind movement of human tiger-passion', but 'a moral Lesson', undertaken with a serious didactic purpose, which as far as I can tell is to warn of the evils of anti-Semitism.

The importance of the story for our purposes is rather different. To begin with, vengeance is visited upon a large number of people of both sexes whose responsibility for the fate of Wyndham's family is never so much as hinted at; and the extraordinarily high body count seems to be treated by the novel as if it only reinforces the lesson Wyndham decided to teach. Second, though the text is keen to point out how careful the vigilantes are to spare the lives of girls and young women, the old people who die are continually described in terms of their sibling relationships, and plenty of sisters get killed along with their brothers. Thus, if the novel provides, in the innocent nieces and young wives, a number of safe places to shelter the surrogates of De Quincey's sister, it provides also some very dangerous places where sisters are brutally murdered. In Margaret, it creates a young woman whose death the hero fails to prevent – it is the unintended by-product of a just vendetta – but in the mother it creates also a woman whose punishment and symbolic death the hero could perhaps (and at the risk of his life, to be sure) have prevented, had he not chosen instead to watch her exposure, and then to 'steal way' secretly so as not to witness her further degradation.

Wyndham's uncertain investment in the scene of his mother's punishment creates an ambiguity in his identity which repeats the ambiguity of Outis and the band of student-assassins, all murderers and pursuers alike.

> Mother, thou art avenged! Sleep, daughter of Jerusalem; for at length the oppressor sleeps with thee! – and thy poor son has paid, in discharge of his vow, the forfeit of his own happiness – of a Paradise opening upon earth – of a heart as innocent as thine, and a face as fair! (12: 278)

Wyndham's narrative, it will be remembered, is composed just before he dies, and is to be read only when he is dead. As his mother had no single oppressor – that is the whole point of the story – the 'oppressor' mentioned here can easily be construed as her own son, who is now dead and who therefore now can be said to be sleeping with his own mother, a consummation no doubt devoutly desired. The passage is reminiscent of various passages which speak of the desire to sleep side by side with Elizabeth or her surrogates in the grave; so that as well as confusing the various roles of aggressor, watcher and avenger, and making them all available to Wyndham, it also, familiarly, confuses Elizabeth and the mother, with the additional complication that the death of Margaret, the wife, and the name of De Quincey's wife (and elsewhere apparently a surrogate of Elizabeth), seems to be offered almost as a sacrifice to the mother, as if to propitiate her. In short, no identity – not aggressor, victim, watcher, avenger, lover – is secure in the novella, and nobody at all is safe – from a wrath which is ultimately that of the novelist himself, in his role as 'the minister of a dreadful retribution' (12: 272).

'The Avenger', especially in the curious parentage it provides for Wyndham, in the sexualised violence of its last pages, calls to mind Freud's paper entitled 'Family Romances' (IX: 237–41), which was published in 1909, the year before he began his analysis of the Wolf Man which was to disclose the central importance of the primal fantasy to the child's understanding of sexual difference. 'Family Romances' is an account of the phases of a fantasy which is of use to individuals in the painful and necessary process by which they liberate themselves from the authority of their parents. The first phase of this fantasy can occur only at the time when the child has begun to realise that its parents are neither unique nor the best parents imaginable. Prompted perhaps by the feeling that it has been slighted by its parents, or does not enjoy an equal or a greater measure of their love to that enjoyed by a sibling, the child may pretend or imagine that it is a stepchild or an adopted child, and that its true, secret parents are of a higher social standing than the impostors who are passing themselves off as its mother and father. The second phase of the fantasy occurs only when the child has found out enough about sexual difference to know that there is more scope for questioning the identity of one's father than of one's mother. In this stage, therefore, it is only the father who is replaced in fantasy by someone more illustrious, and the mother is no longer regarded as an impostor but merely as promiscuous. The second phase of the fantasy is distinguished from the first by being a sexual phase; and the child now tends to picture to itself 'erotic situations and relations, the motive force behind this being his desire to bring his mother (who is the subject of the most intense sexual curiosity) into situations of secret infidelity and into secret love affairs'.

The 'family romance' is a versatile fantasy which can 'meet every sort of requirement' the child may put upon it. For example – and there may be a certain convenience here in relation to De Quincey – it can be used to imagine the eventual downfall of his sibling competitors, for the child can imagine that only s/he is legitimate, and all brothers and sisters, the product of the mother's numerous infidelities, will one day be exposed as bastards. Equally, the boy child can use it to 'get rid of a forbidden degree of kinship with one of his sisters if he finds himself sexually attracted by her'. For the most part, however, the family romance seems motivated by a desire for 'revenge and retaliation', against sibling rivals, or against parents. 'It is as a rule', Freud writes, 'precisely these neurotic children who were punished by their parents for sexual naughtiness and who now revenge themselves on their parents by means of phantasies of this kind'.

If it seems odd that a family romance of nineteenth-century Britain should look to a Jewess to exalt the status of the fantasist, she is after all a princess of the royal house of Judaea. What is more, in the course of the narrative she is provided with a range of possible consorts and lovers, all more exalted than her thoroughly shadowy husband. She was, it will be remembered, beautiful enough to have been 'the favourite sultana of some Amurath or Mahomet'; she 'had been sought in morganatic marriage by an archduke'; and the surname of her son has been bestowed upon him by an English earl. Rather less complimentary were the advances made to her by the French officers when her husband was imprisoned, but such advances are just the thing for ensuring the humiliation of siblings. So too is the sexualised violence inflicted upon her by the executioner, and on Berenice by the jailor. The fantasy of the family romance here seems to combine with the fantasy of the primal scene, which in turn is combined with the memory or fantasy of the violation of Elizabeth's body, to offer a complex sexual pleasure, too painful to enjoy, and too shameful to pass unpunished. As usual, the punishment falls on the woman; the 'exposure' of her body is her crime, and it is her punishment too.

IV

On February 11th 1799, Napoleon left Cairo at the head of an army *en route* for Syria. On March 4th the army invested Jaffa on the coast of Palestine, and two days later the town was stormed and entered. The survivors of the garrison, according to De Quincey some 4,200 Albanian regular soldiers in the service of the Ottoman Sultan, withdrew to a strong defensive position in an 'immense barrack' to make their final resistance. Two aides of Napoleon were sent to treat with them, and the Albanians agreed to lay down their arms, and to submit to have their hands tied behind their backs, in exchange for and implicit promise that their lives would be spared. Once the prisoners had been secured, Napoleon denied that he was bound by the promise of his aides, who had, he claimed, no authority to make it. It was impossible, he argued, to spare the lives of the Albanians. They could not be detained in captivity, for there was insufficient food to feed both them and the French, nor could they be released, for in that case they would certainly have found a way to rearm themselves, and the battle would have had to be fought all over again elsewhere. Napoleon ordered therefore that all 4,200 should be shot. After three fusillades, a few Albanians were still alive, unwounded; and, remarkably, a few of these found that the ropes binding them had been shot apart by the French bullets. These few made a rush for the sea, and managed to swim out to a barren rock, just offshore. The French had no boats and could not follow, and so, unwilling to leave unfinished business behind them in Jaffa, they made signs to the Albanians that if they would return their lives would be spared. Without food and water, and not suspecting that the French would break their word a second time, the Albanians swam back, and were murdered on the shore (8: 315–26).

This is De Quincey's account of Napoleon's Jaffa massacre,[4] an incident which so preoccupied him that he discussed it in his writings no less than four times: in 1832, in a review of G.P.R. James's *The History of Charlemagne*; in 1839, in an essay entitled 'Casuistry'; in 1844, in an article on the first Afghan War (B56 1844 145n.); and in 1847, in his 'Notes on Walter Savage Landor'; in addition, the 1839 account was considerably revised and extended in 1858, and makes reference on a couple of occasions to the Indian Mutiny (8: 319n., 320). The massacre, by any account the act of 'wholesale butchery' that De Quincey describes it as, came to seem still more shocking in De Quincey's judgement as he wrote more about it. He was always outraged that the confidence and the surrender of the Albanians was gained 'by a trick, by a perfidy, perhaps unexampled in the annals of honourable warfare' (8: 319n, 320, 316, 328). But though in his review-essay on Charlemagne he had accepted that Napoleon was indeed placed in a difficult dilemma, by the time of the essay on 'Casuistry' he had decided that there must have been much more food available than Napoleon had acknowledged. He computes that the provisions per head of the French army were actually increasing, because the mortality rate among the French soldiers was high, and he points out that there must have been a reasonable supply of food in Jaffa for the defenders to consider withstanding a siege in the first place. De Quincey became convinced that Napoleon's real motive in ordering the massacre was that 'he wished to signalise his entrance into Palestine by a sanguinary act, such as might strike panic and ghasty horror far and wide . . . and might paralyse the nerves of his enemies', and by the time of his last remarks on the Jaffa massacre, the justification for it by the argument about provisions had become a 'frivolous pretence' (5: 379–80; 8: 316–28).

If De Quincey's account is more or less accurate, it is difficult to imagine how one would challenge his accusation against Napoleon, that he was a 'murderer'; and just because no language is adequate to describe such a massacre, it is hard to claim that De Quincey's description of it, as 'the most damnable carnival of murder that romance has fabled, or that history has recorded', is in excess of the mark, however much it might seem calculated to appeal to an answering violence in his readers. (8: 316–17; 11: 410). To point out that there have been massacres in the past which involved more deaths is to appear to believe that the degree of guilt in such cases can be computed arithmetically, and that to murder 8,000 prisoners is twice as bad as murdering 4,000. To point out that it was at least possible that even more lives might have been lost had the pledge not been given to the Albanians (supposing Napoleon intended it to be given all the time) is to compound the insensitivity of such moral arithmetic with a cynical disregard for the duty of keeping promises. There is something repugnant in the attempt to estimate the degree of guilt attaching to such appalling crimes by comparing them with other appalling crimes, or in imagining that worse outcomes might have resulted from more honourable behaviour.

But this is more or less what De Quincey himself does. He never discusses the Jaffa massacre except to compare it with other massacres which begin to seem, as he describes them, hardly massacres at all. There are three allegedly comparable events that he represents as altogether less culpable than the crime of Napoleon. Of these, the worst is another massacre carried out by the French, in 1845 at Dahra in Algeria; but perhaps because it was uncannily similar to Juan's terrible revenge on the French themselves in 'The Peasant of Portugal', it seems rather to have appealed to De Quincey as an economical means of exacting large-scale retribution than to have shocked him for the same reason. At Dahra, according to De Quincey's version, about 700 'rebellious' Arabs, pursued by the French, took refuge in some caves. The French 'filled up the mouth of their retreat with combustibles, and eventually roasted alive the whole party – men, women, and children'. For various reasons, it appears, this atrocity, though disgraceful, was altogether less culpable than the Jaffa massacre. The officer commanding at Dahra did not 'seduce' his victims from their defensive position by lies, he had no way of getting to his enemy 'without the shocking resource which he employed', and he was massacring *Arabs*, who 'are not rightfully or specially any objects of legitimate sympathy in such a case; for they are quite capable of similar cruelties under any movement of religious fanaticism' (11: 405–12).

I will leave the strength or weakness of these arguments to be evaluated by the reader. The last of them, however, has to be put alongside an argument used against Napoleon in a comparison mounted between the Jaffa massacre of 4,000+ Albanians in the Turkish army, and the massacre of a similar number of Saxons by Charlemagne. In this comparison the argument is that Napoleon, as the leader of a *soi-disant* Christian army, had a particular duty to exhibit Christendom to infidels in the best moral light. Thus though Arabs are especially to be exempted from massacres, to reveal to them the nature of Christian good faith, if it should unfortunately happen that they *are* massacred, it seems they are getting no more than they deserve. De Quincey acquits Charlemagne of murder as wholeheartedly as he condemns Napoleon: Charlemagne's was a 'severe and sanguinary chastisement', admittedly, but it was a 'penalty' . . . which the laws of war in that age conferred' – it was, in short, 'a judicial punishment, . . . designed in mercy, consented to unwillingly, and finally repented' . . . (5: 380).

Why it was repented if it was judicially appropriate and intended as an act of positive mercy is not clear, and it seems more likely that Charlemagne has won De Quincey's approval by virtue of the moral nature of the general cause he was upholding. Napoleon was the leader of 'the armies of Jacobinism', and could get no credit from De Quincey for putting down the infidel armies of the Ottoman Empire if he did it in the name of a politics which was itself imaged by De Quincey as oriental. Indeed, De Quincey's Peninsular War tales, of the wholesale massacre of French soldiers, take on a new significance in the light of the connection we came across in the introduction, between the murderous myriads of the Parisian mob, and the myriads of South-East Asia – especially in view of his opinion that it was above all the Peninsular campaign which saved Britain 'from regicide and triumphant jacobinism'. Charlemagne on the other hand, no upstart corporal but a true king, was engaged, in his wars against infidel Saxons and Moors, in 'the royal tiger-hunt of war' – he was defeating, in the name of royalty and religion, an enemy which De Quincey represented in the form of his worst nightmares as the 'royal', or Bengal, tiger. 'He had a special dispensation for wielding at times a barbarian and exterminating sword, but for the extermination of barbarism; and he was privileged to be in a single instance an Attila, in order that Attilas might no more arise.' John Williams, the murderer and tiger of the East End, was also 'a domestic Attila, or "Scourge of God"', and the parallel is another case of the victim becoming blurred with the avenger, though Williams belonged no doubt to the class of Attilas who are to be put down, rather than to the class of those who are to do the putting down (5: 376, 373–4; B28 1830 963; 13: 75).

V

I am suggesting that De Quincey's accounts of historical events – in all these cases, of massacres of infidels by Christians – are finding expression in a similar vocabulary, and with a similar cast of aggressors and innocent victims, as we have found in his attempts to describe and organise the narratives of his own myth of childhood. The point seems to be reinforced in his comparison of the Jaffa massacre with the lenient treatment offered by Vespasian to the Jews captured after the siege of Tarichae. Vespasian 'gave up to the sword' only 1,200 prisoners. These were 'old and helpless people', for whom death was 'a merciful doom', for there was nothing else to be done with them (though there was no shortage of food); their death, though 'a shocking necessity', was a necessity none the less, for which Vespasian bore no guilt. Napoleon, however, had murdered men almost all in their late teens and early twenties – men not 'old and helpless' but 'helpless as *infants*' (my emphasis); they were 'murdered foully as the infants of Bethlehem', and a footnote manages to imply a connection between Napoleon and Herod, described as 'tiger-like' and 'a bright model for the future sepoy'. As we saw earlier in this chapter, Napoleon had become hooked up somehow with the murder of Elizabeth's innocence; so that Waterloo became the '*victory* that is final', over her oppressors, or over her *other* image, the raving and bloodstained woman risen from the dead (8: 318–20, 317).

The massacre at Jaffa was thus a repetition of the massacre of the innocents, performed by Napoleon in his identity as the Jacobin analogue of Herod, an oriental and tiger-like child-killer, who murdered, in addition to the 'innocents', his wife, her brother, and two of his own sons. Jaffa was an atrocity 'not at all less treacherous than the worst of Asiatic murders', and this point, that such massacres are unchristian, but are not untypical of infidels, accomplishes the implicit orientalisation of Napoleon which seems to be an item on the hidden agenda of all De Quincey's accounts of him. In 1833 De Quincey had written a long and bloody account of the massacre in 1803 of the Suliotes of western Greece at the hands of the Albanians themselves, led by Ali Pacha, who had given the victims a solemn promise that their lives would be spared. De Quincey attached this account to a review of Thomas Gordon's *History of the Greek Revolution* on the grounds that Gordon had failed to mention the matter. One might have imagined that, by the *lex talionis* which governs De Quincey's thinking in such cases, the story of Jaffa – Muslims massacred by Christians – might have performed a reparative function in relation to the story of Suli; and if it does not, that is perhaps because Napoleon is by his very nature incapable of avenging a massacre of Christians by Muslims, for his nature is oriental (7: 216, 319–30).

But perhaps most crucial of all the ingredients of the event and of the narrative possibilities it offered De Quincey was the fact that the massacre took place at Jaffa. Jaffa, De Quincey points out, was the 'Joppa' of the Crusaders; and Joppa was where Tabitha lived, died, and was resurrected in her upper chamber by Peter. It is in the light of this connection between the massacre and the scenery of De Quincey's own psychic life that we should read, I believe, the language in which, in his various accounts of the massacre, De Quincey describes the violation of the promise given to the

Albanians. 'After the faith of a Christian army had been pledged to these prisoners', he writes, 'that not *a hair of their heads* should be touched, the imagination is appalled by the wholesale butchery' (my emphasis). The Albanians, secure in their defensive position, were 'seduced' and 'trepanned' by Napoleon, as the Suliote Giavella had been 'trepanned' by Ali Pacha; as the child-bride Agnes in 'The Household Wreck' was trepanned by her would-be seducer; and as Elizabeth was trepanned by Dr Percival. The regular soldiers of the Sultan have suddenly become feminised and infantilised, with the result that they can be represented as the victims at once of sexual abuse and of dissection (8: 315–16; 11: 410–2; 7: 326).

In the context of this vocabulary of seduction and trepanning, the extraordinary leniency shown by De Quincey in his judgement of Vespasian needs a little more discussion. The massacre, he argues, of 1,200 of the Jews captured at Tarichae, had 'a beneficial effect' on the course of history. In particular it had such an effect on Titus, Vespasian's eldest son, destined to succeed his father as emperor. 'The horror which settled upon the mind of Titus', as a result of his father's reluctant butchery, 'made him tender of human life ever after; made him anxiously merciful, through the great tragedies which were now beginning to unroll themselves'. Though Titus himself, 'an apparition of brightness and of vernal promise' died at a cruelly early age, his exemplary humanity, learned in Judaea, 'availed to plant kindness and mercy amongst imperatorial virtues'. This does seem a case where some moral arithmetic is called for – how many Jews must be massacred to make an Emperor merciful? But if the passage seems to be engaged in a kind of special pleading, it is of a piece with the treatment of Titus elsewhere, who plays a very strange role indeed in De Quincey's account of the subjugation of Judaea, an account in which Josephus's history is tortured into becoming a history, also, of the house of De Quincey (8: 320).

On one occasion, De Quincey's version of the period of Jewish history recorded by Josephus seems to put in question this account of the leniency of Vespasian and Titus. Of the 90,000 prisoners taken at Jerusalem, no less than 10,000, apparently, were 'selected for the butcheries of the Syrian amphitheatres, and the rest were liable to some punishment equally terrific' (7: 132). The fact that these selections were made and these liabilities decided by Vespasian and Titus is passed over. Perhaps De Quincey is entering too thoroughly into the spirit of Suetonius, who sometimes measures the generosity of an emperor by the number of victims he provided for the entertainment of the amphitheatres; or perhaps he thought that the bumper harvest of Jewish deaths in those amphitheatres would inspire an equally bumper harvest of mercy in those who ordered it.

One way or the other, Titus, who according to Suetonius's oddly contradictory account of him was renowned for cruelty as well as kindheartedness (Suetonius 294–5), is always absent from De Quincey's mind when anything brutal is happening, and I want to conclude this chapter by speculating on that absence.

In particular, Titus is oddly absent from De Quincey's account of the triumph he shared with his father Vespasian in celebration of the subjugation of Judaea. That triumph, as we saw in an earlier chapter, was witnessed by Josephus, but according to De Quincey (in one of his most revealingly inconsequential asides: see above, p.69), it would emphatically *not* have been watched by 'many an intelligent girl, not more than seven years old'. That girl, it will be recalled, was dragged into De Quincey's discussion of Josephus's treachery only to be transmuted into the image of Judaea beneath her palm-tree, who was in turn transmuted into Rachel weeping for her children. According to De Quincey, a tableau of 'Judea, in the form of a lady, sitting beneath her palms, – Judea, with her head muffled in her robe, speechless, sightless' formed a part of the triumphal procession as described by Josephus. We know by now what to expect of such images of muffled, sightless heads, though this is De Quincey's only version of Judaea beneath the palm in which her head, almost always described as 'veiled', is described as so thoroughly 'muffled' with fabric. (7: 248, 147).

Though De Quincey makes much of the idea of Josephus sitting 'as a volunteer spectator of his buried country carried past in effigy', and making the tableau of the weeping Judaea a part of his 'picturesque narrative' of the triumphal procession, in fact no such tableau of Judaea is mentioned by Josephus.[5] The image of Judaea weeping either in sorrow or in shame,[6] to which De Quincey so frequently and so obsessively returns, derives from the design of a series of sestertii which began to be issued in AD 71 by Vespasian, in honour of his and Titus's victories in Judaea (Figure 1). But in De Quincey's various descriptions of the image, it becomes another occasion on which Titus is mysteriously absent. There are three very similar versions of the coin. The head of Vespasian or Titus appears on the obverse. On the reverse, all versions bear the legend IVDAEA CAPTA, and all depict a central palm-tree, to the right of which sits a woman, in an attitude of mourning or despair; her head is barely veiled, and certainly not 'muffled'. The area to the left of the tree is differently filled in the different versions. Two show a captured Jew standing with his hands tied behind his back. The third shows an armed figure, sometimes identified as Vespasian but more authoritatively as Titus, in military dress, with his foot on a helmet, and holding a spear and a short sword, a parazonium. De Quincey nowhere mentions any figure as appearing to the left of the tree.[7]

The reasons, if any, why the space to the left of Judaea/Rachel was always left vacant by De Quincey will have been different according to which version or versions of Vespasian's coin he had seen. In the first two versions of the coin I described, the image of the bound Jew can be read as an image of the pariah and captive, unable to prevent the suffering of Judaea; as an image of the bound Albanian innocents massacred by Napoleon and contrasted by De Quincey with the victims of Vespasian and Titus; and as an image, also, of the innocents massacred by Herod – in a veiled reference to the coin in 'Suspiria', Rachel, whom we have already seen represented as related to Judaea, is imagined as weeping for her children, on the night when 'Herod's sword swept its nurseries of Innocents' (13: 364–8). It seems a particularly serviceable version for the purposes of De Quincey's narratives. But he may instead (or also) have known the third version of the coin, in which the armed figure of Titus appears as the aggressor either of Judaea, a regular surrogate of Elizabeth, or of Rachel, the mourning mother, or of both. The repeated eulogies of Titus as the merciful son, and his continual absence from the space allotted to him on the dark side of the coin, would combine to deny and to wish away the son's guilt, for a series of fantasised crimes – seduction, violation, murder – only too close to home.

For De Quincey, the special guilt recalled by the figure of Titus may not have been a matter only of his fantasised participation in a massacre of innocents or of innocence. He may also have evoked in De Quincey the guilt of a fantasised act of incest. The elder sister of Wyndham, the bloodthirsty hero of 'The Avenger', was named Berenice, the same name as the sister and daughter-in-law of Herod himself. But there was another Berenice, the heroine of Racine's tragedy: she was the granddaughter of Herod the Great, and the incestuous lover of her brother Agrippa II. Titus wanted to marry her, and was prevented from doing so only by his fear of offending the Roman people. The common factor of a violated sister seems to propose an identification between Agrippa, Wyndham and De Quincey, and therefore an identification, too, between Berenice and Elizabeth, the violated sisters of Wyndham and Thomas. In this light, Titus may be wished away from the presence of Judaea because he has come to stand for an imagined rival for the love of Elizabeth.

10

Yellow Fever: The Opium Wars

Lady L. made a favourable impression. . . . She was sitting on a large ottoman in the centre of the new saloon, and therefore I can scarcely judge of her figure. She is very little, but her appearance is elegant and delicate. She was most becomingly dressed in a white turban of very *recherché* construction.

Benjamin Disraeli, *Correspondence with his Sister 1832–52*, 96.

At Amoy, for the first time, the so-called tiger soldiers shewed themselves – that is, men dressed up in yellow-coloured clothes, with black spots or stripes upon them, and a covering for the head, intended to be a rude representation of a tiger's head, supposed to look very fierce, and to strike terror into the minds of the enemy.

W.H. Hall and W.D. Bernard, *The Nemesis in China*, 232.

I

The lines by Milton which De Quincey borrows to describe the Orion Nebula introduce the famous paragraph in which, after the Fall, Sin and Death together build a bridge joining Earth and Hell. The bridge is compared with the one built by Xerxes, who

> the Libertie of *Greece* to yoke,
> From *Susa* his *Memnonian* Palace high
> Came to the Sea, and over *Hellespont*
> Bridging his way, *Europe* with *Asia* joind, . . .
> (*Paradise Lost* Book 10: 307–10)

The winter palace of the Persian kings, at Susa east of the Tigris, was known to the Greeks as the Memnonice or Memnonium, and was believed to have been built by Memnon, who was the son of the dawn, Aurora. Milton is conventionally apologetic about this comparison of great things with small, but it may well be the best he can manage – what else on earth can represent hell, it seems to say, if not Asia, especially Asia across the Tigris? De Quincey's essay on the Orion Nebula says the same thing. It produces the grandest example so far of what we can no longer call his geopolitics or his psychic geography, for this new attempt at the moral and political regulation of space extends far beyond the earth and beyond the solar system. The opening remarks on the moral ambiguity of the Earth-as-woman; the invocation of Memnon, now revealed as an ambiguously *cis*- and *trans*-Tigridian deity, both work to suggest that the Orient, Milton's Asia, is here accommodated as the complementary *that* of a European *this*, joined in antagonism against an *other* temporarily projected into outer space. How to describe that other? that hell? that Death? – how else but by invoking the plumes of an oriental Sultan, and the tiaras of trans-Tigridian Assyria? The worst psychic horrors De Quincey can imagine, from all the afflictions of childhood – worse even than those he describes as oriental – are oriental.

In a review-essay of 1843, 'Ceylon', De Quincey quotes again from Milton, this time from *Paradise Regained*. He is discussing the contention of J.W.Bennett, in his book *Ceylon and its Capabilities*, that the Taprobane of the Greeks and the Romans was Ceylon, and not (as has also been argued) Sumatra. If it is either, it is Ceylon, decides De Quincey, and he then quotes a part of the description of the kingdoms of the world as displayed to Christ by the devil; the lines are quoted also in the 'Autobiography' and on various other occasions in De Quincey's writings (7: 430; 1: 165n.–166n.; 3; 99; 10: 321).

> From the Asian Kings, and Parthian amongst these;
> From India and the golden Chersonese,
> And utmost Indian isle Taprobane;
>
> .   .   .   .   .
>
> Dusk faces with white silken turbants wreathed
> (*Paradise Regained* Book 4: 73–6)

Both here and in the 'Autobiography' De Quincey takes care to isolate the last line, which in fact follows immediately after the line about Taprobane; and one effect of this is to exploit the fact that the syntax of the passage allows the various places it mentions to be read as if in apposition with the line about 'dusk faces'. Ceylon itself appears as a 'dusk face' wreathed with a white silken turban, and so – like the various other figures who wear turbans in De Quincey's writings – as a possible oriental surrogate for Elizabeth or William or both. In these final chapters, I want to consider a series of essays by De Quincey in which the Orient no longer features primarily as a metaphor to describe characters from the *dramatis personae* of his own nursery tragedy, but is itself, apparently, the main object of De

Quincey's attention. There are four essays or sequences of essays, on the first Afghan War, on Ceylon, on the Indian 'mutiny', and on British relations with China in 1840 and again in the mid-1850s, where he turns to the discussion of the imperial history and of the imperial future.[1] But as these lines from *Paradise Regained* have already suggested, no easy division can be made between Family and Empire, between the heroes, villains and victims of De Quincey's private afflictions, and the 'horrid enemies' on the other side of the Tigris. The connections run both ways: if the worst traumas of De Quincey's narrative of his family history can be described in their full horror only by being orientalised, the worst of oriental horrors can be represented only by being connected with those personal traumas.

I have said that it is impossible to determine whether it is the fact that these childhood scenarios become orientalised which gives them their particular and terrible force, or whether the Orient becomes an object of terror because it is charged with all the weight of these childhood scenes. The problem of sequence is impossible, and perhaps finally unnecessary, to resolve, in a body of writing characterised by a general instability of narrative positions and identities, and of the relations of repetition and reparation that hold between the different stories that I have described. But as my introduction acknowledged, we must always recognise another possible way of constructing that link between childhood trauma and the Orient, one which seems to begin not in the nursery at Greenhay, but in the most public spheres of British imperial history. For the driving force of this whole saga may be the fully historical and public forms of imperialist discourse, and their image of the terrible Other, which then finds – after the fact as it were – one of its most appropriate embodiments in a childhood myth. It might even be possible to argue that imperialism discovers, in the sexual images of a traumatised nursery, a most convenient, self-exonerating account of its own origins: the personal in this case would serve as a retrospective justification or rationalisation of a fully historical guilt. The relation between the psychical and the historical is finally as indeterminate as everything else we have seen; but it is this relation that I want to attempt to approach in these final chapters. I shall be concentrating mainly on the essays on Ceylon and on the Indian rebellion, but first I shall have something to say about the pieces on China. The essays on the Afghan War are mostly concerned either with the kind of global geopolitical issues examined in my introduction, or with the details of military history; for our present purposes, they are of importance mainly for De Quincey's elaborate interest in Afghan turbans (B49 1841 293, 295), which I notice now in passing, and his curious fantasising about the contents of

Indo-British trousers, to be discussed in prurient detail in Chapter 12.

II

De Quincey's first essay on Sino-British relations, written at the beginning of the Opium War of 1839–42, is as notable as any of his other writings on imperial policy for its belligerence and for the contempt it manifests towards the inhabitants of Asia east of the Tigris. The Chinese are 'incapable of a true civilisation, semi-refined in manners and mechanic arts, but incurably savage in the moral sense'. The objections of the Chinese government to the importation of opium – the profits of the opium trade with China were used by the East India Company to pay for the government of India, to the tune, De Quincey informs us, of over £3 million per annum – are reviewed with impatience and scorn, and the decision of the Chinese government to ban opium imports is treated as evidence of an appalling moral turpitude.[2] At the very beginning of his essay, De Quincey insists that Britain should respond to the interruption of the opium trade with a 'policy of war – war conducted with exemplary vigour' (14: 193, 167, 163).

De Quincey had some degree of interest in the fortunes of the East India Company. His 'Bengal uncle', his mother's brother Thomas Penson, was 'a military man on the Bengal establishment' who had on several occasions helped De Quincey with gifts or loans, and had offered them on several more. Penson was unmarried, and De Quincey hoped to inherit something substantial at his death; but when Penson did die, in 1835, his estate went to Mrs Quincey, with the exception of an annuity of £100, which De Quincey had been receiving for some years, and which on his uncle's death he promptly sold. When Mrs De Quincey died in 1846, a little more of Penson's fortune came Thomas's way.[3] This degree of involvement in the fortunes of the East India Company, and so in the fortunes of war, was not much and certainly not unusual: 'everybody has an India uncle', wrote De Quincey in 1839, and for the English middle class that might not have been far from the truth. In the case of someone as habitually jingoistic as De Quincey there is no need to look for motives of economic self-interest – except as connected, patriotically of course, with the national interest – to explain his views on imperial matters. He was certainly an interested party in the Opium War, but largely as one who wished to see the opium trade made respectable (3: 311–3; 7: 22).

The meandering argument of the essay has great difficulty in maintaining its original insistence on the need to make a belligerent response to the insolence of the Emperor. The difficulty, as De Quincey explains, is that China, as much as it deserves to be 'thumped' and 'kicked' (Afghanistan, he remarks elsewhere, 'needed a cow-hiding for insolence'), is so backward as to be – compared with the highly organised nation states of western Europe – 'an inorganic mass', 'defended by its essential non-irritability'.[4] To raid the odd port on the Chinese coast would therefore communicate no vibration to the seat of government. De Quincey proposes instead that an ambassador be sent to Peking at the head of a column of 14,000 men with appropriate artillery. The idea is that an embassy unsupported by such a show of military force would be disregarded; and that a march on Peking undisguised as an embassy would be 'too openly an expression of coercion to found a settlement that would last' (14: 176; 6: 265; 14: 198, 195).

One of the most remarkable things about the essay is the attempt it makes to represent this belligerent policy as an attempt to forestall a series of acts of revenge certain soon to be perpetrated by the Chinese against the European nations trading in Chinese ports. Still more remarkable, the incidents which the Chinese will certainly treat as the occasions for the prosecution of vengeance have not yet occurred. De Quincey's argument is that the Chinese are by nature a vengeful people, that the more external trade increases, the more 'will the occasions for revenge be multiplied', and that this 'retaliation' will be 'in a twenty-fold proportion' – will be in the grandly excessive manner of De Quincey's own fictions – unless an embassy-in-force can get its own retaliation in first (14: 191).

On at least two occasions we can see De Quincey apparently attempting to describe the future of Sino-British relations in terms of his own narratives of guilt, revenge and reparation. What kind of incident, he wonders, might prompt the Chinese to 'retaliate'? Chinese law acknowledges, he claims, no distinction between offences committed unknowingly or accidentally, and offences committed with malice aforethought. The Chinese themselves 'are bestial enough to think the will and the intention no necessary element in the moral quality of an act' (14: 191–2). An illegal but unpremeditated and accidental landing on the coast would therefore be regarded by them as the British might regard a hostile invasion,

and, if some colonial ship freighted with immigrants, or some packet with passengers, should be driven out of her course, and touch at a Chinese port, as sure as we live some horrid record will convulse us all with the intelligence that our brave countryman, our gentle countrywomen and their innocent children, have been subjected to the torture by this accursed state.   (14: 192–3)

It is to prevent such otherwise inevitable atrocities, it seems, that the British must make to Peking 'an adequate demonstration of our power'.[5]

In fact the shipwreck De Quincey had predicted did occur, in September 1841, hardly a year after his article was published. The transport ship *Nerbudda*, which had sailed from Calcutta with some 300 people on board to join the British expedition, was blown off course and hit some rocks in the Strait of Formosa. About thirty of those on board managed to escape in two lifeboats, and were 'providentially' picked up by a trading schooner bound for Hong Kong. The remainder, after several days on the wreck, made rafts and attempted to land. Many were drowned, or killed as they landed by Chinese villagers in search of plunder; some 200 were imprisoned and almost all of them seem to have been executed by the local authorities. It is not clear that there were any women on board, but the story, as told for example in the contemporary histories of Hall and Bernard, and of Sir John Francis Davis, appears to be exactly the kind of instance of 'Chinese barbarity' against 'British subjects' that made De Quincey so apprehensive (Hall and Bernard 237–8; Davis 2: 5–8)

There were some twenty or thirty Europeans on the *Nerbudda*, all of whom managed to escape in the two lifeboats, while the 240 or 300 natives of India were all left on the wreck – neither Davis, nor Hall and Bernard comment on what might well have appeared to them to have been a still more providential dispensation, or a considerable statistical freak. They ignore the evidence of an earlier, and better informed contemporary historian, Ouchterlony, who had offered enough detail to make sense of the story. The *Nerbudda* was known to be too crowded to make the journey to China in safety. When the ship struck the rocks, the captain, the first and second mates, and all the Europeans embarked on two lifeboats, deliberately disabled the third, and, holding the non-Europeans off with 'fixed bayonets and loaded barrels', they abandoned 'their hapless deserted comrades to their fate' (Ouchterlony 203–7). A story of Chinese barbarity turns out to have been a story, first of all, of British barbarity; and in the game of 'this/that/the other' that Davis, in particular, is playing, the 'natives of India' are not British enough – not *human* enough – to deserve a place with the Europeans in the lifeboat; but they are certainly British enough to serve as instances of the treatment offered to British subjects by the barbarous Chinese.[6]

In an even odder passage, De Quincey argues with particular vehemence that the ambassadorial representatives of Britain in Peking should refuse to perform the 'kotou' – described by De Quincey in a later essay on China as a process of 'knocking' the head

nine times on the floor as a mark of respect to the Emperor (1857
95–6). This was an inexhaustible topic for British writers on
Sino-British relations, beginning with George Staunton's account of
the Earl of Macartney's embassy to China in 1792–4. (Macartney 2:
129–45, 209–19), and culminating in the composition in 1860 of
'The Private of the Buffs', that stirring ballad of a 'poor, reckless,
rude, low-born, untaught' lad from the hopfields of the garden of
England who, while the 'dusky Indians' with whom he had been
captured preferred to 'whine and kneel', himself chose to die rather
than perform the kotou.[7] Its author, the lawyer and poet Sir Francis
Doyle, was no less bloodthirsty a civilian than De Quincey himself,
but even he did not see as clearly as did De Quincey the inevitable
consequence of agreeing to perform the servile act. Writing of Lord
Amherst's 1816 embassy to Peking, when he had refused, like
Macartney, to perform the ceremony of adoration, De Quincey
claims that if, instead, Amherst had 'submitted to such a degradation,'

> the next thing would have been a requisition from the English
> Factory of beautiful English women, according to a fixed
> description, as annual presents to the Emperor. It is painful to add
> that, according to the degradation which too naturally takes place
> in Canton councils, there have been times when such a condition
> would have been favourably received; and the sole demur would
> have been raised on the possibility of trepanning any fit succession
> of their fair compatriots. We know what we are saying.   (14: 184)

And so do we, by now. This is a remarkable example of De
Quincey's pen running away with the essay, hovering between a
sense of humour and a sense of horror, and eventually recurring to
the afflictions of his own childhood. As a result, we get a glimpse of
how, if De Quincey's recommendations are to be followed, future
British policy towards Imperial China will be conducted as an
elaborate attempt to prevent a repetition of the dishonour visited
upon the body of Elizabeth by Dr Percival and his associates.

De Quincey's personal investment in the conduct of the first
Opium War becomes rather clearer in his second essay on China,
'Canton Expedition and Convention', published in November 1841,
and inspired by his disgust that 'her Majesty's forces have been
trepanned into loathing accomplices' in the 'convention' signed by
Captain Elliot and Keshin, the Imperial Commissioner at Canton
(B50 1841 677–88). This essay is briefer and a good deal more
coherent than the first, largely because De Quincey has now decided
– or is no longer concerned to conceal his decision – that Britain must
no longer regard its relationship with China as simply a trading

relationship. China, he believes, must be incorporated into the Empire – a task which seemed no more impossible than the incorporation of India, for De Quincey insisted that all estimates of the Chinese population which put it at more than 80 million were infantile, oriental exaggerations (B50 1841 688, and see also B48 1840 560–1).[8] The justification for annexing China is more or less the same as for the proposal to send an armed embassy: it is to retaliate against Chinese atrocities which have not yet been committed, but certainly *will* be, unless forestalled. The Chinese, it appears, are even more infantile than infants: they cannot be *conditioned* into good behaviour. Their entire inability to connect cause and effect means that they will not understand a punitive act by a British expeditionary force as chastisement for some earlier offence of their own; and so no punitive act can teach them the folly of offending. We can never be sure that 'Chinese treachery will not spring forward with a tiger's bound', and 'not to be crushed by the wheels of the tiger-hearted despot, you must leap into his chariot, and seize the reins yourself' (B50 1841 682,687).

The image of the tiger and the chariot here – anticipating the catastrophe of 'The English Mail-Coach' (see above, p.44) – is evidently the vehicle of a knotting of the public with the personal, and of an Asiatic quarrel', as De Quincey describes the first Opium War, with the remembered or imagined afflictions of childhood. In an extraordinary passage at the end of the essay, he compares the English national character – its 'habitual tendency to bear no malice', its 'indisposition to suspect' – with the vengeful and unforgiving character of 'our hateful enemy', the Chinese (B50 1841 687). The ambiguity of the word 'hateful' there – cherishing hatred or exciting it? – is absolutely appropriate to what follows, a characterisation of 'oriental' attitudes which is only too evidently an act of disavowal, an othering of De Quincey's own highly developed capacity for malice and vengeance:

A [Chinese] mother who does not teach to her children, as her earliest lesson in morality, some catechism of vengeance against the supposed violator of the family rights or dignity, would not take rank in man's esteem as one who realized the ideal of gentle feminine and maternal nature, but as an abject brutified creature, incapable of raising her thoughts to the nobler duties of humanity. Even Greece, in elder days, . . . even the Jews, when removed into captivity . . . adopted that savage maxim, universally binding in the east – 'Exterminate thine enemy root and branch, lest his children, if spared, should hereafter exterminate thine'.

(B50 1841 687)

This writing seems entirely divided between repudiation and identification; between the desire to represent the oriental character as inveterately vengeful and therefore as absolutely un-English, and the desire to justify, even imaginatively to participate in, acts of vengeance amounting even to genocide. In the first sentence, only the word 'supposed' seems to put any degree of distance between the writer and the sentiments he is describing; while the universalising phrase 'man's esteem' is only the clearest of several suggestions that what is being propounded here is a general law of ethics or of the natural history of morals. The appeal to the Greeks and the Jews may be read equally as an instance of how peoples who were otherwise models of humane citizenship or legal rectitude may be infected by the homicidal mania of the Orient, or as evidence that vengeance, even to the point of genocide, is a proper and a prudential act – for even the Greeks and the Jews permitted it. In a later essay on China, De Quincey gives extravagant praise to the British Consul at Shanghai in 1848, who had 'hunted' the murderers of six British subjects 'with the energy of some Hebrew avenger of blood' (1857 17). The ambivalence of the writing makes the point, once again, that it is De Quincey above all who is infected – reinfected – by the horrifying feelings that he has expelled and described as oriental, and by the horrifying images he has invoked in the name of the mother. The implication of the 'oriental' in the domestic – the hybrid, *Eurasian* identity of the writer – is as evident in this passage as anywhere in De Quincey's autobiographical works.

By the time of De Quincey's last outburst on Sino-British relations, in various diffuse essays and memoranda of 1857, the single theme of Chinese policy towards Britain in the 1830s and 1840s has been identified as the Chinese desire to punish the British for refusing to perform the kotou (1857 100–1).[9] This act has now been associated with another anxiety of De Quincey's – the anxiety of the outcast, the pariah, the *Cagot*, which he had discussed at some length in his 'Autobiography' (1: 100–1). In Christendom, he now writes, the people 'most pointedly insulted and trampled under foot' are the Cagots—an outcast people of the Pyrenees, possibly the descendants of medieval lepers.

> The Spaniard never disputed the Cagot's participation in Christian hopes; never meditated the exclusion of the poor outcast from his parish church; he contented himself with framing a separate door for the Cagot, so low that he could not pass underneath its architrave, unless by assuming a cringing and supplicating attitude. But us – the freemen of the earth by emphatic precedency – us, the leaders of civilisation, would this putrescent tribe of

> hole-and- corner assassins take upon themselves, not to force into
> entering China by an ignoble gate, but to exclude from it
> altogether, and for ever.   (1857 iii–iv)

The logic here is evidently very awry; by no stretch of the
imagination is China to the British what their local parish church is
to the Cagots, unless the sobriquet 'the freemen of the earth' is
intended to suggest that the British have an inalienable right to go
everywhere, as other Christians have an inalienable right to go to
church. Equally evidently, however, the comparison with the
Cagots has taken a wrong turning: the concealed point is that even
the Cagots, the most degraded people of Christendom, are not
forced to stoop as low to the Spaniards as the British would have to
stoop to the Chinese, if they are to gain admittance to the Celestial
Empire. To perform the kotou is not simply to acknowledge that
one is a pariah – De Quincey had always claimed that identity with
alacrity – but to be forced to acknowledge it by a people he regards as
having no right (as we shall see in a later chapter) to be regarded even
as human beings.

The 1857 writings on China are mainly of interest for showing De
Quincey's detestation of the Chinese at a new and dangerously
apoplectic level, fuelled no doubt by the fact that his son Horace, an
army lieutenant, had died of fever near Canton in 1842. 'In the case
of China,' he writes, 'this apostrophe – *The nations hate thee!* – would
pass by acclamation, without needing the formality of a vote' (1857
73). That hatred finds its most violent expression by representing the
first Opium War in these terms:

> Not meaning to do more than repress insolence, . . . we probed
> and exposed her military weakness to an extent that is now
> irrevocable. Seeking only to defend our own interests, unavoid-
> ably we laid bare to the whole world, the helpless wreck in which
> China had long been lying prostrate. *The great secret* (whispered no
> doubt in Asia for generations) *was broadly exposed* . . . and . . . it is
> vain to count [amongst the Chinese themselves] upon any filial
> tenderness or reverential mercy towards their dying mother.
>   (1857 38–9; De Quincey's emphasis)

China is now an ageing mother, dying of cancer, whispered about by
her neighbours (and in St Paul's Cathedral, no doubt), abandoned by
her children, her body cancerous, prostrate, naked, probed. What
depths of hatred, and against what or whom – in addition to himself
– could produce such writing? If China is to be attacked again, for
what crime is 'she' to be held responsible? Where was it committed –
in Canton, or in Greenhay?

11

Leontiasis: The Kandyan Wars and the Leprosy of Cowardice

Poor Burnes had made but few friends among the chiefs, who now never mention his name but in terms of the bitterest hatred and scorn. He seems to have kept too much aloof from them; thus they had no opportunity of appreciating his many valuable qualities, and saw in him only the traveller, who had come to spy the nakedness of the land, in order that he might betray it to his countrymen.

Vincent Eyre, *The Military Operations at Cabul*, 312.

My next patient was a young lady, from one of their Zunanas, veiled of course, and in company with other women; but I saw all the lower part of a very pretty face, by assuring her it was quite necessary to see her tongue. I made her uncover both her arms, which were richly ornamented, by expressing a serious anxiety to ascertain the state of both pulses. I advised on her case, and, I suppose, successfully, as she did not visit me again.

G.T. Vigne, *A Personal Narrative of a Visit to Ghuzni*, 76–7.

I

'Ceylon' (1843), a review of J.W. Bennett's *Ceylon and its Capabilities*, develops a double narrative and a double geopolitics. The first narrative offers an account of the relations of coloniser and colonised which is too familiar to demand any very detailed attention. It is an attempt to represent the process of colonisation as an object of scientific study, directed to the question of why colonial enterprises do not always succeed; but De Quincey is too anxious to provide the answer, thoroughly gratifying as it is, to make much of a show of the scientific method used in arriving at it. The first requirement for success, it appears, is the right kind of race of colonisers: the process of colonisation is a 'movement' or a 'machinery' for 'sifting and winnowing the merits of races'. There would be no point in saying this, of course, if it were not to secure the claim that of all nations the British are a 'race of men . . . selected and sealed for an eternal preference in this function of colonising to the very noblest of their brethren'. All the other would-be imperial nations of Europe – France, Holland, Portugal, Spain – have fallen hopelessly behind 'the British race'. The collapsing imperial pretensions of Spain, indeed, enable that country to be represented as one more version of 'Judaea on the Roman coins, weeping under her palm-tree' – as reduced, by the loss of the South American colonies, to the same abject position as the colonised, the tributary state. Correspondingly, Britain now occupies the triumphant position of Titus on the same coins, for Britons can now 'be heard upon every wind, coming on with mighty hurrahs, full of power and tumult, . . . and crying aloud to the five hundred millions of Burmah, China, Japan, and the infinite Islands, to make ready their paths before them'.

This confident prediction of the eventual extent of 'the future Colonial Empire' is made on the basis of an equal confidence in the particular advantages of character enjoyed by 'these Islanders', advantages which 'carry them thus potently ahead' of all other nations. These 'advantages' are not described, except by the singular word 'energy', nor need they be. The race for Empire is quite evidently being represented as a test of virility, a measure of manhood; to ask what makes the British so energetic in their imperial enterprises is for De Quincey the same as to ask what makes them so 'potent'; and the answer, equally evidently, is their potency (7: 427–8).

It is then hardly surprising that the second requirement for success in the process of colonisation turns out to involve a correspond-ing feminisation of the place to be colonised. What has made the 'appropriation' of India in general, and Ceylon in particular, so much the most successful example of the 'colonising genius of the British people', is that both are so thoroughly desirable, and both resisted the initial advances of the British. Too easy a conquest of either would have made them less desirable, and would have made cheap the conquest itself. 'We have prospered by resistance', De Quincey insists; we have been made more potent by it. In the process of elaborating this argument, the sexual undertones of which are hardly concealed at all beneath the discourses of racism and economic geography, an extraordinary image is produced of Ceylon-as-coquette, apparently (or nearly) an innocent virgin – 'she' is 'almost a virgin Eldorado' – but in fact an experienced and a thoroughly sensual woman who knows how to give the British just what they want. This is the kind of thing: 'Great are the promises of Ceylon; great already are her performances'. 'She combines the luxury of the tropics with the sterner gifts of our own climate. She is hot; she is cold. She is civilised; she is barbarous'. 'She has all climates'; she is the 'Pandora of Islands', all-gifted, and ready, if approached properly, to give everything.

The logic that drives this contradiction is the logic that drives the case for the defence (at least by reputation) in so many cases of rape: Ceylon's resistance to the arms of the British was a sure sign of her desire to be embraced, to be subdued by them. By 1843, the year of De Quincey's essay, that resistance had been more or less overcome, and Britain had '*entire* possession of the Island' (De Quincey's emphasis). The danger now was that Britain would become too uxorious, too enervated by the pleasures of possession to maintain the ever-ready potency of the race. 'Ceylon will but too deeply fulfil the functions of a paradise. Too subtly she will lay fascinations upon man . . . ' (7: 454, 429, 453, 430–5, 434).

This is not the only occasion when the connection between rape and imperialism surfaces in De Quincey's writings. There is, for example, a solemnly lubricious passage in his introduction to the sequence of essays on the Roman emperors where he discusses the destruction of the Roman republic by Julius Caesar. The destruction, he argues, was entirely justified: historically appropriate, necessary, beneficial. The justification is that until Caesar crossed the Rubicon, the republic of Rome was a 'minor', but that 'by him she attained her majority, and fulfilled her destiny' (6: 228). The hint that Caesar's relations with the republic amounted to the sexual violation of an under-age girl is made immediately explicit in the argument that follows – though initially it is treated as if the hint came not from De Quincey's imagination, but from some naive republican interlocutor:

> Caius Julius, you say, deflowered the virgin purity of her civil liberties. Doubtless, then, Rome had risen immaculate from the arms of Sylla and of Marius. But, if it were Caius Julius that deflowered Rome, if under him she forfeited her dower of civic purity, if to him she first unloosed her maiden zone, then be it affirmed boldly that she reserved her greatest favours for the noblest of her wooers. . . . Did Julius deflower Rome? Then, by that consummation, he caused her to fulfil the functions of her nature; he compelled her to exchange the imperfect and inchoate condition of a mere *foemina* for the perfections of a *mulier*. And, metaphor apart, we maintain that Rome lost no liberties by the mighty Julius.   (6: 228)

This argument (there is more to come) is something of a classic rehearsal of the contradictions in the classic defence to the charge of rape. 'Rome a virgin when Julius had her? pull the other one! And if she was, she'd been saving it up for him! Made her do it? what if he did, he was doing her a favour!' If it is the obviousness of these contradictions that causes the text to abandon the metaphor at the end of the passage quoted, it may be the pleasures of the same metaphor that hasten its return. A sentence or so later, the text, unable to deny that Rome was indeed raped, offers it as a defence that 'she' had been raped before. Caesar was just finishing the job – it took a man like him, a real man, to do it properly.

> The rape (if such it were) of Caesar, her final Romulus, completed for Rome that which the rape under Romulus, her initial or inaugurating Caesar, had prosperously begun. And thus by one supreme man was a nation-city matured; and from the ever-lasting . . . city was a man produced capable of taming her indomitable nature, and of forcing her to immolate her wild virginity to the state best fitted for the destined 'Mother of Empires'.   (6: 228–9)

The attempt to represent Caesar's brutal treatment of Rome as an attempt to enable her to overcome her youthful wildness, to 'mature', and to fulfil her manifest destiny, is precisely of a piece with De Quincey's attempt to square the rape of Ceylon with a vision of her future perfection, under British colonial exploitation. It does not seem to matter that in the discussion of Rome the rape is of the destined motherland, while the rape of Ceylon is a foreign adventure, an *amour de voyage*: the point is rather that the fantasy of imperialism as a demonstration of a brutal virility is so powerful and so attractive that it turns up everywhere, and sees all political relations, domestic or colonial, in the form of sexual violence.

II

The first narrative of the colonisation of Ceylon is a version – a fairly extreme version – of what was a conventional nineteenth-century attempt to represent imperial conquest and appropriation in terms of a sexualised narrative of the elective affinities of masculine colonisers and feminine colonies. The second narrative developed in the essay on Ceylon is also conventional enough. It turns up everywhere in justification of Britain's imperial adventures, as a tale of Britain saving an oppressed and a feminised people from a tyrannical masculine oppressor – most notably, the Hindus from the Moguls. It is another version of the narrative that Gayatri Spivak has pointed out in the attempts of the British to suppress *sati* – 'white men are saving brown women from brown men' (Spivak 1985a, 121). This narrative involves De Quincey in a more specific account of the history of the British appropriation of Ceylon; and as we shall see, it is a history which comes to be structured almost as an imperial allegory of the narrative so central to De Quincey's representation of his childhood, which manages to twist together what we have called the two stories of De Quincey's guilt – the guilt of failing to prevent the death of Elizabeth, and the guilt of having polluted her body. *Someone has failed to rescue a little girl* – little Ceylon – from the ravages of a ferocious tiger. Someone else must try. If he succeeds, and kills the tiger, Ceylon will be resurrected, and a terrible guilt exorcised. *Someone has polluted a mother*, in a story which also involves a massacre of innocents. A terrible vengeance must be exacted. This second narrative, the colonisation of Ceylon as a process of *saving* 'her' from male violence, coexists with, at times seems even to take the form of, the first narrative, the colonisation as a bold and enterprising act of male violence perpetrated on the resisting body of a female.

Britain gained possession of Ceylon from the Dutch in 1796, but not, as De Quincey would put it, '*entire* possession'; like the Dutch, and like the Portuguese before them, the British were able to control and exploit only the Maritime Provinces of the island, running all the way round the coast.[1] At the centre of the island, however, the Kandyan kingdom, which had resisted all attempts to conquer it before the British came, was not to be finally overthrown until 1815. Until then, De Quincey explains, Ceylon was like a peach, its flesh massed around a central stone. The Sinhalese people of the Maritime Provinces were the 'peach-flesh': they were 'lazy', 'soft, inert, passive cowards', 'silky and nerveless' – effeminate clearly ('strangers often mistake them for women', Bennett informs us), and probably the intention is to raise a question about the sexual orientation of Sinhalese men. The Kandyans, on the other hand, the 'peach-stone' – and once again De Quincey is concerned only with Kandyan men – were a different kind of coward: 'ferocious little bloody cowards'. If the maritime or lowland Sinhalese are effeminate, the highland Kandyans are emphatically masculine. Their king, Sri Vikrama Rajasinha, De Quincey's true villain, whose defeat and exile signalled the victory of Britain in a contest of virility, had 'a peculiarly keen and roving eye, and a restlessness of manner, marking unbridled passions' (7: 437–8, 448; Bennett 97).[2]

The Kandyan is also a 'tiger-man', and it is as tiger that he has to play his part in De Quincey's family version of Spivak's narrative, which for his purposes of course requires a dehumanised enemy: 'brave rescuer saves young woman from tiger' (7: 437, 440). Thus 'the Kandyan' is described at one point exactly as Williams will be, in 'Murder Considered as One of the Fine Arts': in Williams, 'the tiger's heart was masked by the most insinuating and snaky refinement'; the Kandyan is a 'tiger-man, – agile and fierce . . . though smooth, insinuating, and full of subtlety as a snake'. At another point in the essay the McKean murder is evoked, with the Kandyans in the role of the murderers of Elizabeth Bates. But De Quincey's hatred for the Kandyans cannot be satisfied simply by pointing out in them the symptoms of tigridiasis. The Kandyans are also 'tiger-cats', the term functioning, as we have already noted, as an insulting diminutive, and for the same reason they are 'bantams', crowing and flapping their wings on a dunghill (7: 438); they are also snakes, monkeys, hyenas, leopards, and non-specific 'little monsters' (7: 437–8, 441, 444, 450).

It is a good deal easier, however, to identify the aggressor and the rescuer in this second narrative than to decide quite who the victim is, for the early nineteenth-century history of Ceylon offered De Quincey an abundance of possible victims, some of whom seem to be capable of evoking bits and pieces of his personal psychic narrative. Sometimes the lowland Sinhalese occupy the place of the victims of Kandyan aggression, which allows the appropriation of Ceylon to be justified by showing the British as rescuing one part of the island from another. Elsewhere, the victim is a Kandyan woman, the mother of many children, allegedly drowned on the orders of the king of Kandy after a sequence of appalling atrocities; her story seems to evoke that version of De Quincey's narrative in which the female at the centre of his fantasies can appear to participate in the primal scene. Elsewhere again, and especially at the triumphant end of the essay, the part of the victim of the Kandyan tiger is played by Ceylon itself, in the ambiguous character of girlish experience attributed to it in the former of the two narratives of the appropriation of Ceylon.

This ambiguous character of the island, part child part woman, evokes the full range of De Quincey's narratives of personal guilt, at the same time as the coquettishness which results from the superimposition of innocence on experience evokes again the image of the island, or of woman, as complicit with her own violation. Even in the very last lines of the essay, where it is announced that with the defeat of the Kandyans Ceylon is at once resurrected and morally regenerated, the point cannot be made unambiguously. Ceylon 'will be born again: in our hands she will first answer to the great summons of nature, and will become in fact, what by providential destiny she is, – the queen lotus of the Indian seas, and the Pandora of Islands' (7: 456).

To attribute such different identities to the island in the same story can produce other slippages no less disruptive. If what makes Ceylon such an exciting woman in the first story is the resistance she offers to her male admirers, in the second story that resistance is offered by the thoroughly masculine Kandyans, 'standing erect and maintaining perpetual war'. The two stories together develop a more complex homoerotic subtext, in which the text seems to take up – and not for the only time in De Quincey's political essays, as we shall see – the fantasised position of the eager victim of sexual aggression, and its particular preferences become very clear: the Kandyans, it turns out, are altogether 'a more promising race than the silky and nerveless population surrounding them'. This subtext seems to be playing its part in a similar process of juggling a 'this/that/the other' strategy as we discovered in the relations of Thomas, William and the factory boys. Until the Kandyans are defeated, the lowland Sinhalese are needed as victims and therefore as allies, however inert and cowardly, against the ferocious other. But as soon as their defeat is accomplished, the greater masculinity and more 'promising' character of the Kandyans can be used to propose a guarded affinity between them and their British conquerors, in which they may unite to despise the effeminate lowlanders.

These shifting alliances and identifications speak very clearly of that dynamic within racism whereby each tentative reconciliation requires an exclusion somewhere else; and in this essay, and in the essays on Afghanistan, the game of this/that/the other is complete, it seems, when the masculine British are in a position to make common cause with an inferior but masculine subject race, to exclude another subject race represented as effeminate: the British and the Sikhs versus the Hindus; the British and the Kandyans versus the coastal Sinhalese. That these exclusions may speak (among other things) of a confusion in De Quincey about his own sexual orientation; that his identification with the masculine may be more like a desire for it; that his contempt for the effeminate may be functioning as a disavowal of identification with the feminine – all this will be still clearer in the next chapter (7: 438, 430; see below p.174).

Throughout the essay on Ceylon, the indications of De Quincey's own psychic investment in the recent history and the future of the island are unmistakable. He repeats for example the story of an atrocity attributed to the king of the Kandyans, the most appalling details of which were probably a fabrication put into circulation by the British to justify their conquest and annexation of his kingdom. According to this story, the wife of Ähälëpolä, the Kandyan *adigar* or Prime Minister, who had been discovered to be in secret negotiation with the British, was obliged to watch the decapitation of her children: 'the eldest boy shrunk [shrank] from the dread ordeal, and clung to his agonised parent for safety; but his younger brother stepped forward and encouraged him to submit to his fate, placing himself before the executioner by way of setting an example'. When the children had been murdered, their mother was forced, in order 'to save herself from a diabolical torture and exposure', to pound their heads in a rice-mortar. She was then drowned (7: 446; De Quincey's correction).

This shocking story is rehearsed in virtually all nineteenth-century descriptions and histories of Ceylon, as an example of the savage and oriental barbarity from which the British had rescued the island – though as the historian Henry Marshall pointed out in 1846, the punishment inflicted on Ähälepolä's wife was not obviously more barbaric than the punishment in Britain for high treason, which had been inflicted without mitigation in the previous century. The story had been eagerly repeated by the colonisers of Ceylon, who were frustrated, in the decades around 1800, by the reluctance of the British government to allow them to proceed with the complete conquest of the island.[3] The need for such a conquest, the story suggests, is urgent: the policy of restraint meant that the colonists had already failed to rescue one brown woman from brown men; surely it was time to rescue another, in the form of the whole island? In the official declaration of March 1815 by which the British announced their willingness to accede to the wishes of the Kandyans and to take over the government of the kingdom, the tale of the *adigar*'s nameless wife was offered as a reason for the British refusal to restore the fugitive king of Kandy to his throne. Just as in connection with *sati*, according to Spivak, 'the British . . . construct the woman as an *object of slaughter*, the saving of which can mark the moment when not only a civil but a good society is born out of domestic chaos', so the announcement of regret at the failure to save the *adigar*'s wife marks the moment of official determination to save Ceylon, to shield her from the violence of the Kandyans by placing her under the protective body of the British (Marshall 137n.–9; Tolfrey 42–3; Spivak 1985b 144; and see Spivak 1985a, 127).[4]

The anecdote's more specific appeal to De Quincey himself will also already be clear – an elder brother who 'shrinks' from his task of protection, a younger brother whose manhood is vindicated, the ruined heads, and in particular the threatened exposure of the mother. This threat enables a story about the guilt of failing to prevent a death to function at the same time as a story of the guilt which attends the violation of a woman, a violation which (as we saw in the previous chapter) demands retribution on a very large scale. De Quincey's desire for revenge is not at all qualified by the reflection that this atrocity happened (if it had happened at all) thirty years earlier, in an independent sovereign state; and he manages to represent the subsequent annexation of the kingdom, and exile of the king, as acts of 'vengeance' taken by the British in punishment specifically or especially for this crime.

III

But the capacious history of early nineteenth-century Ceylon offers another person, along with the king of Kandy, to fill the role of polluter/pariah, on whom De Quincey seems to take a thoroughly personal literary revenge. In 1803 a British contingent had managed to occupy Kandy. Finding themselves surrounded, they negotiated with the Kandyans for a safe passage out (this is the British version of events), but were massacred when they had completed only 3 miles of their march. A few of the British escaped the massacre by being kept as hostages, and these included the commanding officer, a Major Davie. The only survivor of the massacre itself, a Corporal Barnsley, later reported that Davie had, with much indecision, ordered his men to lay down their arms before the Kandyan 'tiger-cats'. The suspicion was produced that Davie had sacrificed the life of his men to save his own; and the story seems to have become connected with De Quincey's dream of 'impotence' – connected with his failure to prevent the death of Elizabeth – and of lying down before the lion.

De Quincey was probably first attracted to this portion of the history of Ceylon by the narrative of the survivor, Corporal Barnsley, which he had read in *The Life of Alexander Alexander* (1830).[5] Barnsley had been left for dead by the Kandyans, after receiving one chop on the back of his neck, which severed the sinews but not the spinal column; throughout the long and difficult walk to Trincomalee and safety he had been obliged to support his head in his hand (Alexander 112–24). De Quincey makes an elaborate comparison between the 'resurrection' of Barnsley and the briefer resurrection of the young woman murdered by the McKeans, who after her throat was cut, briefly stood up, walked, and finally collapsed. The story of the massacre seems to connect a demand for revenge against the Kandyans with what can obscurely be shaped as the death of De Quincey's sister, also wounded in the head: the young woman murdered by the McKeans was called Elizabeth (7: 441–2; 13: 121).

It is also the story of a pollution and a pariah. There is general agreement among historians of Sri Lanka that Davie died in captivity at Kandy in 1810, without being able to give his version of events. De Quincey however will have none of this, and in the violence of his denunciation of Davie he exceeds all other commentators on the affair, most of whom in fact regard the charge of cowardice against

Davie as not proven.[6] 'He could have made no apology', De Quincey insists, and if he could have done, he had the opportunity to make it. For De Quincey has somehow heard a rumour that Davie was subsequently seen alive, in Colombo or Trincomalee, where, because he had 'shrunk' from his 'duty', and 'polluted the British honour', he lived as an outcast (7: 442). He was, writes De Quincey, in his most vindictive, and apparently most self-hating vein,

> encrusted with the leprosy of cowardice, and because upon him lay the blood of those to whom he should have been *in loco parentis*, made a solitude wherever he appeared: men ran from him as from an incarnation of pestilence; and between him and free intercourse with his countrymen, . . . there flowed a river of separation, there were stretched lines of interdict heavier than ever Pope ordained, there brooded a schism like that of death, a silence like that of the grave; making known for ever the deep damnation of the infamy which on this earth settles upon the troubled resting-place of him who, through cowardice, has shrunk away from his duty, and, on the day of trial, has broken the bond which bound him to his country.   (7: 443)

Davie here is acting as the white double of Sri Vikrama Rajasinha, the polluter of honour, the exile, the *massacreur* of innocents or the one responsible (*in loco parentis*) for their massacre. He becomes like the exiled Napoleon, a white oriental outcaste: throughout this essay, the king of Kandy (like other oriental 'villains', Herod and Nadir Shah) is compared with Napoleon: they were both finally defeated and exiled in 1815 (7: 439, 449, 453; B305 1841 281). And as in the case of De Quincey's treatment of Napoleon, his language becomes especially violent, especially outraged. It is as if such characters are imagined not only as the surrogates of William, but as doppelgangers of De Quincey himself, his fellow-pariahs.

What is above all else disturbing, therefore, about the essay on Ceylon, is that this language and these fantasies occur in a piece of writing which everywhere, implicitly and explicitly, is recommending a severe policy of repression towards the native population. Britain should not repeat the mistakes of 'our Eastern rulers' hitherto, who have been '*too* long-suffering, and have tolerated . . . many miscreants, when their duty was . . . to have destroyed them for ever'. There is, indeed, a language of genocide in the essay, though displaced on to the religion of the Kandyans. The first step for the 'regeneration' of this 'demoralised race' is 'to exterminate their filthy and bloody abominations of creed and of ritual practice'. And unless and until the 'subtle savage' proves himself 'docile', and 'becomes capable of Christianity', 'we must not transfer to a Pagan island our own mild code of penal laws' (7: 446, 448, 451, 453). It is not clear what limits, if any, De Quincey's recommendation would impose on the behaviour of the colonisers towards the colonists; but it appears to give them *carte blanche* to exact whatever retribution they please, on the tigers whose crimes seem somehow to include the murder and mutilation of his sister, and the exposure and violation of his mother; to inflict on them the punishments that somewhere De Quincey believes should be inflicted on himself.

12

Phallalgia: India in 1857

They are the true composite of monkey and tiger, those Orientals,
W.H. Russell, *My Diary in India*, 1: 288.

Yes, ye vile race, for hell's amusement given,
Too mean for earth, yet claiming kin with heav'n
God's images, forsooth! – such gods as he
Whom INDIA serves, the monkey deity; . . .
Soon shall I plant this foot upon the neck
Of your foul race, and without fear or check,
Luxuriating in hate, avenge my shame,
My deep-felt, long-nurst loathing of man's name!

Thomas Moore, *Lalla Rookh*,
'The Veiled Prophet of Khorassan', 1: 508–19.

I

The concatenation and confusion of the public and the personal in De Quincey's writings is nowhere more evident than in his articles on the rebellion in India in 1857. At the outbreak of the rebellion, De Quincey's married daughter, Florence Baird Smith, was with her infant daughter and her husband Richard, an engineer in the Indian army, in Rurki, 150 miles or so from Delhi, which was then in the hands of the rebels.[1] It was as if his visions of young women and girls menaced by an oriental death had been prophecies, rather than the refractions of the experiences of his childhood that he believed them to be. The visions had suddenly become realised: not projected on to India as if on to a blank screen, but actually happening there, three months and many thousands of miles away; the 'horrid enemy from the infinite deserts of Asia', feared by all those who lived west of the Tigris, was now 'moving over the plains of Hindostan'. The fears were not imaginary: British women had been killed at Delhi, though the stories of the 'public violation' of wives and daughters, believed implicitly by many in Britain, seem mostly to have been British fabrications. But the reciprocal massacres at Cawnpore and Jhansi, for example, were to show that British women had no less cause to fear the rebels than Indian women had to fear the 'English fury' (10: 177; U1: 303; Kiernan 47; Majumdar 90).[2]

In December 1857, by which time he knew that Florence was safe, De Quincey wrote to another of his daughters, Emily.

> Every night, oftentimes all night long, I had the same dream – a vision of children, most of them infants, but not all, the *first* rank being girls of five and six years old, who were standing in the air outside, but so as to touch the window; and I heard, or perhaps fancied that I heard, always the same dreadful word *Delhi*, not then knowing that a word even more dreadful – Cawnpore – was still in arrear . . . now every night, to my great alarm, I wake up to find myself at the window, which is sixteen feet from the nearest side of the bed. The horror was unspeakable from the hell-dog Nena or Nana [Nana Sahib]; how if this fiend should get hold of FLORENCE or her baby (now within seventeen days of completing her half-year)?
>
> (U1: 299; P2: 132)

'Horrible! that a man's own chamber – the place of his refuge and retreat – should betray him!' – perhaps no passage poses so completely the unanswerable question of determination than does this letter to Emily. Is the rebellion represented by De Quincey as a repetition, in the public sphere, of a personal psychic trauma? or is the evocation of personal trauma an act of displacement, and a rationalisation, of a political, an imperialist guilt that cannot be avowed in that form? The dream seems to recall, once more, the bedroom of Elizabeth: the window; De Quincey standing between the window and the bed (as if to stand between the sun [son] and its [his] female victim); the sound he hears, no longer the Memnonian wind but the one reiterated word '*Delhi*'; the identification of the aggressor, the agent of death, as a 'hell-dog'. In relation to Florence at Rurki, De Quincey finds himself in two superimposed positions: as father of a threatened daughter, and as the brother of the sister that in this crisis Florence seems in part to represent (P1: 329).

The doubling is evident elsewhere in the language of the three essays De Quincey wrote about the rebellion in 1857–8. His imagination, in common with that of many (but not all) British writers on the rebellion, was much troubled by the vision of 'female relatives, separated from their male protectors in the centre of a howling wilderness, now dedicated as an altar to the dark Hindoo goddess of murder'. Fantasies such as this, whatever else they did, gave expression to fears which were understandable enough, however manipulated by the British press and however tragically in

5 *English Homes in India*, from *Narrative of the Indian Revolt* (1858).

excess of the event they may often have been; and they are to be
found everywhere in Britain in the autumn of 1857. We can put De
Quincey's vision alongside the illustration of 'English Homes in
India', for example, which repeats his fantasies of British woman
exposed to the gaze, and worse, of furious sepoys (Figure 5);[3] or
these lines from the *Edinburgh Review*:

> Women, whose slightest caprice had been law to their followers,
> and who had lived in a mixture of English refinement and Oriental
> luxury, found themselves at once exposed to the frenzy of a
> lawless soldiery, tracked naked through burning jungles, thrown
> to the merciless populace of maddened cities, or consigned to the
> worst brutality of man, until they met a death worthy of the early
> martyrs. Many of them, we know, endured with sublime energy
> and faith that tremendous trial, the last to which humanity can be
> exposed.   (E106 1857 572–3)

What is special though not unique about De Quincey's fantasies,
perhaps, is that these women are to be thought of as 'sisters' ('our
dear massacred sisters', 'our dear martyred sisters', and so on) at least
as often as they were 'innocent daughters' and 'dying daughters' (U1:
320, 304–5, 324).

De Quincey's narrative of his childhood appears to return, too,
when he attempts to find consolation in the deaths of British women
and children, and even in the possible death of Florence – for this first
essay of the three was published before he knew she was safe. There
is no one so base, he begins, as to be willing, like Agamemnon, to
sacrifice his daughter on the pretence of achieving a public benefit.
But if 'some calamity, or even some atrocity, *had* carried off the
innocent creature under circumstances which had involved an
advantage to her country . . . the most loving father might gradually
allow himself to draw consolation from the happy consequences of a
crime he would have died to prevent'. The sepoys of the Indian
army, he points out, were almost all Brahmins or Rajputs; when
eventually they are defeated, the British must take the opportunity of
inflicting an 'everlasting retribution' on the rebels, must revenge the
death of their sisters by an entire destruction of the caste system. The
revenge of the British will be sweet to the self-styled pariah.

One of the grounds of Thomas's identification with Elizabeth,
Ann, and their surrogates, was their shared status as pariahs or as
outcastes: the visible degradation of Ann, and the visible deformity
of Elizabeth, whether by scrofula, hydrocephalus or both, were
'pollutions' which Thomas, by kissing them both, took to himself.
They all therefore became the victims of caste – pollutants in a
system which is itself now classified as polluting. One of De

Quincey's hopes for the end of the rebellion was that there would soon be inscribed, on a solitary monument standing where Delhi itself once stood, that by sisters martyred and massacred, 'by women and children', was 'the pollution of caste cleansed from the earth for ever!' (U1: 304–5). The self-inflicted degradation of Thomas's identity as pariah now functions as a new form of inoculation, in a new game of 'this/that/the other': the polluting kiss seals an alliance with the pariahs of India, against the evil of the higher castes.

Like many commentators on the rebellion, De Quincey at first discounted the possibility that it could have been the result of an organised conspiracy, uniting Muslim and Hindu soldiers and civilians of both religions; later, however, and like many other commentators, he came to see conspiracy everywhere. [4] In September 1857, accordingly, he is contemptuous of the notion that the rebellion should be thought of as a conspiracy: the 'oriental mind', he argues, has always been characterised by a 'defect of plan and coherent purpose'. There is no evidence in the actions of the rebels of any foresight; 'no concert between remote points; no preparation; no tendency towards combined action'. By October, however, he is beginning to find this stereotype of the oriental, as childish and as incapable of consecutive thought and joint action, less serviceable than the stereotype of the oriental as wily, indeed as fiendishly cunning. It now appears that there has been 'a great sepoy conspiracy'; and not until January does he manage to accommodate both stereotypes, by representing the sepoys as 'brutally ignorant', foolish dupes as well as 'incarnate demons', murderous puppets whose strings were pulled by an organising cabal of 'Indian princes and rajahs, standing in the background' (U1: 309, 320, 342–8).

For the most part, the language of the essays works to infantilise the rebels, to represent them as characterised by the same 'childishness' as De Quincey had everywhere detected in the Chinese. And the effect of this is to cast the British as fathers – fathers not just in their severity, not just in their mildness, but in their possession of the phallus. As surely as the class struggle is fought out between groups distinguished by their different relation to the means of production, so in the race war (that is what it is to De Quincey) the participants are differentiated by their various relations to the means of reproduction, and in this process of differentiation the Hindus may be equally well be represented as children, who have not yet acquired the phallus, or as women, who have lost it. To make the point most clearly, I want to turn first to two of De Quincey's articles on the first Afghan war, 'The Dourraunee Empire' and 'Affghanistan', contributed to *Blackwood's* in the early 1840s.

'The Dourraunee Empire' is heavily dependent on Mountstuart

Elphinstone's *An Account of the Kingdom of Caubul*, first published in 1815, but reprinted in 1840 as an aid to understanding the ill-conceived British invasion of Afghanistan. To a far greater extent than his source, however, De Quincey is everywhere preoccupied by an image of the proud masculinity of the Afghans. 'Their countenance has an expression of manliness and deliberation, united to an air of simplicity, not allied to weakness'; 'what strikes every body at first sight, on coming amongst the Affghans, is their manliness and simplicity of demeanour, by comparison with all eastern nations'; 'of all oriental races, the Affghans had best resisted the effeminacy of oriental usages . . . their strength lay in their manly character', and so on and so on (B49 1841 297, 291; B56 1844 139). Though this great manliness distinguishes them from *all* other oriental peoples, it especially divides them from the Hindus. The Afghans 'have always been a name of power amongst the feeble Hindoos'; they are 'a nation of men; whilst the timid and submissive Hindoo suggests a painful feeling that here is a people meant to be conquered'; consequently ' "the stern Afghan" ' has 'a slight shade of contempt for the supple Hindoo' (B49 1841 291–2).

It may have been to provide a pratical demonstration of the truth of this gendered account of Asian ethnography that De Quincey discusses an incident from 'Mr Durie's Narrative' of a journey through Afghanistan, published as an appendix in Elphinstone's *Account*. Durie was a member 'of that very interesting (some think dangerous) class, called the Indo-British children, that is to say, of Hindoo mothers and British fathers'; he was an 'avowed mendicant', and rambled through Afghanistan with no means of support other than the hospitality of the inhabitants (B49 1841 299). In the course of his narrative Durie notes that, when his trousers were worn out, he was given another pair by an Afghan, but that (presumably because of the cold) he wrapped some pieces of his old trousers round his waist, and as a result was often searched in his travels, as if his valuables were kept in the roll of cloth round his waist.[5]

Out of this incident, De Quincey produces a strange fantasy, which was to return to haunt him at the time of the rebellion in India:

From his journal . . . it does not appear that he ever felt himself in danger from mere want of food; but, on the other hand, he had his pockets felt and probed with equal fervour. In his case there was nothing to rob; the pockets were empty; but it happened ludicrously enough that mere excess of poverty had left about him one sole delusive indication of wealth: various trowsers, which had successively fallen away in rags from the lower parts, remained as so many zones or belts in their upper portions (which had been more strongly lined) about his hips. Suffering much from cold in the winter, as a native of Bengal, he could not resolve to sacrifice these accumulated strata, these northern frontiers of ancient trowsers; and dire was the suffering which he thus created to himself and to many of his kind hosts. Often he was called out into the dark by an affectionate friend, who would entreat to know what treasure it was that he carried about him, causing this regular swell about the equator of his person; and then a search would commence, terminating of course in disappointment; but this disappointment never led to any bad feeling, or to any interruption of the hospitality. . . . Thus the simple traveller revolved amongst this simple nation, every man giving him food, every man feeling his pockets, until his perfidious trowsers became as well known in Affghanistan as the Hindoo Koosh, or Cape Disappointment to sailors in Baffin's Bay.   (B49 1841 299–300)

This delightful fantasy seems to manage to combine (and, as usual in De Quincey's writings, without any indication of priority) the personal and the political in two narratives whose pleasures are oddly contradictory. On the one hand, the private pleasure of vicarious homoeroticism: an affectionate friend in the darkness, a swelling in the trousers, a probing and a being probed – all ending in disappointment, but not in 'bad feeling'. On the other hand, an anxiety about the potency of the Indo-British (some think them 'dangerous') which is laid to rest by the discovery that the swelling in their trousers is 'delusive' – there is *nothing there* – the Indo-British are as childlike or as effeminate as the Hindus themselves. Durie was a native of Bengal, and compared with the 'brave men' beyond the North-West frontier, the 'Bengalees', as we learn from another of the Afghanistan articles, are 'Phrygian' (B56 1844 136).

But if in 1841 it gave De Quincey a 'painful feeling' to reflect that the Hindus were 'a people born to be conquered', it gave him a still more painful feeling in 1857 to contemplate the possibility that they were not. And in his essays on the Indian rebellion that possibility is entertained by a return to thoughts of Hindu trousers, and of whether there might be something dangerous concealed in them after all. Indeed, all the protagonists in the rebellion are contemplated in the light of their sexual potency. 'It is perfectly dazzling'. writes De Quincey, shaping in his mind the spectacle of all spectacles, 'to review over the whole face of India, under almost universal desertion, the attitude of erectness and preparation assumed by the scattered parties of our noble countrymen . . . No matter how small the amount of the British force may be, . . . it holds its own' – which is almost as good as having it held by an affectionate friend. No useful help is to be expected, however, from 'the *native* associations formed in Calcutta': 'either the members will be sleeping at the moment of outbreak, or will be separated from their arms'. Fortunately, some of the rebellious sepoys have already been disarmed, and even (De Quincey's inexplicable emphasis) '*stripped of their private arms*'; and still more fortunately, the task of the British forces is facilitated by an extraordinary distinguishing mark which visibly betrays the most guilty among the remainder.

The rebels have been plundering the coffers of the East India Company, but because the Company's cash is mostly in silver, not gold, it is extremely difficult to carry away discreetly in large quantities, for 'money, carried in weighty parcels of coin, cannot be concealed. Swathed about the person, it disfigures the natural symmetries of the figure.' The innocent sepoy, therefore, or the guilty but unsuccessful, 'having no money, . . . had no swollen trousers'. The worst offenders, on the other hand, will only too visibly have acquired, have *stolen*, the swelling denied them by De Quincey's wishes, if not by his fears; so that 'if his robberies had been very productive and prosperous, in that proportion he became advertised to every eye'. For one hundred years the British in India had expressed their contempt for Hindu men by representing them as infantile or as feminine. All the major commentators on the history of India – Robertson, Orme, Mill, Macaulay, Elphinstone – had concurred on the effeminacy of the Hindus, and in Calcutta University Hindus reading for the BA degree were obliged to study Elphinstone's *History of India*, in which they would have discovered that they were members of an effeminate race – indolent, timid, mendacious, frivolous, and vain.[6] In what other form, therefore, could the British fantasise the revenge of the Hindus, if not of bulging trousers? And what other punishment could have been as appropriate, for this mutiny of the lower members, as dismemberment, by being 'blown away' from the guns? – the punishment preferred by many of the British, if time and ammunition allowed (U1: 309–10, 334, 328–30; Majumdar 199–200).

II

In 1853 De Quincey had claimed that the single greatest advance, the most 'absolute conquest over wrong and error won by human nature in our times' was 'the mighty progress made towards the suppression of brutal, bestial modes of punishment'. In 1858, in company with various other commentators on the rebellion, he was considerably exercised by the question of the appropriate mode of punishment to be meted out to captured rebels; and, like others, he thought that mere hanging was too lenient, insufficiently brutal and bestial a punishment for those he described variously as 'pagan hounds', 'a bloody kennel of hounds', 'hell-born destroyers', and 'a mass of carrion from a brotherhood of thugs' (1: 293; U1: 338–9, 314, 324, 315). John Nicholson proposed the flaying alive, impalement, and burning of the rebels; [7] more merciful British commentators were content that the most guilty of the rebels should be 'blown away', as the phrase delicately put it, a 'mode of death' which had the advantage for those who suffered it of being (according to Henry Fane) 'perhaps, the quickest and least cruel of any', and the further advantage, for those inflicting it, that it prevented the dead from being buried intact, and mixed together the fragments of Hindu and Muslim. If this mode of execution caused a 'murmur of horror' among native troops, that was what it was meant to do; but if the repeated scenes of 'legs, arms, and heads, flying in all directions' were at first too much for a delicate European sensibility to bear, 'such is the force of habit,' a British officer reassured a British journalist, that 'we now think little of them'. Another detailed account of this form of execution was published in *Blackwood's* in November 1857, a couple of months before De Quincey turned his mind to the problem; and it would be surprising if he was unaware of it (Fane 2: 148; *Indian Revolt*, 36; B82 1857 609–10). [8]

His own preference, however, was for hanging, followed by decapitation, but it seems unlikely that he favoured this method on humanitarian grounds. For De Quincey, as for the advocates of 'blowing away', the essence of the punishment was the religious terror it would strike, he believed, in men who believed 'that to suffer any dismemberment of the body operates disastrously upon the fate in the unseen world'. But for De Quincey, in search of as 'degrading' a punishment as he could think of, 'mutilation' by decapitation was perhaps the worst or the most appropriate imaginable. 'It will sometimes have been noticed,' wrote Freud in 1916, 'that patients suffering from obsessions express an amount of abhorrence of and indignation against punishment by beheading far greater than they do in the case of any other form of death; and in such cases the analyst may be led to explain to them that they are treating being beheaded as a substitute for being castrated' (XIV: 339). In these terms, to decapitate the rebels of 1857, as well as symbolically 'breaking the neck of the mutiny' (to borrow a phrase from Richard Baird Smith, De Quincey's son-in-law) would also ensure that never again would they be able to flaunt their swollen trousers; but their punishment may also be read as a punishment for something that happened in the upper chamber at Greenhay in June 1792, sixty-five years earlier (U1: 338–9; Vibart 131). It is as if somewhere De Quincey imagined that to stage a repetition of that event would be to repair the 'painful feeling' associated with the discovery of the grounds of sexual differentiation.[9]

The precise nature of the crime for which this retribution is to be exacted is as obscure here as it is elsewhere. When first he heard news of the capture of Delhi by the rebels, he was unimpressed by the stories of a 'universal and undiscriminating' massacre. He wrote to Emily (perhaps to reassure her) that 'everything will have been dreadfully exaggerated' (P2: 130). Soon, however, he seems to have become willing to believe anything that is alleged against the sepoys. But it may be that the real crime attributed to the rebels is, once again, the half-imagined, half-suppressed dissection of Elizabeth. It may equally have been the fantasised primal scene which seems to be inextricably linked to that scene of dissection. The alleged atrocities of Delhi are described by De Quincey as '*aporreta* (απορρητα) things not utterable in human language or to human ears – things ineffable – things to be whispered – things to dream of, not to tell' (U1: 303). The last phrase here had been used to describe (among other things) the terrors of the Orion Nebula; in Coleridge's 'Christabel' it describes the sight of the lady Geraldine's 'bosom, and half her side', as, watched by Christabel, she undresses for bed. The line seems to attach the events at Delhi to those other images and fantasies we have encountered of maternal 'exposure' – of the corpse of Mrs Williamson, 'exposed' to the 'gaze' of the young journeyman; of Agnes in 'The Household Wreck', 'exposed in the bloody amphitheatre'; of the evil mother in 'The Love-Charm', who murders her child *en déshabillé*; of Wyndham's mother, exposed and scourged; of mother China, 'laid bare to the whole world'; of the wife of the Kandyan *Ádigar*, threatened with exposure and worse; of 'Milton's "incestuous mother"', exposed to mortal gaze in the essay on the Orion Nebula itself.

The displacements here are multiple, and speak at the same time of shared imperial fantasies and of the domestic fantasies of De Quincey's private world. The sepoys must suffer for exposing the nakedness of European women, for appropriating and reversing the European privilege of exposing the colonial woman, or the colonial *as* woman – of revealing the nakedness of Ceylon, imagined as Pandora inspected by the lords of Olympus; of China, exposed to the world as a cancerous and dying mother; of Afghanistan, imagined in one of the epigraphs to Chapter 11 as naked and so as incapable of defending 'herself'; of the woman in the other epigraph to that chapter who came to ask the traveller Vigne for medical advice, and was tricked into removing her veil and exposing her arms. And the sepoys must suffer too for what Dr Percival did to Elizabeth, and for what someone else – Thomas's father? his brother? his Bengal uncle? – is imagined to have done to De Quincey's mother. But as we have repeatedly seen, all those guilty men from De Quincey's childhood are the bearers of a guilt which, however urgently he tries to pass it elsewhere, is always also his own. The demand that the sepoys be decapitated, in obedience to a perverse *lex talionis*, is another version of the demand that someone should be punished for something De Quincey himself has done, or for something he *is*.

III

Thirty or more years before the outbreak of the rebellion, De Quincey had begun to translate the satire *Niels Klim* from the Danish of Ludvig Holberg; the incomplete manuscript of his translation is in the Auckland Public Library. *Niels Klim* is a Gulliveresque fantasy which begins when Klim decides to engage in some speleological investigation; arming himself with a boathook, he descends one day into a 'crater' or 'abyss' in a range of Norwegian mountains. His rope breaks, he falls for a long long time, and eventually lands on one of the planets which are to be found in the 'subterraneous heavens' (1953 16–17). It is inhabited by a race of 'rational trees', Holberg's houyhnhnms, who identify Klim as an *'Extraordinary Ape'*, teach him their language, and eventually decide that he has the intellectual capacities of a 'booby'. The planet has its yahoos too, 'troops of wild apes', who had 'the presumption,' Klim complains, 'to mistake me for one of their own species'. As he travelled across the planet, these apes 'were continually making snatches' at him as he passed, as if to claim him as one of their own; and in his vexation he lays into 'these infernal monkeys' with his boathook, so as 'to revenge the horrid affront they were putting on the whole species overhead, which I had the honour to represent in the subterranean world' (1953 22–3, 29–31). What follows is almost entirely De Quincey's free expansion of Holberg's story:

> With the perseverance of flies or gnats however, as often as they were brushed off, back they swarmed again; so that I was obliged to keep in continual readiness for action; and the whole latter part of my progress was a running fight, in which I had the satisfaction of bestowing innumerable raps and fractures on some thousands of empty skulls, and strewing the road with heaps of chattering baboons whom I had smashed in vindication of my own insulted honor and that of my species.   (1953 31)

Two sentences later the manuscript breaks off.

This vengeful attack is reminscent of the soliloquy of Ahasuerus in

the notes to Shelley's *Queen Mab*, who smashes the skulls of his
father, wives and children, in his anger that they could die, but he
could not – I have already suggested this version of Ahasuerus as De
Quincey's role model when he took to himself the identity of
Wandering Jew.[10] But as Nigel Leask has pointed out, the attack also
has the effect of turning Holberg's satire into as imperialist fantasy,
or rather an imperialist nightmare, of the swarming hordes of Asia,
the innumerable millions out there, beyond the Tigris, where all
identity is lost. It may equally be read as a bourgeois fantasy of the
underworld east of Aldgate, the sea of faces where all are faceless.
'Once let them', writes De Quincey of the Chinese, 'in any one
pursuit, manifest a sense or a love of anything really intellectual . . . then first will they rise out of that monkey tribe' (1857
12).[11] In De Quincey's version of Holberg, Klim is determined to be
recognised, as a differentiated individual, and as the representative of
a superior race in this underworld. But that very determination
suggests that he is only too aware of sharing a common humanity, or
a common guilty bestiality, with this subordinate and subject race,
this demonised underclass. The fury of Klim – or of De Quincey
rather, for this is his narrative now, not Holberg's – is the rage of
Caliban seeing his own face in the glass. The baboons, like the
sepoys, are punished in an act of displaced self-hatred and self-
accusation, as is evident from the mode of punishment inflicted upon
them, a head for a head, their skulls rapped, fractured and smashed.
They are punished, indeed, as the sepoys must be, as if to
demonstrate that no suspicion of guilt can fall on De Quincey for
what happened at Greenhay, or on the class he claims membership
of, or on the British in general, for what was happening in London,
or India, or anywhere else in the British Empire.

The mutual and inextricable implication of the personal and the
public in De Quincey's writings on the rebellion is demonstrated,
finally, by the fate he envisaged for Delhi, which in common with
others he insisted should be utterly destroyed, in retribution for
having welcomed the first rebels from Meerut and for having
permitted or participated in the massacre of its European inhabitants.
The plea of those who have lost their lives in the rebellion, he writes,
is that Delhi should be 'swept by the ploughshare and sown with salt'
(U1: 305). There is a reference here to Judges 9.45, which describes
how Abimelech fought all day against the city of Shechem, 'and he
took the city, and slew the people that *was* therein, and beat down
the city, and sowed it with salt.' By the end of the chapter, God has
punished Abimelech by the hand of 'a certain woman', who 'cast a
piece of millstone upon Abimelech's head, and all to break his skull'.

The passage from Judges had been in De Quincey's mind a few

years earlier, when he was describing the occasion when, fighting alongside his brother William in the stone-throwing wars against the factory boys of Manchester, he was captured and handed over to the factory girls for safe keeping (see above, p.95). Their kindness threw his ideas of soldierly duty into complete confusion. Surely, he writes (the passage is a long one, and needs quoting at length)

> the assumption of warlike functions pledged a man . . . to *storm* his enemies; . . . to storm the houses of these young factory girls; briefly, and in plain English, to murder them all; to cut the throats of every living creature by their firesides . . . neither the guiltless smiles of unoffending infancy, nor the grey hairs of the venerable patriarch sitting in the chimney corner; neither the sanctity of the matron, nor the loveliness of the youthful bride; no, nor the warlike self-devotion of the noble young man, fighting as the champion of altars and hearths; none of these searching appeals would reach *my* heart; neither sex nor age would confer any privilege with me; that I should put them all to the edge of the sword; that I should raze the very foundations of their old ancestral houses; having done which, I should probably plough up the ground with some bushels of Nantwich salt, mixed with bonedust from the graves of infants as top-dressing; – that, in fact, the custom of all warriors, and therefore of necessity of myself, was notoriously to make a wilderness, and call it a pacification.
>
> (H6 1851 235)

This passage, as bloodthirsty as any in the earlier revenge fiction, seems to change direction as it goes on, so that the 'should' which describes what it is the duty of the soldier, however reluctant, to do to his enemies, becomes a 'should', a 'should probably', a 'would', describing what De Quincey would like to do to everyone, given half the chance. It is a fantasy of running amok, of slaughter on the scale of Delhi or Cawnpore, which greedily appropriates to its own pleasurable elaboration all that 'oriental' violence which it was also De Quincey's pleasure to abhor and to denounce. The playful detail about top-dressing – 'bonedust from the graves of infants' – makes the connection, across these two passages, between a private guilt and a public punishment. The bonedust and the graves of infants were left out when De Quincey revised this passage for the 1853 version of the 'Autobiography', in a rare moment of awareness on his part that such fantasies of violence could perhaps be taken too far (1: 80). But along with the salt, they were certainly present to his mind as he contemplated the future destruction of Delhi. The plea for the destruction of the city is one that De Quincey imagines arising from the 'bloody graves' of 'dying daughters and their perishing infants'; the sequence of Abimelech's story has been reversed; and the destruction of Delhi is figured as one more act of revenge for the wound in De Quincey's head (U1: 305).

13

Concussion

She turns, and turns again, and carefully glances around her on all sides, to see that she is safe from the eyes of Mussulmans, and then suddenly withdrawing the yashmak, she shines upon your heart and soul with all the pomp and might of her beauty. . . . You smile at pretty women – you turn pale before the beauty that is great enough to have dominion over you. She sees, and exults in your giddiness; she sees and smiles; then presently, with a sudden movement, she lays her blushing fingers upon your arm, and cries out, 'Yumourdjak!' (Plague! meaning, 'there is a present of the plague for you!').   A.W. Kinglake, *Eothen*, 40.

I live and have borne my misery as best I could. To most I appear calm and cheerful, but the wound rankles in my heart; and could you but know my sufferings, sahib, you would perhaps pity me. Not in the daytime is my mind disturbed by the thoughts of the past; it is at night, when all is still around me, and sleep falls not upon my weary eyelids, that I see again before me the form of my unfortunate sister; again I fancy my hands busy with her beautiful neck, and the vile piece of coin for which I killed her seems again in my grasp as I tore it from her warm bosom, Sahib, there is no respite from these hideous thoughts; if I eat opium – which I do in large quantities, to produce a temporary oblivion – I behold the same scene in the dreams which it causes, and it is distorted and exaggerated by the effects of the drug. Nay, this is worse to bear than the simple reality, to which I sometimes become accustomed, until one vision more vivid than its predecessors plunges me into despair of its ever quitting me.
                    Meadows Taylor, *Confessions of a Thug*, 432–3.

I

Let me begin to end by putting together a by now familiar involute – a secret book, a locked space, an intrusion, a head wound – and a by now equally familiar geopolitical terrain, Afghanistan, the barrier-state between almost everywhere and almost everything. 'The Dice', another of De Quincey's translations from the German, is the story of a bailiff's son, Rudolph, whose father has a secret book which he keeps in an elaborately secure safe. The whole family, intensely curious about the contents of the safe, had attempted to discover what it contained, but only Rudolph had succeeded: once, when he was 12, he burst in upon his father reading a large black folio volume, and was brusquely ordered away. Six years later he intrudes upon his father again, to find him burning the book. It had contained, explains his father, two prophecies concerning Rudolph: that he would be made an offer by the Evil One, tending much to his advantage, and that he would be the last of the family. In circumstances too complicated to describe, Rudolph later finds himself in a position where the roll of a die is to determine whether he, or a 'brother' officer, is to face a firing squad. With the aid of dice supplied by the devil, Rudolph saves himself, and proceeds to make his living by playing at dice. But one day, believing his wife has stolen the devil's dice, he stabs her to death; and shortly afterwards his only son accidentally treads on a die. He 'fell with such violence against the edge of the stove that he died in a few hours of the injury inflicted on the head' (12: 364–90).[1]

In his discussion of the absurdity of British fears of a Russian attack on India, De Quincey remarks, light-heartedly enough, that 'the Russian drummer-boys, by the time they reach the Khyber Pass, will all have become field-marshals, seeing that, after three years' marching, they have not yet reached Khiva'. An invading Russian army, travelling across the great spaces between their homeland and India, would never be able to put up with the snows, the thirst, the inevitable famine, the continual harassment from the local warriors. Russia, he remarks, in a passage we glanced at earlier,

> is a colossus, and Bokhara, Khiva, Kokan, &c., are dwarfs. But the finger of a colossus may be no match for the horny heels of a dwarf. The Emperor Tiberius could fracture a boy's skull with a *talitrum*, (or fillip of his middle finger;) but it is not every middle finger that can do that; and a close kick from a khan of Toorkistan might leave an uglier scar than a fillip at arm's length from the Czar.   (B56 1844 138)[2]

That Russia, attempting to bite off Afghanistan, would bite off more than it could chew, has turned out to be an entirely accurate prophecy; but that of course is not my concern.[3] What intrigues me is how the image of the drummer-boy suddenly conjures up one of the most brutal of Roman emperors, playfully drumming on the thin and vulnerable skull of an imaginary boy, and how this in turn has come to represent the behaviour of an aggressive eastern superpower towards its weaker neighbours. The sentence about Tiberius is not an invention of De Quincey's – it comes from Suetonius – but how on earth has it found its way into an essay on the imperial policy of the East India Company?

In another of De Quincey's accounts of the political history of Russia we can discover a version of perhaps the most private, and the most complex involute of all, which came to be attached to his memory or invention of the scene in Elizabeth's bedroom: the involute 'sister/kiss/trance/shaft,recess,abyss/Memnon/wind/ sudden noise (perhaps a footstep)/face of terror'. A version of this involute appeared also in the narrative of Thomas's departure from Manchester Grammar School, and in the account of the bust of Memnon and of the nebula in Orion. In 1841, De Quincey published in *Blackwood's* a *rifacimento* of a portion of Ernst Moritz Arndt's *Erinnerungen aus dem Äusseren Leben* (1840). It is called 'Russia As It Was in The Summer and Winter of 1812', and it translates and embellishes the experiences of Arndt as he observed, from the Russian side, the French invasion of that year – the 'precipitation', as De Quincey calls it, 'of the West upon the East', for in his version Russia is represented as an Asiatic and an exotic land, hardly European at all.[4] At one point the article describes the atmosphere, patriotic but light-headed, that developed in Smolensk prior to the French attack on that city. Women – even 'the most innocent and lovely' – took to caressing total strangers, in 'an expression of a sisterly recognition towards every known participator in Russian sentiments'; they manifested 'an air of sisterly love' in the most 'fervent' kisses, freely bestowed.

This emphasis on sisterliness is entirely absent from the original German, and the next paragraph owes almost nothing to Arndt, almost everything to De Quincey's own accounts of the scene in Elizabeth's bedroom. The narrator describes how, one hot day, he rode up to an eminence outside the town to enjoy the 'Pan-like' silence of the landscape, reminiscent (it seems) of the equally 'Panlike' smile on the face of Memnon, as described in a long note to the account of the last visit to Elizabeth (1: 41n.). His eye is suddenly caught by the 'gloomy recesses' of a distant woodland, and their utter stillness prompts in him a thought of death. The world, he reflects, is shaking beneath the 'resounding tread' of the soldiers gathering for battle; but what of the approaching 'tread' of death, the 'common abyss of darkness' that waits in turn for them? Suddenly he hears 'a solemn breathing of wind from the forests, so sad, so full of woe in its sound, half between a sigh and a groan, that I was really startled . . . It was a sound, beyond all I ever heard, that expressed a requiem and a lamentation.' The sister, the silence, the face imagined as calm and in repose, the recess and abyss, the footstep, the sound of the wind, the thought of death – all are to be found within that complex of images that constitutes the memory or fantasy of the last visit to Elizabeth's bedroom; and there is more to come. As Thomas turned to look at Elizabeth, he fell into a reverie, from which the footstep awoke him; he then approached nearer to Elizabeth's face – a face which, in the reparations or repetitions of this scene, may be a countenance calmly beautiful or a ruined skull – and kissed her. Similarly, in 'Russia as it was', the narrator falls into a reverie, only to be woken by the sound and sight of the local Russian militias converging in thousands of waggons upon Smolensk – they resembled, he suggests, a dance of death, led by a 'marrowless and eyeless skeleton'. The whole scene was – De Quincey quotes once more that line from 'Christabel' which seems to be associated with the scenery of primal fantasy – ' "a sight to dream of, not to tell", and even for dreams too like delirium and frenzy' (B49 1841 742–4; Arndt, 143–5).[5]

What are we to make of the appearance, in public writings about public and most often oriental topics, of involutes and patterns of narrative which occur also in the most private contexts?[6] At the end of my introduction, I announced my intention of avoiding the attempt to establish 'a hierarchy of precedence' in De Quincey's writings, 'an organisation into the manifest and the latent, the surface and the depth, among the various objects of fear'. As a result the question of primacy has been begged over and over again throughout this book – perhaps most evidently when I spoke of an 'archaeology' in his writing, and of 'strata of anxiety' whereby a racial or a class fear may be thought of as in turn concealing, or as concealed by, a sexual fear. Which comes first? Where is the fundamental layer, the earliest moment, in the story De Quincey has to tell? What *is* the story? Is it the tale of a private and secret guilt, whose origin, private, unknown, unapproachable, is figured first in the primal scene and in the sister's bedroom, and only thereafter in Cawnpore, the Khyber Pass, Kandy? Or have we been discovering in the narratives of De Quincey's childhood what I called earlier a fully social guilt? – a guilt at his own participation in the fantasies of imperial conquest and subjugation, and a guilt which, because it cannot be avowed, can find a voice only by being relocated in the terrain of the family, where it is both more usual to find it acknowledged and (from reticence or discretion) to find it concealed. It may be worth making, in this conclusion, one more attempt, not to answer those questions, but to explain, or to describe, my reluctance to offer any answers.

There is an early scene in John Frankenheimer's film *The Manchurian Candidate* where a group of bored GIs are discovered sitting around in what appears to be a large ornamental glass-house, the palm court of an old-fashioned New Jersey hotel. They are listening to, or rather they are languidly ignoring, a talk on the cultivation of hydrangeas, delivered by an expensively dressed woman who is old enough to be their mother. The rest of the audience consists of other expensively dressed women who are old enough to be their mothers. Suddenly everything changes. A group of bored GIs are discovered sitting on the stage of a lecture theatre. They are listening to, or rather they are intermittently aware of, a lecture on how thoroughly and successfully they have been brainwashed, delivered by an oriental communist who is also a psychologist. The rest of the audience consists of other oriental communists who are also psychologists. The narrative switches, back and forth, from New Jersey to Manchuria, from conditioning back to cultivation, from hard-faced American matrons to hard-faced oriental communists.

As the film develops, so we discover that the leading character, apparently a hero of the Korean War, has been brainwashed by the Chinese, and is controlled by his apparently all-American but actually communist mother. The danger to America is twofold: it comes from home, the very centre of the family, from mom; it comes from the Far East. But even after we discover that these two threats are both 'real', and are operating in tandem, we still seem able to hold on to a reading of the film by which one is a mask, a figure, a hallucination of the other. The Communist Menace is merely an externalisation of the enemy within, a momism which emasculates the American male. Or momism is just an internalisation of the enemy without, the Communist Menace and its plans for world domination. There is nowhere in the wide world where you can escape from mom; in every chamber, no matter how private and protected, there are reds under the bed. De Quincey may turn in horror from his sister's bed, and the white turban of bandages, and he may turn from the imagined brutality of the Orient; but where can he turn from each except to the other?

'The Turkish troops began to appear in considerable force', he writes, of an engagement in the Greek War of Independence, 'and . . . an alarm was suddenly given "that the white turbans were upon them".' The white turban, to most Europeans, was the badge of the Muslim in the Ottoman Empire, sometimes forbidden to be worn, on pain of death, by the members of other religions.[7] But for De Quincey it was rather more. The inhabitants of Afghanistan wear white turbans; so do the Sinhalese; so do Malays; so do brothers and so do sisters. There are white turbans *everywhere*, objects of unutterable terror. But equally, wherever we turn to in the East, we find mothers – mothers exposed to insult, mothers exposed in punishment, mothers with heads muffled in veils or in turbans – all objects of unutterable terror (7: 305).

II

The point I am trying to make is that, whether in Frankenheimer's film or in De Quincey's *oeuvre*, both worlds are horrifying, the inner and the outer, and that the attempt to rationalise one in terms of the other, to establish one as primary to the other, has the effect of making each of them doubly horrifying, for each is then the double of the other. If the dangers that threaten the British constitution and the British Empire are to have a chance of destroying either, writes De Quincey,

> whether at home or abroad, it is essential that the danger should mask itself, should approach us in disguise, and should act upon us by what, in Scottish or Roman law, is called 'concussion' – in a sudden cumulative surprise upon all our means of resistance.
>
> (B52 1842 271)

It is the *co-operation* of internal and external terrors, each disguised as the other, that makes De Quincey's world such a terrifying place; and the secret of safety and happiness, it seems, is to distinguish one from the other, to move one terror or the other from one column to another, and so to prevent them from acting cumulatively or in concert, or rather to prevent either one revealing the face of the other that it both wears and hides. The 'this/that/the other' structure could then be seen as an attempt to force a terrifying presence ever further afield; a presence constantly rediscovered, however, in the devices which should conceal it – in the very features of the mask, in the very pattern of the curtain.

What can we say, then, about the apparent 'normality' of De Quincey's life? – for throughout the period that he was writing his most ferocious and brutal denunciations of the Chinese, of the Kandyans and of the rebels in India, he seems to have enjoyed, not exactly a 'normal' family life (apart from anything else, his debts, for much of that period, made that impossible), but still a happy one. In that context, both the private and the public narratives can perhaps be understood as, if not serving a purpose, still as producing an effect, of 'normalisation': the family space becomes safe, happy even, because the fears and phantoms of De Quincey's personal and political life are expelled beyond it, into De Quincey's own past, or into the Far East.

6   James Archer, *Portrait of Thomas De Quincey with his daughters Emily and Margaret* (1855).

In fact, if we look at one of the most striking portraits of De Quincey – it is of De Quincey as 'family man' – we can see the extent to which the Far East is present, present precisely as a conspicuous absence, at the very heart of the family scene. At the end of 1855 De Quincey's daughter Florence commissioned from James Archer a pastel group portrait of her father and his children (Figure 6). None of De Quincey's sons was present to be portrayed along with their father. The eldest, William, had died in 1834, of what looked to De Quincey like hydrocephalus, but was probably chloroleukaemia (L319–20), and the youngest, Julius, had died in infancy. The other three had embraced or submitted to the customary fate of the sons of the genteel but impecunious. Horace had become a lieutenant in the

Cameronian regiment, and had died of a fever in 1842 at Canton; Francis had emigrated to Brazil in 1851; and Paul Frederick had also become a soldier, who served in the Indian Mutiny and then in New Zealand, eventually settling there. In 1855 therefore there were only daughters (and granddaughters) left in Scotland to surround the 70-year-old patriarch: Florence herself, her two sisters Emily and Margaret, and Eva, Margaret's daughter. The portrait was intended as a reminder and a consolation to Florence when she too left with her husband for India.

There is a pleasing informality about the grouping and the poses. One might have imagined that the guilts, hatreds and fantasies of revenge we have been tracing out in this book would somehow show on De Quincey's face, as he himself seems to have feared they would (see above, pp.16–17). That face is the most sharply focused area of the whole image: there should surely be some mark of Cain, some identifying outbreak of leprosy or scrofula? No such thing. He looks alert, but also relaxed – he has claimed the old man's, and the writer's privilege of looking scruffy even in his best clothes. He is almost if not quite smiling, and he assumes no posture of authority in relation to his daughters. It is indeed the portrait of a man who had enjoyed, by all accounts, the most enduring and affectionate relations with his wife and daughters (if not, perhaps, with his sons: L347). The women of the family had sustained him, and he them, through years and years of poverty (by middle-class standards) and of the most exhausting drudgery on both sides, domestic and literary. He has now finally achieved some kind of modest financial stability, helped by gifts from his East-India uncle, by a small inheritance from his mother, and by contracts with American and Scottish publishers for collected editions of his writings.

Should we find it odd, then, that a family man, so apparently happy and at ease with himself and others, should harbour such terrifying aggression, and should dream of exacting such a terrible retribution from those on whom he has projected his own self-hatred? I don't think so. Among the various styles of racism in the 1830s, 1840s and 1850s, De Quincey's is one of the more violent, but we cannot therefore assume that he was *more* racist than those whose racism may have taken a less violent fantasmatic form. It is not hard to imagine that if we were to ask the same questions of other Victorian writers as this book has asked of De Quincey, we might well find ourselves regarding the story this book has told as a typical, rather than an unusual, one. There may have been something about that identity – the 'family man', the man brought up in, and eventually taking his place at the head of, the middle-class and aristocratic British family in the period of imperial expansion at the end of the eighteenth and beginning of the nineteenth centuries – there may have been something in the coincidence of family history and imperial history which emerges as the characteristic racism – as the common characteristic of the different racisms – of a whole generation of authors.

The styles of that racism are indeed very different. To pick instances only from accounts of the Near and Middle East, there is not at first sight very much of De Quincey in the manner of, for example, A.W. Kinglake's or Thackeray's progress through the Levant and Egypt. Both seem to offer us their racism – light-hearted, deftly ironic, condescending – as a part of their enormous charm. In their dealings with Jewish and Muslim men, they behave like friendly, pipe-smoking prep-school masters: they *tolerate* them, and are prepared to forgive even the error they have committed in failing to be European. Kinglake judges the women of the East entirely according to their looks: the one oversight he cannot forgive is that of a woman who has 'grossly neglected the prime duty of looking pretty' (155). On the other hand there is, if anything, too little charm in Lord Lindsay's racism for it to look much like De Quincey's: Lindsay travels through the Ottoman Empire in the style of a British bulldog: he is always on the look-out for Muslim 'curs' to quarrel with, and he prides himself on his ability to make them 'fawn' like 'spaniels'. Compare and contrast this with the compassion of Godfrey Thomas Vigne, ever willing to take on himself the sufferings of oriental others (and to manifest his boundless belief in the magical power of *baksheesh*). 'On two or three occasions', he writes on his travels in Kashmir and further north, 'I have had the misfortune to pepper a peasant's legs with small shot (which by the by, with all caution, it is sometimes really difficult to avoid, on account of their extreme carelessness)'. In all such cases, however, he has 'made them perfectly happy with a few rupis' (Vigne 1842 2: 212). Or there is the scientific racism of E.W. Lane, one of a number of British men of the period (David Urquhart was another) to 'go native' in the Middle East, whose writing is entirely dependent (as Edward Said points out) on a racial stereotyping of both the European and the oriental, which situates one as the cold, neutral observer of the overheated passions of the other (Said 158–64).[8]

But almost wherever we look, in the writings of British men about the 'Orient' from Egypt to China, we come across a strange triangulation of ideas and images that expresses, more than anything else, their fear of the East and the irrationality of that fear. It is a triad we have found repeatedly in De Quincey, and which combines in a single image the East, the body of the woman, and death. It is everywhere in British writing on *sati*. It is evident in both the epigraphs to this chapter. Though Meadows Taylor certainly knew how very rare were the instances (or those known to the British) of women being killed by thugs, the paragraph from his novel which stands at the beginning of this chapter is only the most extreme version of a scene repeated several times through the work: the murder of a beautiful woman, and the memory of her face distorted by the effects of strangulation.[9] Kinglake, who like so many other British travellers to Islamic countries is desperate to *see* women – to see behind their veils, to see into the harem – is granted his wish in Istanbul, and what he sees is the face of death. At Smyrna, he finds in the 'rare beauty' of the women 'a terrible stillness', like that of 'the young Persephonie . . . Queen of Shades', or like 'the stillness of a savage that sits intent and brooding day by day on some one fearful scheme of vengeance' (61).

The same triad is evident in the epigraph to Chapter 2, where Lindsay, arriving at Palmyra, can find no more apt image to describe that city than the body of a beautiful, dead woman.[10] It is evident also in the epigraph to Chapter 5, where W.H. Russell describes his first night in Calcutta, where he had gone to cover the rebellion for *The Times*. Just as he is on the point of going to sleep, he hears what he thinks is the scream 'of a dying woman close at hand, which chilled the marrow in my bones'; it turns out to be 'only a pack of jackals'. The elaborate comparison offered by Eliot Warburton, in his bestselling travel book *The Crescent and the Cross* (1845), between 'the Odalisque of the Hareem' and 'the Arab woman of the street' is offered as a comparison of absolute contraries, as different as Memnon and the nebula in Orion. But there is one thing, in addition to their oriental character and their femininity, that the two have in common: both are inseparable from the idea of death. Merely to look upon the woman of the harem 'is danger or death'; the body of a prostitute is at once concealed and advertised by 'a mass of white, shroud-like drapery' (Warburton 1: 65, 73–6). Most of the rest of his chapter 'Woman – The Hareem' is occupied with tales of two Egyptians whom Warburton claims to have come across on a trip up the Nile , both of whom have just murdered their wives. This is the kind of thing:

> Not a palm-tree raised its plumy head, not a shrub crept along the ground; the sun was low, but there was nothing to cast a shadow over the monotonous waste, except a few Moslem tombs with their sculptured turbans; . . . As I paused to contemplate this scene of desolation, an Egyptian hurried past me with a bloody knife in his hand; . . . my groom, who just then came up, told me he had slain his wife.   (Warburton 1: 69)

This triad (it could be exemplified over and over again) is ubiquitous enough to be 'normal', and its repeated occurrence seems to make the apparently strange pathology of De Quincey – the repeated linking of the same three notions, the East, the woman's body, and death – look 'normal' too. Apart from that, I have no more to say about it than I had earlier about the question of what comes first, for it raises the same question, which we can now put, however, a little more directly: what comes first for the masculine psyche in the texts of this period, aggression towards women, or aggression towards the people of 'other' cultures? Once again that aggression seems to shuttle between its two objects, representing each as a mask or metaphor for the other. It is a repeated theme of British writing on imperial issues in the late eighteenth and nineteenth centuries that the stage of civilisation a people has reached can be judged by the way its women are treated. The idea may not have been British in origin – De Quincey himself seems to have found it in Kant (14: 57–8) – but it was especially serviceable to an imperialist nation at a stage when it was both inventing the Victorian ideal of virtuous womanhood and, by virtue of its imperial adventures, making itself more vulnerable to anxieties about the hostility and violence of 'other' peoples. Did the image of violence against women in the East, did the notion of eastern woman as the image of violence, serve to confirm the English gentleman in his sense of his sexual civility at home? And does that same civility reveal, in these imperialist and woman-hating fantasies, its 'true' face, its 'true' other?

That ideal of womanhood, as Carol Christ has argued (162), 'left the man who embraced it in an impossible dilemma, for to him woman was both a perpetual reproach and a perpetual temptation'; the idealisation is at once an act of aggression towards women, a negation of their sexuality, and the cause of more aggression, as women come to be blamed – and punished – for the masculine sexuality they both excite and reprove. Time and time again we have come across the trope that holds together that double character of woman, her power at once to inflame, and to freeze male sexuality into a 'languishing impotence' – the trope whereby the exposure of the woman's body – as object of desire or as image of horror – is both her crime and her punishment. But it is a punishment which, if it does not directly lead to her death, always *stands for* death: to 'expose' the nebula in Orion was also to 'cut the lovely throat' of the nebular hypothesis.

'That no Asiatic state has ever debarbarised itself', writes De Quincey in relation to the 'Chinese Question', 'is evident from the condition of WOMAN at this hour all over Asia' (14: 357). It is in the light of the secret history of that claim, as it emerges not only in his writings but in so much Victorian writing on Woman and Empire, that we must view his belief in the superiority of European civilisation, and in the manifest destiny of Britain especially to conquer and civilise the East. It may be appropriate to end, therefore, with a passage from the essay 'Joan of Arc' which shows De Quincey at his most reverential towards the ideal of European womanhood:

> Woman, sister, there are some things which you do not execute as well as your brother, man; no, nor ever will. Pardon me if I doubt whether you will ever produce a great poet from your choirs, or a Mozart, or a Phidias, or a Michael Angelo, or a great philosopher, or a great scholar . . . . Yet, sister woman, though I cannot consent to find a Mozart or a Michael Angelo in your sex, cheerfully, and with the love that burns in the depths of admiration, I acknowledge that you can do one thing as well as the best of us men – . . . you can die grandly, and as goddesses would die, were goddesses mortal.   (5: 406–7)

The passage goes on to meditate on the voyeurism of extra-terrestrials. The 'grandest sight' that Earth has to show to the telescopes of other worlds, it suggests, is 'a scaffold on the morning of execution', and *especially* if 'the poor victim of the morning's sacrifice is to be a woman' – a Marie Antoinette, a Charlotte Corday (5: 407). The civilisation of Europe – for it is the civilisation of Mozart, of Phidias, of Michelangelo that is at stake here – is to be judged by its treatment of women; and the 'grandest' example of that, it seems, are the scenes of decapitation or the images of mutilated heads that fill De Quincey's fantasies. The most disturbing of De Quincey's images of horror – often of *oriental* horror – are here rediscovered as the measure of European grandeur, of the immense superiority of Europe over the East.

III

It may, as I say, be appropriate to end there, but it will not seem so to many readers of De Quincey. Thus Hillis Miller, for example, ends his fine essay in *The Disappearance of God* with a death, but with the triumphant death, as he believes it to be, of De Quincey himself, and with his last words. 'De Quincey's penultimate speech', he writes, 'is apparently a confession of the guilt he felt towards his mother for his disobedient flight from school into a life of wandering. The last words of all show, across the widening gulf of death, that De Quincey found his sister again at the last moment of his life, and that he did indeed "rise again before he died":

'Twice only was the heavy breathing interrupted by words. He had for hours ceased to recognise any of us, but we heard him murmur, though quite distinctly, "My dear, dear mother. Then I was greatly mistaken". Then as the waves of death rolled faster and faster over him, suddenly out of the abyss we saw him throw up his arms, which to the last retained their strength, and say distinctly, and as if in great surprise, "Sister! sister! sister!" The loud breathing became slower and slower, and . . . [he] fell asleep for ever'.

    (J.H. Miller 79–80, quoting Florence Baird Smith in P2: 305)

I have never understood why critics and biographers of De Quincey treat this 'reunion' with his sister as beyond question a restorative event, a final reparation for sixty and more years of strife and affliction. It seems equally available to be read as the (let us hope) final nightmare, the final appearance of the terrifying and two-faced figure of the woman, at once, or ambiguously ('I was greatly mistaken') mother and sister. Miller reads these last words through De Quincey's conclusion to his essay 'Joan of Arc', which promises to Joan 'a second childhood, innocent as the first' (J.H. Miller 79; 5: 414). But De Quincey's essay does not quite end there. The last two pages describe the death of the Bishop of Beauvais, who has Joan's death on his conscience.

> Bishop of Beauvais! because the guilt-burdened man is in dreams haunted and waylaid by the most frightful of his crimes, and because upon that fluctuating mirror . . . most of all are reflected the sweet countenances which the man has laid in ruins; therefore I know, bishop, that you also, entering your final dream, saw Domrémy. That fountain, of which the witnesses spoke so much, showed itself to your eyes in pure morning dews; but neither dews, nor the holy dawn, could cleanse away the bright spots of innocent blood upon its surface. By the fountain, bishop, you saw a woman seated, that hid her face. But, as *you* draw near, the woman raises her wasted features. Would Domrémy know them again for the face of her child? Ah, but *you* know them, bishop, well!   (5: 414–5)

It is hardly necessary by now to point out the presence here of so many of the images that compose the involutes associated with Elizabeth's death: the face laid 'in ruins', the dews, the dawn, the seated woman who hides her face.[11] Hardly necessary, either, to point out De Quincey's conscious identification with the bishop: *I know* what you saw in your final dream, he seems to be saying, because I also am burdened with guilt; I also have seen *my*

Domrémy. *my* muffled woman, *my* vision of a child's face in ruins.

The bishop turns his own face away, as if to escape the image of the woman 'whom once again he must behold before he dies'. The scene of the dream changes: there is 'a tribunal that rises to the clouds'; the bishop is 'the prisoner at the bar' – and there is no one who will defend him. But De Quincey knows of just one person who will:

> Who is this that cometh from Domrémy? Who is she in bloody coronation robes from Rheims? Who is she that cometh with blackened flesh from walking the furnaces of Rouen? This is she, the shepherd girl, counsellor that had none for herself, whom I choose, bishop, for yours. She it is, I engage, that shall take my lord's brief. She it is, bishop, that would plead for you: yes, bishop, SHE, – when heaven and earth are silent.   (5: 415–16)

This second passage attributes to De Quincey a privileged knowledge and vision which now serve to differentiate him from the bishop: my vision, not yours; your guilt, not mine. But what is that separation or privilege if not the ground of an ever more self-revealing identification: I choose what you see? To call up the dead martyr from the shades of death may be another of De Quincey's fantasies of the woman as horrific and threatening – like the image of the 'sister unknown' at the end of 'The English Mail-Coach', who rose like a martyr in crimson robes, only to be described as 'raving, as despairing'. It may equally be another of his acts of hatred and revenge – a curiously double revenge, for the threatening appearance of the woman may not be at all at odds with her mission of mercy – De Quincey was fascinated by the kind of revenge which rendered a valuable service in return for evil.[12] The woman who waits on the threshold of life and death may intend restoration, or retribution, or both. We cannot repair De Quincey's life by choosing for him the death we would like him to have had.

Notes

1 Introduction

1. I am indebted to Raphael Samuel for information on the Saturday night markets in London. When Monday was treated as a day of rest, or 'holy day', it was referred to by artisans, labourers and their critics at 'St. Monday'. The term 'ghoster' may be anachronistic in the context of De Quincey: when East-End artisans of the 1880s and 1890s worked very late on Friday evening, or even all night, to complete their piecework by Saturday, they described themselves as working a 'ghoster'. The practice, if not the term, must have been as common at the beginning of the century as at the end.

2. For another example of De Quincey claiming to converse with 'poor men', and discovering that almost all are 'jacobins at heart', see 'Anti-Corn-Law Deputation to Sir Robert Peel', B52 1842 272. A hatred of Jacobinism, and a disposition to regard as Jacobin all political positions (and especially Brougham's) that could not be accommodated within the Tory party, is a feature of De Quincey's writing as early as 1818, if he is indeed the author of *Close Comments upon a Straggling Speech* (De Quincey 1818; attributed by Axon). For more of De Quincey's views on Jacobinism before 1830, see 1966, 51–2, 78, 284, and 366 and 391, where Lord Brougham's Jacobinism is again unmasked (as it is also in 'The Present Cabinet in Relation to the Times', B29 1831 148–9, 153–6). De Quincey's fear of Jacobinism was reawakened, though not immediately, by the events in France in 1830. His *Blackwood's* article 'French Revolution' of September 1830 (542–58) is relatively temperate; but in a series of articles thereafter his fear of popular Jacobinism became intense: see 'France and England' (B28 1830 699–718; 'Political Anticipations' (B28 1830 719–36); 'The Late Cabinet' (B28 1830 960–81); 'The Present Cabinet in Relation to the Times' (B29 1831 143–58); 'On the Approaching Revolution in Great Britain' (B30 1831 313–29); 'The Prospects for Britain' (B31 1832 369–91); 'Mrs Hannah More' (T4 1833 293–321). In 'Hints for the Hustings', Chartism is unmasked as another form of 'the fierce Jacobinism which growls for ever in the lower strata of our . . . domestic population' (B48 1840 309–13). In 'Secession from the Church of Scotland' (1844), we hear of 'Christianity prostituted to the service of Jacobinism' (14: 259).

3. On the figure of London as labyrinth in De Quincey's writings, see J. H. Miller 24–5.

4. Disraeli made the remark in a speech in the House of Commons on March 15th 1838.

5. For cabinets of curiosities and oriental collections, see Impey and MacGregor 251–80; for the early history of the British Museum, see E. Miller, esp. 19–90, 191–244; for a general history of the development of museums as instititions, see Murray.

6. For Palmer's coaches, see Copeland 109–14.

7. 'Raffs', according to Grose, is 'an appellation given by the gownsmen of the university of Oxford to the inhabitants of that place'. It was at Cambridge, according to the Oxford English Dictionary (OED), that townsmen were called 'snobs'. Other early to mid-nineteenth-century meanings of 'snob' include a person of the lower classes; an ostentatious person without breeding; one who seeks to associate with those of a higher class. 'Raffs', more generally, refers to the lowest class of society. In a note to the passage (13: 275n.) De Quincey suggests that the application of the term 'snobs' to shoemakers did not become current until some ten years after the incidents described in 'The English Mail-Coach'.

8. For a useful survey of theories of colonial discourse, see Parry.

9. For Frankistan, or 'Frangistan', see also Lindsay 283.

10. There are several other such imaginary tripartite geopolitical divisions of the globe in De Quincey's writings. For example, if a belief in the unity of God is a crucial test, then Persia in the period of Xerxes and of Herodotus should be seen as belonging with the Jews of Israel to its west, rather than with the superstitious peoples of the further East. At that period Asia can be understood as divided by the river Tigris into Asia *cis*-Tigritana; and Asia *trans*-Tigritana; and although the Persian Empire was established on both sides of the river (7: 178), *true* Persia was to be found between the two great rivers, that is to say, it was cis-Tigritanian (J2: 242). For contemporary attitudes to the Afghanistan campaign, see Bearce 191–9. For another account of the differences that structure De Quincey's imaginary Orient see Maniquis 96–7.

11. In De Quincey's essay 'The Opium Question with China in 1840', he too had talked of 'a monomania in this country as regards the Emperor of Russia' and his ambitions in south central Asia (14: 203). De Quincey's *Blackwood's* article 'Affghanistan' is a review of Lushington's book (B56 1844). The main sources of De Quincey's knowledge of Afghanistan in the earlier articles were the writings of Burnes and Elphinstone's *Caubul*: by 1844 he is aware also of Eyre's, Havelock's and Nash's accounts of the war, as well as Lushington's. In 'The Prospects for Britain' (B31 1832 577–81, 89–90), the supposed territorial ambitions of Russia are regarded as altogether more dangerous, though it is conceded that Russia is (perhaps) 'the "hammer" employed by the Supreme Ruler for crushing the Mohammedan faith'. By 1842, such anxieties are dismissed as 'mere phantoms of crazy fear' (B52 1842 271; see also below, pp.183–4. In De Quincey's essay 'National Temperance Movements' (1845) Bokhara has come to fill the intermediate position, barrier between everywhere and everything, that had also been filled by Afghanistan; see 14: 277 and n. For other European accounts of the Indus as Forbidden River, see for example Moore 1910 435n., J. Burnes 11–13.

12. 'Farther East' – the phrase is W.H. Russell's – 'I am once more on my way to the East – another and a farther East' (1: 1; i.e. farther than the Crimea, Russell's previous assignment).

13. For a different use of inoculation, as it were in the reverse direction, see 1857 12, where De Quincey despairs at the fact that the ignorant Chinese have never been 'inoculated' with true (i.e. with European) science.

14. The economic dependence of Britain on the East was a fact that came to be acknowledged by De Quincey in 1857, if not before: 'Without tea, without cotton, Great Britain, no longer great, would collapse into a very anomalous sort of second-rate power' (U2: 25); see also for example Osborn 10. This issue is an organising theme of Nigel Leask's forthcoming essay on De Quincey (see Acknowledgements).

15. On the 'inexhaustible power of self-reproduction' of the oriental images in De Quincey's opium dreams, see J.H. Miller 68ff.

16. For the production of De Quincey's autobiographical writings see Whale, *Thomas De Quincey's Reluctant Autobiography*, and his essay ' "In a Stranger's Ear": De Quincey's Polite Magazine Context', in Snyder, 35–53.

2 Hydrocephalus

1. For the accounts by Hillis Miller and Robert Maniquis of the effect on De Quincey of Elizabeth's death, see below, pp.207–8, note 6.

2. There is an interesting variant of the lion dream in De Quincey's review, 'Gillies's German Stories' (B20 1826 844). He refers to a meeting between Mungo Park and a lion in the Bilidulgerid, and compares the meeting to that between a young aspirant for literary honours and a periodical reviewer – in this case himself. The effect is of a playful reparative narrative, making good what was painful in the dream. It is possible that the lion dream, or the idea of it, derived from this anecdote from Park (163–4, July 28th 1796), whom De Quincey read in August 1800 (P1: 51).

3. For De Quincey and the Brocken-spectre, see Robert M. Maniquis, 'The Dark Interpreter and the Palimpsest of Violence: De Quincey and the Unconscious', in Snyder, 109–39.

4. The portrait was of the Duchess of Somerset; see 1985 236. For further references to the Whispering Gallery, see 3: 313, 314, 317, 347–8; 1: 187.

5. According to the OED, the word 'pariah' is applied to outcastes only by Europeans; it

offers no instance of 'untouchable' meaning 'outcaste' earlier than 1921; the imagined 'taint' involved in touching a pariah (as = outcaste) seems very clear however in the instances I have cited from De Quincey.

6. For the history and grounds of the attribution of *The Stranger's Grave* to De Quincey, see Grevel Lindop, 'Innocence and Revenge: The Problem of De Quincey's Fiction', in Snyder 213–38.

7. See below, p.206, n.10.

8. For De Quincey's materialism, see Nigel Leask's forthcoming study, referred to in my acknowledgements. De Quincey had read some version of what we know as the 1805 *Prelude* in Wordsworth's manuscript; he retained it all in his memory, so he claims; and he certainly seems to have been able to quote it at will.

9. Maniquis (96) writes extremely well on 'De Quincey's Near East'. It is 'crime and love, Christ among mysterious Jews, Easter palms and strangling vegetation all mixed together. His exoticism is not like that of Byron, Moore, Chateaubriand, or even Goethe. His forbidden tastes are not so much sensual as funereal.' As my own argument develops, however, it is precisely that distinction – between the sensual and the funereal – which will appear as the problem which De Quincey has displaced or discovered in his imaginary Orient.

10. For a rather different account of the 'involute' see Hayter 125–8. On De Quincey's fear of discontinuity, and on his writing as an attempt to construct an innocent unity of self, see J.H. Miller 38–42, 66, 72, and Maniquis, esp. 53–60.

11. For 'lawn', 'lawny' as referring either to meadow or fabric, in the context of versions of involutes associated with Elizabeth's death, see 1: 37, 47, 50; 13: 321, 357–8; B49 1841 743). Much of the involute of Elizabeth's bedroom seems to have been present to De Quincey's imagination as early as 1803. In his diary for that year he writes (May 5th) 'Last night I imagined to myself the heroine of the novel [he had been reading the first volume of Clara Reeve's *The Memoirs of Sir Roger de Clarendon*] dying on an island of a lake, her chamber-windows (opening on a lawn) set wide open – and the sweet blooming roses breathing ye odours on her dying senses' (1828 156).

12. 'Strange fits of passion' is quoted by De Quincey on 2: 285 immediately next to another poem by Wordsworth, ''Tis said that some have died for love'.

3   Nympholepsy

1. For De Quincey's interest in, and echoing of, Wordsworth's poem 'She was a phantom of delight', see John Beer's excellent essay, 'De Quincey and the Dark Sublime: the Wordsworth – Coleridge Ethos', in Snyder 164–98, and esp. 175–6. At 2: 229, the word 'nympholepsy' is used of De Quincey's passion for pure intellectual pursuits, and in the context of his desire to meet Wordsworth, and see the lake landscape.

2. According to Rees (18: article on 'Hydrocephalus'), digitalis had been employed 'with apparent advantage' in some cases, but its uncertain operation had to be 'cautiously and unremittingly watched'.

3. In a similar way he reduces the age of the girl speaker of Wordsworth's 'We are Seven ' from nine to eight (3: 462).

4. Fanny is also connected, whether by identity or antagonism, with Ann of Oxford Street. De Quincey's last meeting with Ann preceded his departure from London on the Bristol coach, which he points out shared much of its route with the Bath coach (3: 368n.).

5. When De Quincey was writing 'The English Mail-Coach' he may have been reminded of the incident in Humboldt by Archibald Alison, who had quoted it in 1845 in a *Blackwood's* essay on Humboldt (B58 1845; Alison 3: 190). The essays later collected as 'The English Mail-Coach' appeared in *Blackwood's* in October and December 1849.

6. For De Quincey's interest in palmistry, see also 5: 357n. It may be linked in his mind with Palm Sunday and the palm-trees in one of the involutes associated with Elizabeth's death; for Palm Sunday as a day of evil omen, see 7: 311.

7. In the chapter of St Paul used in the funeral service, and against which De Quincey's heart rebelled, we find the verse 'If after the manner of men I have fought with beasts at Ephesus, what advantageth it me, if the dead rise not?' (1 Cor. 15. 32)

8. For another example of De Quincey's hydrocephalus scares, see Jordan 323–4.

4 Tigridiasis

1. Reproductions of some of these paintings appear in Forrest. In addition to the works listed by Forrest, J.M.W. Turner made three watercolours of the siege of Seringapatam (see Egerton 178).

2. For Tipu as Jacobin, and as anti-imperialist Muslim revivalist, see K.M. Ashraf, 'Muslim Revivalists and Revolt'. in Joshi 73–5; for more on Tipu as Jacobin, see Wilks 3: 342–3.

3. According to a letter reproduced by Jordan (273) De Quincey was at East India House on July 1st 1813.

4. But Lord Robert Jocelyn, in his contemporary account of the first Opium War, assures us that the Bocca Tigris was not at all tigerish, on account of the military incompetence of the Chinese: 'Nature has here done her utmost to strengthen the place, and if it was held by a European power there is no doubt it would indeed be a tiger's mouth, and nearly impregnable to an invading foe' (Jocelyn 138).

5. See *Encyclopédie* 17: article 'Tigre'.

6. In the course of her elopement Emily, in *The Stranger's Grave* (Chapter 20), also gets away with dropping her luggage; the connection between this incident and the dropping of the trunk at Manchester is noted by Lindop (Snyder 218).

7. In H8 1852 275, 'on the banks of the Tigris' was 'on the banks of an Asiatic river'.

8. In an earlier version, an 'old female servant' (1985 102).

9. Thus De Quincey indentifies with the two pariah girls, who die unmourned, and prompt reflections on 'noonday tragedies' (1: 109), and on the particular guilt of being passive in advance of – of failing to prevent – the deaths of young girls. One can become a pariah by failing to prevent the death of a pariah; as a pariah, one identifies with those who die as pariahs.

10. For other translations of 'Der Freischütz', see Apel and *Tales*.

11. For De Quincey on the virtues of free translation, or *rifacimento*, see his review, 'Gillies's German Stories' (B20 1826 857–8); see also Goldman, 82–153.

12. There are skulls and/or wounded heads in most of De Quincey's translations or *rifacimenti*. Thus, in addition to 'The Fatal Marksman', 'The Dice' (see p.183), and *Niels Klim* (see p.178f.), 'The King of Hayti' provides a hero who attends a masked ball in the character of a death's head (and thus attired kisses the heroine, 12: 404–8), and 'The Love-Charm' (see p.100ff.) contains these verses:

> I know that face so fair and full
> Is but a masquerading skull;
> But hail to thee, skull so fair and fresh!

and so on, in similar vein (12: 448–9), expanding freely on a brief reference to a skull in Tieck's original poem in 'Liebeszauber' (Tieck 2: 98).

13. I am indebted for the detail about the change in Williams's hair colour to the excellent essay on the Williams murders by A.S. Plumtree, 'The Artist as Murderer: De Quincey's Essay "On Murder Considered as One of The Fine Arts"', in Snyder (140–63). There is also an immensely suggestive essay on De Quincey and murder by Josephine McDonagh, 'Do or Die: Problems of Agency and Gender in the Aesthetics of Murder'. For painted horses in the Punjab see Fane 1: 127–8. For a comparison of De Quincey's account of the Williams murders and the contemporary newspaper accounts, see Burke, and Goldman 140–53. The fullest and most thoroughly researched account of the Williams murders is P.D. James and T.A. Critchley, *The Maul and the Pear Tree*, which also provides a full bibliography of the case. The book reveals De Quincey's account of the murder of the Marr family to have been mistaken on various matters. In particular, the murdered baby was three and a half months old, not eight months, and he was in fact a little boy, Timothy. All of the victims – not just the baby – had been battered to death with a ship's carpenter's maul, or hammer; only the baby's throat had also been cut (James and Critchley 14–15).

14. For an account of the full range of the possible significances of Williams's name to De Quincey, see Plumtree in Snyder 157–8. Among those he considers is, appropriately enough, the name of William Wordsworth, who can arguably be represented as De Quincey's big brother, protective and frightening, during De Quincey's Grasmere days in particular, and who in that sense becomes along with Williams another surrogate of William; and as John Beer (Snyder 181–2) points out, De Quincey writes of Wordsworth's resemblance to 'Mrs

Ratcliffe's Schedoni and other assassins' (8: 291). I have not pursued the theme of Wordsworth as surrogate of William, largely because it does not appear to have much to do with the oriental theme of my study, except as suggested on p.56 and p.132 (Wordsworth as an equivalent of the magician in the story of Aladdin, who can hear footsteps or the sound of hoofs at a great distance).

5 Hydrophobia

1. 'Am I not a man and a brother', with the image as I have described it, appeared for example on a Wedgwood medallion of 1787; for a little about the history of the sentiment, see Walvin 104; for De Quincey's views on the slave trade and slavery – he approved of the abolition of the first but not of the second – see for example 'Political Anticipations' (B28 1830 726–9; 1: 18–19 and 19n.; 14: 307–8; and 1966 358–83).

2. In the last years of his life, De Quincey came to regard the Chinese as dogs too: see 1857 26, 27, 78, etc. The Jesuit missionaries, he remarks, were to China as Prospero to Caliban – 'the carnal dog' (11).

3. A 'pariah dog' is a vagabond dog of uncertain or undistinguished breed, found scavenging in the towns and villages of India. Pariah dogs make frequent appearances in the English literature of nineteenth-century India, where they seem to focus the mixture of contempt, guilt and violence which so many of the British felt towards the Indian poor. See for example W.H. Russell 2: 353, Sale 401, and (especially) Acland 101.

4. For Thomas and the mad dog as 'kindred souls', see Martin Bock, 'De Quincey's Retrospective Optics: Analogues of Intoxication in the Opium-Eater's "Nursery Experiences"', Snyder 74.

5. There seems to be a memory here of a scene of 'people running after a mad dog' that De Quincey had observed on Whitsunday 1803 at St Ann's (1928 184).

6. The story of Turk may be compared with the story of the monstrous dog Juno, in De Quincey's translation from the German, 'Mr. Schnackenberger; or, Two Masters for One Dog' (1823). Juno twice terrorises a defenceless kitten (12: 329,353).

7. In 'Mr. Schnackenberger', opium is suggested as a cure for canine overeating (12: 356). The idea of dosing animals with opium was not unheard of in countries where the use of the drug was more regular and more acceptable. Here for an example is an anecdote told by Charles Masson, from one of his journeys across the North-West frontier:

> My conductor was, like all the Lúmrís, an opium eater, and not only took a dose himself on starting but administered one to his camel. The animal became in consequence very wild for a time, and ran here and there, little troubling itself about the path, until the exhilaration of the opium had past. . . . My Búlfút ate opium with every man he met. The ceremony observed on such occasions may be noted. The opium, formed into pills, is placed by the fingers of the one into the mouth of the other, so that no man, unless alone, employs his own fingers.   (Masson 2: 160–1)

8. A similarly reparative narrative is offered by the medal struck by the British after the fall of Seringapatam, which is exhibited in the same case as Tipu's tiger at the Victoria & Albert Museum. It shows a tiger, representing Tipu, flat on his back, and in the position of the East India Company soldier in the clockwork toy: over it – in the attitude and position adopted by the tiger itself in the toy – stands a British lion.

9. De Quincey's source for 'The Spanish Military Nun' was Alexis de Valon's essay 'Catalina de Erauso' in the *Revue des Deux Mondes* 17 (February 15th 1847), which was itself a summary and *rifacimento* of a Spanish text: see 13: 245–50 and Goldman 127–40. De Quincey invents some of the topographical features of the Andean landscape, but he found much of what we may feel to be the most significant details of the story – the act of fratricide, the frozen corpse – ready-made in Valon's text.

7 Diplopia

1. My thanks to Geoff Hemstedt for calling my attention to the appropriateness to De Quincey's obsessions of these speeches from *Othello*.

2. On Williams as the double as well as the enemy of De Quincey – as an 'artist' in murder – see 13: 75, and Plumtree (Snyder 157).

3. That it is Elizabeth too who is drowned is suggested by 3: 435n., where De Quincey tells the story of a female relative of his, who had lived to the age of 99, and who had, when 'about nine years old', nearly drowned (predictably enough, through the negligence of her nurse – and see 13: 347).

4. For another wounded face described as in 'ruins', see also 'Russia As It Was in The Summer and Winter of 1812' (B49 1841 756) and 'Joan of Arc' (below, p.194).

5. In this connection, it is worth recalling that Margaret, De Quincey's wife, is described in terms which recall this cottage-woman, as having 'arms like Aurora's' and 'smiles like Hebe's', and also as his sister, Electra to his Orestes (3: 409, 377). Equally, the passage may envisage the relationship of mother and son.

6. The horror on the face of the cottage-woman, as she warned De Quincey away from the cottage, may be a reflection of the horror which, in another posthumous fragment of 'Suspiria', is experienced in childhood when 'we find ourselves torn away from the lips that we could hang on for ever', the lips of a dead 'mother or sister'. But in 'Who is this Woman', that horror appears on the face of the woman herself, and is represented, perhaps, as the reaction to a kiss. There is an expression of terror, perhaps a blush, which seems to connect cheek and lips alike with the June rose: 'horror . . . now rose, as with the rushing of wings, to her face' . . . 'a horror that rose to her lovely lips'; a horror, perhaps, in which the rose is an emblem of some guilty relation of death and sexuality, foreshadowed earlier in the fragment by the image of 'the saintly odour of corruption' that sweeps from 'a bed of violets' (Wordsworth's Lucy, of course, was a violet as well as a rose; see 'She dwelt among the untrodden ways') (J1: 20, 18, 13; for more roses in June, see J1: 26). For an early example of De Quincey's interest in the ambiguous gestures of welcome and dismissal, see the 1803 journal, where he quotes two lines from William Shenstone's 'Pastoral Ballad' –

> So sweetly she bid me adieu,
> That I thought that she bade me return. –

and offers as a parody of them;

> He kick'd me downstairs with such a sweet grace,
> That I thought he was hand^g me up. (1928 149)

8   The Plague of Cairo

1. De Quincey is rewriting here some pages on 'our "common mother's" age' which had appeared in his 1833 essay 'Kant on the Age of the Earth(14: 69–70). His views on the question are discussed by Robert Lance Snyder in ' "The Loom of *Palingenesis*": De Quincey's Cosmology in "System of the Heavens" ' (Snyder 338–59).

2. Hillis Miller (210–2) also discusses the Memnonian wind. The melodious statue of Memnon became a favourite motif of Romantic literature: see for example Byron, *Don Juan* III, xii, 64, 3; Keats, *Hyperion* 2: 374 and 376, Moore, *The Epicurean* (Moore 1827 165); Tennyson, 'The Palace of Art', 171, and *The Princess*, iii, 116; Wordsworth, *Descriptive Sketches*, 11. According to which authority you believe, the original of Shelley's Ozymandias may have been the head in the British Museum, or another, larger head left lying in the Memnonium at Thebes, or an amalgam of the two. For a list of references in classical writers to the musical Memnon, see de La Barre de Baumarchais 44.

3. I cannot resist quoting Nichol's whole sentence, for it is an extreme example of the representation of phallogocentric power by means of sentence length (here appropriately deployed on the question of the relative sizes of different instruments) which I have discussed (and at very great length, I am proud to say) in my book *Poetry, Language and Politics* – see Barrell 55–77:

Tried by the standard of comparison, it is surely no wonder that the rude tube of GALILEO sufficed to unveil the spots of the Sun; changed the surface of the Moon from a mottled, unintelligible disc, into a world checkered by mountains, valleys, and extensive plains; that to an instrument which one can carry in the hand, that speck of brilliant light, the planet

Jupiter, reveals himself as a majestic globe, the centre and ruler of a large scheme of dependent satellites; – that Mars tells us of his continents and oceans, and polar snows; and the distant Saturn displays his gorgeous ring: – less marvel still, that HERSCHEL, by gradually enlarging his metallic discs with the growth of his experience and mechanic skill, until he reached the perilous adventure of the four feet mirror, passed, by gigantic strides, through regions of the universe to which not even imagination, in its wildest moods, had essayed to penetrate before; – or that now, after enjoying their peaceful triumphs through the third part of a century, even *his* discoveries must again, in some directions, hide their heads, and speculations among the loftiest to which human reason will probably ever attain, and which seemed also among the surest, are doomed to undergo change or destruction, because of the achievements of a tube whose vast eye is SIX FEET in DIAMETER!'

(Nichol 5–6)

On the increases in telescope size in the nineteenth century, Snyder (357n.) refers us to Clerke 142–9, Lovell 118–19, Ronan 114–15 and Rousseau 259. See also Herrmann Chapter 4.

4. For the shape of Assyrian tiaras, see Layard 2: 320–1.

5. 'A sight to dream of, not to tell': 'Christabel', l.253. The quotation is used also of Indian atrocities during the 1857 rebellion (see below, p.177); of the Turkish fleet at the Battle of Navarino, as exaggerated by newspaper reports (1966, 185); and of the arrival of the Russian militia at Smolensk in 1812 (see below, p.185).

6. The adventure of the mail-coach and the girl in the reedy gig took place on the road from Manchester, through Lancaster, to Kendal; the quicksand may be displaced from the nearby oversands coach route across Morecambe Bay.

7. I have preferred the looser punctuation of 1985 199 to the later text at 13: 290n.; Lindop (232) also connects Humboldt's crocodile story with Fanny and suggests that it refers to some unspoken sexual theme.

8. On Burke's sublime as a masculine category, as 'swelling', the best account I know is by Tom Furniss (82–4, 92–5); a revised version of the chapter in which this discussion appears is soon to be published as 'Edmund Burke: Bourgeois Revolutionary in a Radical Crisis', in Osborne, *Socialism*.

9. Hillis Miller (38–9, 66, 72) also discusses the motif of the chasm or abyss in De Quincey's writing: for him it is the place and sign of existential discontinuity.

9   Homicidal Mania

1. For De Quincey's uses of 'doppelganger', see 1966, 276.

2. Newbold, writing of the Straits Settlements in 1839, is more reassuring:

Running Amok rarely occurs on the Peninsula . . . . To wipe out a stain on his honour by shedding the blood of an offender, even if assassination be the means employed, is accounted as little disgraceful by him as the practice of duelling by others in civilised Europe. Should the offender's rank be much superior, the injured party in despair has recourse to opium, and the desperate Amok, slaying indiscriminately all he can lay hands on.   (Newbold 2: 185–6)

In W.H.G. Kingston's *The Three Midshipmen*, the young heroes have a good deal of trouble from Malays running 'a-muck' – see Chapters 24–5. For more on running amok, see Kiernan 83.

3. De Quincey's interest in the Peninsular War was especially kindled by his experience of seeing through the press Wordsworth's pamphlet on the convention of Cintra (see Jordan 97–202); on the theme of revenge in the context of that war, see Jordan 259, where De Quincey says of Sir Samuel Ford Whittingham, then a Major-General in the Spanish army, that 'a general impression has gone out amongst the Spaniards who know him that he is destined to act some great part among them – and to become one of their first-rate avengers'. A part of the context of 'The Caçadore' is the controversy about the value of the contribution made to the war by the Spanish and Portuguese guerrillas. This had been attacked in Napier's history of the war on the grounds that the guerrilla forces were incapable of discipline. 'The Caçadore' seems to confirm this view of the indocility of the Iberians, though not necessarily to regard it as a liability. In his article 'The Aristocracy of England' (B54 1843 51–66), De Quincey offers a brief discussion of this controversy, and places a high valuation on the guerrilla contribution (52–3).

4. For the Jaffa massacre, and various estimates of the numbers of those who died, see Napoleon items 4012, 4013, 4019; Chandler 236; J. Thompson 132. Napoleon was allegedly responsible for another massacre at Jaffa: of French soldiers infected with plague, whom he ordered to be given a fatal dose of opium. This death by treating plague with opium is so much closer to De Quincey's preoccupations than the massacre he repeatedly refers to that one wonders whether his anger at the killing of the Albanians has not become displaced on to that incident from the other.

5. The spectacles staged in the joint triumph of Vespasian and Titus are described at length by Josephus, 384–6.

6. Compare the figure of the doomed Alethe, as she manifests herself at one moment in Thomas Moore's *The Epicurean* (1827), a tale as obsessed as anything written by De Quincey with the triangular relation (to be discussed briefly in my final chapter) of the East, death and the body of the woman: 'I could perceive, not far from the spot where we sat, a female figure, veiled, and crouching to earth, as if subdued by sorrow, or under the influence of shame' (Moore 1827 87).

7. See Stevenson 490–91 and Carson items 476 and 477.

10   Yellow Fever

1. A few of De Quincey's writings on China – those republished by Masson – are discussed by Maniquis, 105–11.

2. On opium sales to China 'as a means of raising an Indian revenue' see E105 1857 537. The whole article (517–51) offers a very different (Whig) view to De Quincey's; and see E107 1858 15, on the opium trade with China as 'the principal resource to cover the deficiency of the public revenue of India'. For a detailed account of the issues raised by the opium traffic with China, see Fay 41–53 and *passim*; for a neat summary and unintentional exposé of British motives in fighting the Opium War, see Kingston Chapter 34; and for a full account of Sino-English relations through the period covered by De Quincey's essays, see Graham.

3. On money lent or given by Penson, see L139 (1806); P1: 137 (1808), 180 (1813); 205, and L234–6 (1819); on money contributed in 1809 to Mrs Quincey's estate by Penson, L181; on Penson's legacies, and the sale of the annuity, L320–1; on Mrs Quincey's legacy (1846), L360. See also L123–4, for a rather tenuous early connection between the Pensons and opium trade.

4. Russia too is treated as made invulnerable by its lumpishness (14:177). On China as an inorganic lumpish mass, see also 'Sir Robert Peel's Position on Next Resuming Power', where, however, it is treated as a delusion of the Chinese to believe that the British were able only 'to tease the outlying extremities' of the Chinese Empire (B50 1841 408). See also Oliphant 1: 413–17, and especially:

> But if these incidents went to show how impossible it was to influence the Court of Pekin by coercion applied at remote parts of the Empire, still more hopeless was it to effect this object by diplomacy exercised at a distance from the seat of government . . . Lord Elgin's observation had therefore led him to this conclusion, that it was necessary to be at the heart to affect the extremities, and that it was impossible to affect the heart through the extremities.   (1: 416)

5. An excellent article in Q102 1857 126–65 compared the atrocities of British penal system unfavourably with those of the Chinese.

6. Hall and Bernard (237–8) also tell of the wreck of the brig *Ann*, in which were embarked some 57 souls; of whom, '14 were natives of Europe or America, 4 Portuguese [not Europeans?], 5 Chinaman, and 34 natives of India'. These all seem to have shared the fate of the captured Indians from the *Nerbudda*.

7. 'The Private of the Buffs' which originally appeared in Doyle's *The Return of the Guards, and Other Poems* (1860), is based on the report in *The Times* of an incident of 1860. It is the verse tale of a Private Moyse of the Buffs, or East Kent Regiment, who along with some Sikhs was captured by the Chinese. They were all told to perform the kotou before a Chinese dignitary. The Sikhs obeyed, but Moyse refused, 'was immediately knocked on the head, and his body thrown on a dunghill' (*The Times*, November 3rd 1860). Much is made in the poem of Moyse's Kentish origins; in fact he was a Scot. For more information see Holt 262–3 and Turner 248–9. I am grateful to Tom Raworth for all the information in this note.

8. On overestimation of the population of China, see 1857 47, 123–4.

9. Apart from government publications and newpapers, De Quincey's main source on recent Chinese history and especially on the Tae-ping rebellion appears to have been Meadows (cited 1857 102) and Fortune (cited U2: 27).

11 Leontiasis

1. For the history of Ceylon in the early days of the British presence, see Davy 311–34, Ludowyk 18–56; de Silva 3: 12–33; Tennent 63–96.

2. 'The higher castes of the Sinhalese', according to Bennett,

> are, generally, speaking, a fine handsome race, but the men are notorious for the effeminacy of their appearance and habits, . . . [they] allow their hair to grow its full length, and support it with tortoise-shell combs of an extravagantly large size; this, together with their very prominent breasts and effeminate costume, but more particularly when returning from bathing, at which time they wear their hair loose upon a handkerchief, spread over their shoulders and back, and tied upon the forehead, gives them such a feminine appearance, that even at a moderate distance, strangers often mistake them for women; and their light white jackets and clothes (Sarongs), wrapped round the waist and descending to the ankles like a petticoat, heightens the deception (97).

The distinction Bennett and De Quincey make between the *masculine* Kandyans and the *effeminate* coastal Sinhalese seems to go back in British writing at least as far as Robert Knox's history of Ceylon (1681), where it takes the standard form of a distinction between mountain people (say the Swiss or the Highlanders) and a valley people. Among nineteenth-century historians of the island and commentators on it, the distinction is rehearsed in one form or another by Robert Percival and Henry Marshall. According to Percival,

> the countenance of the Candian is erect, his look haughty, his mien lofty, and his whole carriage marked by the pride of independence. The humble yielding deportment of the Cinglese, on the other hand, with the patient or rather abject endurance which is painted on their faces, plainly denotes the dependent and helpless state to which they are reduced.
> The looks of the Cinglese even denote a degree of effeminacy and cowardice, which excites the contempt of the Candians.   (R. Percival 233)

According to Marshall (19–20), the character of the Kandyans is marked by manliness, a 'love of liberty', and a 'detestation of foreign conquest'; the lowlanders he describes as (quoting Knox) 'kind, pitiful, helpful, honest, and plain'.

3. Bennett's account of the fate of Ähälëpolä's wife, which introduces the theme of exposure elaborated by De Quincey, is much more graphic than any other (she was obliged to use the pestle 'to save herself from the *most diabolical* torture and ignominious exposure', 391). There are less sensational versions in Davy (322–3), Tolfrey (4), Marshall (136–9), Knighton (322), Forbes (1: 350–1), Tennent (2: 88–9; Knighton and Forbes both claim to have verified the story by consulting eye-witnesses). Marshall (137n.–9n.) points out that the sufferings inflicted on the *adigar*'s wife, and deplored by the British as acts of savage and oriental barbarity, were no greater than the punishment in Britain for high treason, which had been inflicted in full as recently as the eighteenth century. According to de Silva (3: 23), the Ähälëpolä's wife and children suffered 'the penalty meted out by Kandyan law to relatives of traitors. The precise mode of the execution . . . has been transformed by legend into a story of incredibly horrid sadism'. According to Pieris, the story of the mode of execution and its accompanying circumstances was 'fabricated as a piece of political propaganda . . . and was intended not merely to estrange the minds of the Sinhalese from their king, but also to counter the declared policy of Downing Street against territorial expansion' (see Pieris, Appendix H, 104–11).

4. The cases are not equivalent of course: in the case of the execution of the '*adigar*'s wife', the objectification is less a matter of denying the woman any position where she can appear as active in relation to events, for as a prisoner to be executed she was already without such a position. It is more a question of using her – nameless as she is, and with no history outside the story of her death – as the mere occasion of a demonstration of the virtue of the imperial

power and the viciousneess of natives. Nor is there any question of an oppositional 'nativist argument', in the form 'the women wanted to die' (see Spivak 1985a 122).

5. For Barnsley's original deposition on returning to Trincomalee, see R. Percival 435–6.

6. Davie's conduct is represented as beyond palliation by Knighton (316–17), and by Heber (2: 257), whose version of the story is rather garbled. Otherwise contemporary commentators offer a very much less severe account of Davie than does De Quincey. His conduct is treated as 'strange' by Davy (314), but not censured; nor is he censured by Cordiner (2: 215–16), by Bennett (419), by Tennent (2: 83–4), or by Marshall (100–8), who makes clear the impossible position in which Davie found himself. Forbes (1: 34) speaks of his 'errors of judgment' and of his own 'severe opinion' of Davie's 'indefensible acts', but suggests that his mind was affected by the scenes of suffering he had witnessed, and that his superiors were more culpable than he was. None of these writers suggests, as De Quincey does, that Davie may have survived his captivity, nor does the suggestion appear in De Quincey's other acknowledged source, *The Life of Alexander Alexander*. There is a full discussion of Davie's case in Methley (92–125) who (like Forbes) suggests his culpability was grossly exaggerated to shield others more responsible; see also Mills 149–53.

12 Phallalgia

1. On the events at Rurki, see Vibart 4–8; for De Quincey's knowledge of events in India as they concerned his son and daughter, see P2: 129–39.

2. On British atrocities, see Joshi, '1857 in our History', in Joshi 159–66. See also Edwardes 58, 80–9, 120–1, 163–4; Majumdar 192–225; E. Thompson, 58–66; for a contemporary view see W.H.Russell 1: 162, 222; 2: 42–3, 82, 402. On Indian atrocities, see Majumdar 90, 192–4; on the exaggeration of Indian atrocities, and the lack of evidence to support the most highly coloured accounts of Indian savagery, see James Byrne, 'British Opinion and the Indian Revolt' (Joshi 291–300). For a supporting contemporary view, see W.H.Russell, 1: 2, 92, 117, 135, 191. On Cawnpore, Russell points out (1: 164) that 'the peculiar aggravation of the Cawnpore massacres was this, that the deed was done by a subject race – by black men who dared shed the blood of their masters, and that of poor helpless ladies and children'. For a recent account of the massacres at Cawnpore, see Gupta. For an excellent account of representations of the rebellion (and of Cawnpore in particular) in British fictional writing, see Brantlinger 199–224.

3. On the claim that British women were 'made to walk about naked in the streets' of Delhi, see P.C.Joshi, '1857 in our History', in Joshi 161.

4. Among the leading British periodicals of the period, the *Edinburgh Review* at first flatly denied the possibility of a 'sepoy conspiracy': the sepoys were characterised by 'low animal propensities', 'bestial superstitions', and they surpass 'the wild animals of the Indian jungle in bloodthirstiness and treachery'. There could be no 'vast political conspiracy' among such people (E106 October 1857 554, 581), but by January it had discovered a fairly sizeable one (E107 1858 34ff). *Blackwood's* did not believe in a conspiracy until January 1858 (B83 1858 94–8). The *Quarterly* detected a conspiracy straight away (Q102 October 1857 535, 539–40, 549).

5. On keeping money in the waistband of one's trousers as a normal thing in Afghanistan, see Fane 2: 136.

6. For set books at Calcutta University, see Q104 1858 238n. De Quincey had dismissed the Hindus as 'effeminate' and 'cowardly' in 'Hints for the Hustings' (B48 1840 293) and in various other contexts. Among historians, see Orme 1: 5 (the 'enervated' character, and the 'pusillanimity' of the Hindus are summarised in the index to volume 1 – see the entry 'Indians' – as 'effeminacy'); see also Robertson 332 and Mill 1: 467. Elphinstone, 1857 195–201, offers to distinguish the manly Marathas from the effeminate Bengalis, but quickly represents the supposed characteristics of the Bengalis as those of all Hindus. Macaulay, the most anxiously macho of all these writers, makes a similar move: the Bengalis may differ from other Hindus as feminine to masculine, but they give their feminine character to all Hindus (1: 562–3, 568, 594), as contradistinguished from 'the English breed, the hereditary nobility of mankind', the 'master caste' (1: 528, 555); and see 1: 503, 513, 581. See also Kiernan, 33–4, and the review of Elphinstone's *The History of India* in Q68 1841 377: 'a feeble and unwarlike race, who live on

rice, and meekly submit to every kind of oppression'. For the attitudes to India of British historians, see Bearce 263–71, and C.H.Philips, 'James Mill, Mountstuart Elphinstone, and the History of India', 217–29, in Philips. Bolt (178–86) is informative on attitudes to the 'Indian temperament' after 1857, though to me she seems to overestimate the change in attitude precipitated by the rebellion. Guest 36ff. offers some brilliant reflections on the implications of the feminisation of the Hindus of Madras in the writing of the artist William Hodges.

7. For Nicholson; see Edwardes 156–7, Majumdar 219–20. For evidence of more humane attitudes among the British to the question of retaliation and revenge, see W.H. Russell 2: 43 (for example), or Q102 1857 548, 552–3, 557, 549, 558, 570.

8. De Quincey broke with *Blackwood's* around 1850, but he was still on the complimentary list in 1855 when the quarrel was made up. No doubt he continued to get his free copy thereafter (P2: 106).

9. For British belief in the Chinese terror of beheading, see Hall and Bernard 262–3, and Meadows 651–6: in the latter case especially, as in De Quincey, it is rather the British fear that comes across. De Quincey recommends decapitation for Chinese murderers of British subjects in the last of his essays on China. Decapitation is preferable to hanging, he argues, 'since in that case the corpses, being headless, would in Chinese estimation have been imperfect' (U2: 19n.).

10. The relevant section from the notes to *Queen Mab* is as follows:

Ahasuerus crept forth from the dark cave of Mount Carmel – he shook the dust from his beard – and taking up one of the skulls heaped there, hurled it down the eminence: it rebounded from the earth in shivered atoms. 'This was my father!' roared Ahasuerus. Seven more skulls rolled down from rock to rock; while the infuriate Jew, following them with ghastly looks, exclaimed – 'And these were my wives!' He still continued to hurl down skull after skull, roaring in dreadful accents – 'And these, and these, and these were my children! They *could die*; but I! reprobate wretch! alas! I cannot die! Dreadful beyond conception is the judgement that hangs over me. Jerusalem fell – I crushed the sucking babe . . .

Shelley claims that this 'is the translation of part of some German work, whose title I have vainly endeavoured to discover. I picked it up, dirty and torn, some years ago, in Lincoln's-Inn Fields' (Shelley 1967 818–9). Thomas Medwin (vii–viii) seems to hint that he was the author of the note, which however is in part adapted (as Medwin certainly knew – see Shelley 1887 xxvi) from the speech of Ahasuerus in Matthew Lewis's *The Monk* (169), or which shares a common source with that speech.

11. Compare De Quincey: 'To return to the Peninsular news – I am very much rejoiced that the armies of the Supreme People have again drifted the "tyger-monkey" nation (as Walking Stewart calls them); though I am sorry that Sir A.[rthur] W.[ellesley] should be carrying away the glory' (Jordan 177, letter to Dorothy Wordsworth of 25th–27th May 1809. 'Drift' seems to mean 'hold up, delay, obstruct' in this context.

13   Concussion

1. De Quincey discusses 'The Dice' briefly in his review 'Gillies's German Stories', in B20 1826 854; he attributes it to Frederick Laun. My moderately diligent search has failed to locate the original story.

2. For other statements on the impossibility of Russia's threatening India, see 1966 95–6 and 14: 204, 277–8.

3. At the time of writing (December 1989), another of De Quincey's predictions about Russia, made during the Crimean War, seems to be still more strikingly true: 'it is well to remember . . . that hereafter against Communists and Red Republicans we shall need to invoke the aid of Russia, and to *rejoice* that she is strong' (P2: 92). But no doubt it was the power of the Czar, and of the feudal system, that were expected to come to the aid of a western Europe overrun with Jacobins.

4. At one point De Quincey elaborates into a grand epic paragraph Arndt's brief account of the Asiatic soldiers of the Czar mustering at Smolensk, prior to the capture of that town by the French in August: Tartars, Kalmucks, Cossacks, Bashkirs, Circassians, flying past his eyes 'like a hurricane' (B49 1841 742).

5. Finally Arndt is made to tell us that after all 'this scene occurred not at Smolensko, but some stages further to the east – either at Wiasma or at Gschat'. In fact, in Arndt's narrative,

only the mustering of the Asiatic armies happened at Smolensk. The kissing (which as we have seen Arndt does not connect with sisters) occurred at Wiasma, and the rural excursion at Gschat (B49 1841 744; Arndt, 143–5). Goldman (83–91) also discusses these passages from the translation of Arndt. His concern, however, is with correspondences between De Quincey's writings and those of other authors, not with correspondences within the writings of De Quincey himself, and so he does not point out the relation between the paragraphs I have discussed and the passage in the 'Autobiography' and 'System of the Heavens'.

6. Almost precisely the same question is asked by Robert M. Maniquis in his superb monograph 'Lonely Empires: Personal and Public Visions of Thomas De Quincey': ' . . . his fantasy contains *both* a communal, imperial ethic and a dream eroticism. Is either the cause of the other or are they both together causes and effects?' (103). Maniquis does have an answer to this question, but before I say what it is, it will help if I give a brief account of the argument of his monograph, which is, along with J. Hillis Miller's essay in *The Disappearance of God*, one of the two most exciting discussions of De Quincey's work I know.

According to Miller (20), when Elizabeth dies, 'three things . . . happen simultaneously. God withdraws to an infinite distance, . . . De Quincey becomes aware of the infinity of space and time' and these events together 'bring about the initial moment of self-awareness'. It is the last two of these events that most concern Maniquis. The fear released by the death of Elizabeth was 'fear of the infinite, of disappearance into time and space, of memory that both identifies and fragments the self, of inner, isolated space, where identity is reflected in the dark mirror of death, into which he gazes, trying to understand both his fear and his guilt' (50). De Quincey identifies in Elizabeth a 'wholeness' which is also innocence; with her loss, De Quincey himself experiences a fragmentation of the self which is experienced as a loss of innocence, and therefore as 'existential' guilt (58, 71). Thereafter his writing becomes for Maniquis (as it was also for Hillis Miller, 38–9) a search to unify the discontinuities of self, to construct a real or a surrogate self which by being unified will also be innocent.

It is in the context of this search that Maniquis turns to the themes of nation and empire. For De Quincey hopes to find in the nation 'a surrogate self, indeed like his sister, an image of wholeness and innocence' (76). This is not easily to be found in the industrial chaos of contemporary Britain (69), though De Quincey's Toryism does look to the nation as the place of an imagined organic community. He could more easily believe that he could recover the wholeness (and therefore the innocence) he had lost in the idea and destiny of Britain as an imperial nation, giving its own ideal unity to the world it conquers, becoming the head of an organism whose body sprawls over Asia from the Mediterranean to the China Sea (76–7, 110–11, 96–7). For De Quincey this movement from the personal to the historical is a movement from 'an unreal inner time' which expands and contracts unpredictably and frighteningly, to a sublime 'historical time', time as process, in which 'the self, the political individual, nations, and empires are in a process of individuation' and 'self-consciousness is always being reborn' (82, 84).

Guilt cannot be 'absolved' in history; it 'is born of self-consciousness, where also it must be absolved' (60). For Maniquis, De Quincey turns to history in search of the resolution of an existential problem, and history remains only ever a symbolic language in which the existential fears and hopes attendant on the birth of self-consciousness are represented. The same is true of the psychosexual narratives in De Quincey's writings: they are the symbolic language in which existential anxieties find expression. De Quincey, 'we can be sure, has incest on his mind', but incest 'is one of the most common motifs of late eighteenth-century and early nineteenth-century literature', where it can be 'a sign for all that is forbidden . . . whatever incestual guilt he may feel does not explain . . . how all forms of guilt keep turning back upon themselves, into one form of guilt in the divided consciousness' (102).

That seems to be the appropriate place to point out where I part company from Maniquis's study; for to me, this last sentence begs a series of questions which Maniquis treats as if they are settled. What if one does not choose to believe that the existential is unquestionably prior to the social and the psychosexual, unquestionably a deeper stratum of being than they are? Why shouldn't we say that the meditations on being and existence, the acknowledgements and declarations (if they can be found) of an existential guilt, are the symbolic language in which a psychosexual and/or a social guilt are represented, displaced, mystified? It all seems rather to depend on the assumptions you start with, on your point of entry into De Quincey's texts, on the kinds of question you find yourself asking. Maniquis regards the kinds of narrative of guilt that I have been concentrating on as symbolic illustrations of existential anxieties and dilemmas; when I started reading De Quincey, my attention was first drawn to what I saw as the extraordinary incidence of narrative repetition in his writing; and I found myself treating the narratives as prior to the meditations on space, time and identity, which were so often offered as commentaries upon those narratives.

To return then to Maniquis's question, which is also my question, though not quite in my terms: 'Is either [viz. the communal, imperial ethic; the dream eroticism] the cause of the other or are they together both causes and effects?' My answer is not exactly that they are causes and effects of each other, but that each may be both what it is and a representation of the other: a fear of the Orient, for example, may be a fear of the Orient and the site of a different, a displaced fear. Maniquis's answer is that 'all "causes" of [De Quincey's] fantasy seem to re-solve themselves into the unending symbolic process, a constantly functioning structure of oppositions at work in the *Ur*-dream of self-identity' (103). I am much in sympathy with this answer until its very last phrases; the issue of what is *Ur* is surely what we cannot decide.

7. According to Eliot Warburton, in his remarks on Egyptian dress, though the green turban was restricted to descendants of the Prophet, and the black turban to Copts, the turban of white muslin 'is open to any who chooses to adopt it' (1: 85). But as the epigraph to my tenth chapter suggests, a feared return of Muslim fundamentalism was imaged in the form of a restriction of the white turban to Muslims; the same is suggested by this passage from E.W. Lane: 'The Christians at that time had reverted to the habit of wearing the white turban; and the Sultán caused it to be proclaimed that every person of this sect who was seen wearing a white turban, or riding a horse, might be plundered and killed' (Lane 556).

8. For Lindsay's canine entanglements with Muslims, see 208 and 213, where he reduces 'a most uncourteous dog' to the condition of 'a beaten spaniel'; 316–7, where a Turkish soldier, one of five 'cowardly dogs', takes a licking at British hands, and afterwards 'the slave fawned like a spaniel'; and 333–4, where some 'quarantine officers (common soldiers)' announce that '"the English are dogs!"' but their commanding officer is soon 'fawning', I suppose like a spaniel again. Vigne's belief in the magical power of *baksheesh* was evident also when he had the misfortune to come across a widow about to engage in *sati*: 'At Lahore I once, taking a Sepahi with me, threaded my way up to the pile, and offered the unhappy victim a sum of money, if she would not burn. I should perhaps rather say that I mentioned it to the bystanders; for I am not certain that she was told of it, or that she would quite have comprehended my meaning' (Vigne 1842, 1: 83). Indeed not. There is a very good discussion of the casual yet unremitting racism of early nineteenth-century British travel writing (in the context of Africa) by Mary Louise Pratt, 'Scratches on the Face of the Country; or, What Mr Barrow Saw in the Land of the Bushmen', in Gates 138–62.

9. On the (very exceptional instances of) killing of women by thugs, see Sleeman 79–80, 146–9, 190; Meadows Taylor (viiin.) claims to be indebted to Sleeman for 'much valuable information' about Thuggee. For examples of the recurrent image of the distorted faces of women strangled or about to be, see Taylor 7, 203–5, 255, 366, 383.

10. Lindsay's description of Palmyra appears to be heavily dependent upon Volney (see Volney 1: 3–5). Both in turn are dependent on Robert Wood's description of Palmyra in *Ruins of Palmyra*. In John Hall's print after Gavin Hamilton, *James Dawkins and Robert Wood Esqrs, First discovering Sight of Palmyra* (1773–5) (reproduced in Llewellyn 18–19), the sculptured corpse of a voluptuous woman in classical draperies appears on the sepulchre in the top right-hand corner, above a funerary inscription in Greek. This image, and the classical dress of Wood and Dawkins, form a contrast with the bearded and beturbaned expedition auxiliaries, and help establish a cultural sympathy between the classical ruins of Palmyra and its British 'discoverers', and a cultural contrast between the ruined Greek city and its Islamic environment. The presence of the sculptured corpse in a scene thus racially coded gives to the triad Orient/woman's body/death a poignancy (to western sensibilities) similar to the reverential hush of Lindsay's description of Palmyra.

11. The figure of Judaea/Rachel now appears, perhaps, as the woman of Samaria who sits with Jesus by the side of Jacob's well (and beneath a canopy of palms) in so many early nineteenth-century biblical illustrations – the much-married woman, who when Jesus met her was living in sin (John 4. 3–30).

12. In the chapter of his 'Autobiography' called 'Infant Literature', De Quincey rehearses at length such an instance of revenge: it is a story from Dr Percival's *A Father's Instructions*, in

which a private soldier who has been struck by an officer and is prevented by military discipline from returning the blow, says to the officer that he would ' "make him repent it" '. After a hot action in which the private soldier distinguishes himself, he finds himself embraced in congratulation by the officer, who does not at first recognise the man he is embracing. ' "Sir," says the private. "I told you before that I would *make you repent it*." The story has echoes of the end of the Joan-of-Arc essay. The officer kisses the private, who is 'crimsoned with glorious gore', 'as if he were some martyr glorified by that shadow of death from which he was returning' (1: 132–3).

References

Acland

Rev. Charles Acland, *A Popular Account of the Manners and Customs of India*, London (John Murray) 1847.

Alexander

The Life of Alexander Alexander: written by himself and edited by John Howell, 2 vols, Edinburgh (William Blackwood) and London (T. Cadell) 1830.

Alison

Archibald Alison, *Essays Political, Historical, and Miscellaneous*, 3 vols, Edinburgh and London (William Blackwood) 1850.

Apel

The Original Legend of Der Freischütz, or the Free Shot, translated from the German of A. Apel, London (A. Schloss) 1833.

Apel and Laun

Gespensterbuch. Herausgegeben von A. Apel und F. Laun, 4 vols, Leipzig (G.J. Göschen) 1811.

Arndt

Errinerungen aus dem Äusseren Leben, von Ernst Moritz Arndt, Leipzig (Weidmann'sche Buchhandlung) 1842.

Axon

William E.A. Axon, 'The Canon of De Quincey's Writings, with References to Some of his Unidentified Articles', *Transactions of the Royal Society of Literature*, 2nd series, vol. 32 (1914), 1–46.

Bakhtin

Mikhail Bakhtin, *Rabelais and His World*, trans. Hélène Iswolsky, Bloomington (Indiana University Press) 1984.

Barrell

John Barrell, *Poetry, Language and Politics*, Manchester (Manchester University Press) 1988.

Barthes

Roland Barthes, *Mythologies*, selected and translated by Annette Lavers, London (Paladin) 1973.

Baudelaire

Charles Baudelaire, *Oeuvres Complètes*, ed. Claude Pichois, 2 vols, Paris (Gallimard; Bibliothèque de la Pléiade) 1975–6.

Bearce

George D. Bearce, *British Attitudes towards India 1784–1858*, London (Oxford University Press) 1961.

Bennett

J.W. Bennett, *Ceylon and its Capabilities; An Account of its Natural Resources, Indigenous Productions, and Commercial Facilities*, London (W.H. Allen) 1843.

Bhabha

Homi K. Bhabha, 'The Commitment to Theory', *New Formations* no. 5, Summer 1988.

Bolt

Christine Bolt, *Victorian Attitudes to Race*, London (Routledge and Kegan Paul) 1971.

Brantlinger

Patrick Brantlinger, *Rule of Darkness: British Literature & Imperialism. 1830–1914*, Ithaca (Cornell University Press) 1988.

Buffon 1775–6

Georges Louis Leclerc de Buffon. *The Natural History of Animals, Vegetables, and Minerals; with the Theory of the Earth in General*, trans. W. Kenrick et al., 6 vols, London (T. Bell) 1775–6.

Buffon 1791a

Georges Louis Leclerc de Buffon, *Buffon's Natural History Abridged*, London (for C. and G. Kearsley) 1791.

Buffon 1791b

Georges Louis Leclerc de Buffon. *The System of Natural History, written by the celebrated Buffon, carefully abridged*, 2 vols, Perth (for R. Morison and son et al.) 1791.

Burke

Thomas Burke, 'The Obsequies of Mr Williams: New Light on De Quincey's Famous Tale of Murder', *Bookman*, vol. 28 (1928).

Burnes A. 1834

Lieut. Alexander Burnes, *Travels into Bokhara; being the Account of a Journey from India to Cabool, Tartary, and Persia; also Narrative of a Voyage on the Indus. &c.*, 3 vols, London (John Murray) 1834, reprinted in facsimile, ed. James Lunt, Karachi (Oxford University Press) 1973.

Burnes A. 1842

Lieut.-Col. Sir Alexander Burnes, *Cabool: being a Personal Narrative of a Journey to, and Residence in that City, in the Years 1836, 7, and 8*, London (John Murray) 1842.

Burnes J.

James Burnes, *A Narrative of a Visit to the Court of Sinde: A Sketch of the History of Cutch, . . . and Some Remarks on the Medical Topography of Bhooj*, Bombay (Summachar Press) and Edinburgh (John Stark) 1831.

Carson   R.A.G. Carson, *Principal Coins of the Romans*, vol. 2, London (British Museum Publications) 1980.

Caseby   Richard Caseby, *The Opium-Eating Editor: Thomas De Quincey and the Westmorland Gazette*, Kendal (Westmoreland Gazette) 1985.

Chandler   David G. Chandler, *The Campaigns of Napoleon*, London (Weidenfeld and Nicolson) 1967.

Christ   Carol Christ, 'Victorian Masculinity and the Angel in the House', in Martha Vicinus (ed.) *A Widening Sphere: Changing Roles of Victorian Women*, London (Methuen) 1980.

Clerke   Agnes M. Clerke, *A Popular History of Astronomy during the Nineteenth Century* (1885), 3rd edn, London (Adam and Charles Black) 1893.

Collins   Wilkie Collins, *The Moonstone* (1868), Harmondsworth (Penguin Books), 1966.

Copeland   John Copeland, *Roads and their Traffic, 1750–1850*, Newton Abbot (David and Charles) 1968.

Cordiner   Rev. James Cordiner, *A Description of Ceylon, containing an Account of the Country, Inhabitants, and Natural Productions*, 2 vols, London (Longman, Hurst, Rees and Orme) 1807.

Damer   The Hon. Mrs G. L. Damer, *Diary of a Tour in Greece, Turkey, Egypt, and the Holy Land*, 2 vols, London (Henry Colburn) 1841.

Davis   Sir John Francis Davis, Bt., *China. During the War and Since the Peace*, 2 vols, London (Longmans, Brown, Green and Longmans) 1852.

Davy   John Davy, *An Account of the Interior of Ceylon and its Inhabitants*, London (Longman, Hurst, Rees, Orme and Brown) 1821.

De Quincey 1818   [Thomas De Quincey?], *Close Comments upon a Straggling Speech*, Kendal (Airey and Bellingham) 1818.

De Quincey 1823   [Thomas De Quincey], *The Stranger's Grave*, London (for Longman, Hurst, Rees, Orme, Brown and Green) 1823.

De Quincey 1827   [Thomas De Quincey], *The Peasant of Portugal: a Tale of the Peninsular War* (1827), London (Aporia Press) 1985.

De Quincey 1828   [Thomas De Quincey], *The Caçadore: A Story of the Peninsular War* (1828), London (Aporia Press) 1988.

De Quincey 1857 — *China, by Thomas De Quincey: A Revised Reprint of Articles from 'Titan', with Preface and Additions*, Edinburgh (James Hogg) and London (R. Groombridge) 1857.

De Quincey 1889–90 — *The Collected Writings of Thomas De Quincey*, ed. David Masson, 14 vols, Edinburgh (Adam and Charles Black) 1889–90.

De Quincey 1890 — *The Uncollected Writings of Thomas De Quincey*, ed. James Hogg, 2 vols, London (Swan Sonnenschein) 1890.

De Quincey 1891–3 — *The Posthumous Works of Thomas De Quincey*, ed. Alexander H. Japp, 2 vols, London (William Heinemann) 1891–3.

De Quincey 1928 — *A Diary of Thomas De Quincey, 1803*, ed. Horace A. Eaton, London (Noel Douglas), no date [1928].

De Quincey 1953 — 'Niels Kilm, being an incomplete translation, by Thomas De Quincey, from the Danish of Ludvig Holberg, now edited from the manuscript by S. Musgrove', *Auckland University College Bulletin*, no. 42, English series no. 5, 1953.

De Quincey 1966 — *New Essays by De Quincey: his Contributions to the Edinburgh Saturday Post and the Edinburgh Evening Post, 1827–8*, ed. Stuart M. Tave, Princeton (Princeton University Press) 1966.

De Quincey 1970 — Thomas De Quincey, *Recollections of the Lakes and the Lake Poets*, ed. David Wright, Harmondsworth (Penguin Books) 1970.

De Quincey 1971 — Thomas De Quincey, *Confessions of an English Opium Eater*, ed. Alethea Hayter, Harmondsworth (Penguin Books) 1971.

De Quincey 1985 — Thomas De Quincey, *Confessions of an English Opium-Eater and Other Writings*, ed. Grevel Lindop, Oxford and New York (Oxford University Press) 1985.

Disraeli — *Lord Beaconsfield's Correspondence with his Sister 1832–1852*, London (John Murray) 1886.

Doyle — Sir Francis Doyle, *The Return of the Guards, and Other Poems*, London (Macmillan) 1866.

Edwardes — Michael Edwardes, *Red Year: The Indian Rebellion of 1857*, London (Hamish Hamilton) 1973.

Egerton — *Wright of Derby*, London (Tate Gallery) 1990.

Elias — Norbert Elias, *The Civilizing Process*, [vol. 1] *The History of Manners* (1939), trans. Edmund Jephcott, Oxford (Basil Blackwell) 1978.

Elphinstone 1815   The Hon. Mountstuart Elphinstone, *An Account of the Kingdom of Caubul, and its Dependencies in Persia, Tartary, and India: comprising a view of the Afghan Nation. and a History of the Douraunee Monarchy*, London (for Longman, Hurst, Rees, Orme, and Brown and J. Murray) 1815.

Elphinstone 1857   The Hon. Mountstuart Elphinstone, *The History of India. The Hindu and Mahometan Periods* (1841), 4th edn, London (John Murray) 1857.

Encyclopédie.   [Diderot, Denis, D'Alembert, Jean le Rond. et al.], *Encyclopédie, ou Dictionnaire Raisonné des Sciences. des Arts et des Métiers. par une Société de Gens de Lettres*, 35 vols, vols 1–7 (text) and 18–28 (plates) Paris (Briasson et al.) 1751–72, vols 8–17 (text), Neufchastel (Samuel Faulche) 1765, 4 supplementary volumes Amsterdam (M. Rey) 1776–7, 2 further volumes (*Table Analytique*), Paris (Pancoucke) and Amsterdam (Marc-Michel Rey) 1780, and a supplementary volume of plates, Paris (Pancoucke et al.) and Amsterdam (M.M.Rey) 1777, reprinted in facsimile, 5 vols, New York (Readex Microprint Corporation) 1969, reissued New York and Paris (Pergamon Press) no date.

Eyre   Lieutenant Vincent Eyre, *The Military Operations at Cabul, which ended in the Retreat and Destruction of the British Army, January 1842* (1843), 2nd edn, London (John Murray) 1843.

Fane   Henry Edward Fane, *Five Years in India, &c.*, 2 vols, London (Henry Colburn) 1842.

Fay   Peter Ward Fay, *The Opium War 1840–1842*, Chapel Hill (University of North Carolina Press) 1976.

Forbes   Major [J.] Forbes, *Eleven Years in Ceylon. Comprising Sketches of the Field Sports and Natural History of that Colony and an Account of its History and Antiquities*, 2 vols, London (Richard Bentley) 1840.

Forrest   Denys Forrest, *Tiger of Mysore: The Life and Death of Tipu Sultan*, London (Chatto and Windus) 1970.

Forster   *The Arabian Nights' Entertainments*, trans. Rev. Edward Forster, revised by G. Moir Bussey, London (Joseph Thomas; T. Tegg; Simpkin, Marshall) 1840.

Fortune   Robert Fortune, *A Journey to the Tea Countries of China; including Sung-Lo and the Bohea Hills*, London (John Murray) 1852, reprinted in facsimile, London (Mildmay Books) 1987.

Freud   *The Standard Edition of the Complete Psychological Works of Sigmund Freud*, ed. James Strachey and Anna Freud, 24 vols, London (The Hogarth Press and the Institute of Psycho-Analysis) 1966–74.

Furniss   Tom Furniss, 'Edmund Burke's Revolution: The Discourses of Aesthetics, Gender, and Political Economy in Burke's *Enquiry* and *Reflections on the Revolution in France*', unpublished Ph.D. dissertation, University of Southampton, 1989.

Gates   Henry Louis Gates, Jr., (ed.) *'Race', Writing, and Difference*, Chicago and London (University of Chicago Press) 1986.

Goldman   Albert Goldman, *The Mine and the Mint: Sources for the Writings of Thomas De Quincey*, Carbondale (South Illinois University Press) 1965.

Goldsmith   Oliver Goldsmith, *A History of the Earth and Animated Nature* (1774), 6 vols, London (for F. Wingrave *et al.*) 1805.

Gordon   Thomas Gordon, *History of the Greek Revolution*, 2 vols, Edinburgh (William Blackwood) 1832.

Graham   Gerald S. Graham, *The China Station: War and Diplomacy 1830–1860*, Oxford (Clarendon Press) 1978.

Grose   *A Dictionary of Buckish Slang, University Wit, and Pickpocket Eloquence. Compiled Originally by Captain Grose*, London (for C. Chappel) 1811.

Guest   Harriet Guest, 'The Great Distinction: Figures of the Exotic in the Work of William Hodges', *The Oxford Art Journal*, vol. 12, no.2, 1989.

Gupta   Pratul Chandra Gupta, *Nana Sahib and the Rising at Cawnpore*, Oxford (Clarendon Press), 1963.

Hall and Bernard   *The Nemesis in China, comprising a History of the Late War in that Country; with an Account of the Colony of Hong Kong, from the notes of Captain W.H. Hall, R.N., and personal observations by W.D. Bernard, Esq., A.M. Oxon.* (1844), 3rd edn, London (Henry Colburn) 1847, reprinted in facsimile, New York and London (Praeger Publishers) 1969.

Havelock   Captain Henry Havelock, *Narrative of the War in Affghanistan. In 1838–9*, 2 vols, London (Henry Colburn) 1840.

Hayter   Alethea Hayter, *Opium and the Romantic Imagination*, (1968) London (Faber and Faber) 1971.

Heber   Amelia Heber, 'Journal of a Tour in Ceylon', vol. 2, pp. 222–66 in Rt. Rev. Reginald Heber, *Narrative of a Journey through the Upper Provinces of India, from Calcutta to Bombay, 1824–1825*, 2 vols, London (John Murray) 1828.

Herrmann   Dieter B. Herrmann, *The History of Astronomy from Herschel to Hertzsprung*, trans. and revised by Kevin Krisciunas, Cambridge (Cambridge University Press) 1984.

Herschel   Sir John F.W. Herschel, Bart., *Outlines of Astronomy*, London (Longman, Brown, Green and Longmans) 1849.

Hodson   *Twelve Years of a Soldier's Life in India: being extracts from the letters of Major W.S.R. Hodson, B.A., . . . edited by his brother the Rev. George H. Hodson, M.A.* (1859), 3rd edn, London (John W. Parker) 1859.

Hofland   Mrs Hofland, *The Young Cadet; or Henry Delamere's Voyage to India, &c.*, London (John Harris) [1827].

Holt   Edgar Holt, *The Opium Wars in China*, London (Putnam) 1964.

Humboldt   Alexander von Humboldt, *Personal Narrative of Travels to the Equinoctial Regions of America during the years 1799–1804*, trans. Thomasina Ross, 3 vols, London and New York (George Routledge) no date.

Hyde   Ralph Hyde, *Panoramania! The Art and Entertainment of the 'All-Embracing' View*, London (Trefoil Publications) 1988.

Impey and MacGregor   Oliver Impey and Arthur MacGregor (eds), *The Origin of Museums: The Cabinet of Curiosities in Sixteenth- and Seventeenth-Century Europe*, Oxford (Clarendon Press) 1985.

Indian Revolt   *Narrative of the Indian Revolt from its Outbreak to the Capture of Lucknow, &c.*, London (George Vickers) 1858.

James   T.G.H. James, *The British Museum and Ancient Egypt*, London (British Museum Publications) 1981.

James and Critchley   P.D. James and T.A. Critchley, *The Maul and the Pear Tree: The Ratcliffe Highway Murders 1811* (1971), London (Sphere Books) 1987.

Jocelyn   Lord [Robert] Jocelyn, *Six Months with The Chinese Expedition; or, Leaves from a Soldier's Notebook*, London (John Murray) 1841.

Jones   Sir William Jones, 'The Gods of Greece, Italy, and India', *Asiatic Researches*, vol. 1, 1789.

Jordan   John E. Jordan, *De Quincey to Wordsworth: A Biography of a Relationship*, Berkeley and Los Angeles (University of California Press) 1962.

Josephus   Josephus, *The Jewish War*, trans. G.A. Williamson, revised and ed. E. Mary Smallwood (1981), New York (Dorset Press) 1985.

Joshi   P.C. Joshi (ed.) *Rebellion 1857; A Symposium*, New Delhi (People's Publishing House) 1957.

Kiernan   V.G. Kiernan, *The Lords of Human Kind: Black Man, Yellow Man, and White Man in an Age of Empire* (1969), London (Century Hutchinson; The Cresset Library) 1988.

Kinglake   A.W. Kinglake, *Eothen* (1844), new edn, London (Longman, Brown, Green and Longmans) 1851.

Kingston   W.H.G. Kingston, *The Three Midshipmen* (1873), numerous editions.

Kinnear   John G. Kinnear, *Cairo, Petra. and Damascus, in 1839. With Remarks on the Government of Mehemet Ali, and on the Present Prospects of Syria*, London (John Murray) 1841.

Knighton   William Knighton, *The History of Ceylon from the Earliest Period to the Present Time*, London (Longman, Brown, Green, and Longmans) 1845.

de La Barre de Beaumarchais   [Antoine de La Barre de Beaumarchais], *The Temple of the Muses . . . represented in sixty sculptures . . . by Bernard Picart . . . and other . . . masters*, etc., Amsterdam (Zacharias Châtelain) 1733.

Lane   Edward William Lane, *An Account of the Manners and Customs of the Modern Egyptians, written in Egypt during the years 1833–1855* (1836), Paisley and London (Alexander Gardner) 1896.

Laplanche and Pontalis   Jean Laplanche and Jean-Bertrand Pontalis, 'Fantasy and the Origins of Sexuality', in Victor Burgin, James Donald and Cora Kaplan (eds) *Formations of Fantasy*, London and New York (Methuen) 1986.

Layard

Austen Henry Layard, *Nineveh and its Remains* (1849), 6th edn, 2 vols, London (John Murray) 1854.

Lewis

Matthew Lewis, *The Monk* (1796), ed. Howard Anderson, Oxford and New York (Oxford University Press) 1980.

Lindop

Grevel Lindop, *The Opium-Eater. A Life of Thomas De Quincey*, London (J. M. Dent) 1981.

Lindsay

Lord Lindsay (Alexander William Crawford), *Letters on Egypt, Edom, and the Holy Land* (1838), 4th edn, London (Henry Colburn) 1847.

Llewellyn

Briony Llewellyn, *The Orient Observed: Images of the Middle East from the Searight Collection*, London (Victoria & Albert Museum) 1989.

Lovell

Bernard Lovell, *Emerging Cosmology*, New York (Columbia University Press) 1981.

Ludowyk

E. F. C. Ludowyk, *The Modern History of Ceylon*, London (Weidenfeld and Nicolson), 1966.

Lushington

Henry Lushington, *A Great Country's Little Wars; or England, Affghanistan, and Sinde*, London (J. W. Parker) 1844.

Macartney

Earl of Macartney, *An Authentic Account of an Embassy from the King of Great Britain to the Emperor of China. . . taken chiefly from the papers of His Excellency the Earl of Macartney. . . by Sir George Staunton, Baronet*, 2 vols, London (for G. Nicol) 1797.

Macaulay

Thomas Babington Macaulay, *Critical and Historical Essays* (1843), 2 vols, London (J. M. Dent) and New York (E. P. Dutton) 1907.

McDonagh

Josephine McDonagh, 'Do or Die: Problems of Agency and Gender in the Aesthetics of Murder', *Genders*, no. 5, Summer 1989.

Majumdar

R. C. Majumdar, *The Sepoy Mutiny and Revolt of 1857* (1957), 2nd edn, Calcutta (Firma K. L. Mukhopadhyay) 1963.

Maniquis

Robert M. Maniquis, 'Lonely Empires: Personal and Public Visions of Thomas De Quincey', in Eric Rothstein and Joseph Anthony Wittreich, Jr. (eds) *Literary Monographs*, vol. 8, Madison (University of Wisconsin Press) 1976.

Marsden	William Marsden, *The History of Sumatra*, London (for the author) 1783.
Marshall	Henry Marshall, *Ceylon: A general Description of the Island and its Inhabitants; with an Historical Sketch of the Conquest of the Island by the British*, London (William H. Allen) 1846.
Martineau	Harriet Martineau, *Eastern Life, Present and Past* (1848), new edn, London (Edward Moxon) 1850.
Masson	Charles Masson, *Narrative of Various Journeys in Balochistan, Afghanistan, and the Panjab; including a residence in those countries from 1826 to 1838*, 3 vols, London (Richard Bentley) 1842.
Maurice	Thomas Maurice, *The History of Hindostan, its Arts, and its Sciences*, 3 vols, London (for the author) 1795–8.
Mayhew	Henry Mayhew, *London Labour and the London Poor* (1851), 2nd edn, 4 vols (1861–2), reprinted in facsimile, London (Frank Cass) 1967.
Meadows	Thomas Taylor Meadows, *The Chinese and their Rebellions. . . to which is added. An Essay on Civilization and its Present State in the East and West*, London (Smith, Elder) 1856, reprinted in facsimile, Shannon (Irish University Press) 1972.
Medwin	[Thomas Medwin], *Ahasuerus, The Wanderer: A Dramatic Legend in Six Parts. By the Author of Sketches in Hindoostan, and Other Poems*, London (for G. and W. B. Whittaker) 1823.
Methley	V. M. Methley, 'The Ceylon Expedition of 1803', in *Transactions of the Royal Historical Society*, 4th series, vol. 1, 1918.
Mill	James Mill, *The History of British India*, 3 vols, London (Baldwin, Cradock and Joy) 1817.
Miller, E.	Edward Miller, *That Noble Cabinet: A History of the British Museum*, London (André Deutsch) 1973.
Miller, J. H.	J. Hillis Miller, *The Disappearance of God: Five Nineteenth-Century Writers*, Cambridge Mass. (Harvard University Press) 1975.
Mills	Lennox A. Mills, *Ceylon under British Rule, 1795–1932* (1933), London (Frank Cass) 1964.
Moor	Edward Moor, *The Hindu Pantheon*, London (Joseph Johnson) 1810.
Moore 1827	Thomas Moore, *The Epicurean, A Tale*, Paris (A. and W. Galignani) 1827.

Moore 1910   *The Poetical Works of Thomas Moore*, ed. A. D. Godley, London (Henry Frowde, for Oxford University Press) 1910.

Mure   William Mure of Caldwell, *Journal of a Tour in Greece and the Ionian Isles*, 2 vols, Edinburgh and London (William Blackwood) 1842.

Murray   David Murray, *Museums, Their History and Their Use*, Glasgow (John MacLehose) 1904.

Napoleon   *Correspondance de Napoléon 1ᵉʳ Publiée par ordre de l'Empereur Napoléon III*, 32 vols, Paris (Henri Plon, J. Dumaine) 1858–70.

Nash   Charles Nash (ed.) *History of the War in Affghanistan, from its Commencement to its Close. . . from the Journal and Letters of an Officer of High Rank*, London (Thomas Brooks) 1843.

Newbold   T. J. Newbold, *Political and Statistical Account of the British Settlements in the Straits of Malacca, viz. Pinang, Malacca, and Singapore*, 2 vols, London (John Murray) 1839.

Nichol   John Pringle Nichol, *Thoughts on Some Important Points relating to the System of the World*, Edinburgh (William Tait) 1846.

Oliphant   Laurence Oliphant, *Narrative of the Earl of Elgin's Mission to China and Japan in the Years 1857, '58, '59*, 2 vols, Edinburgh (William Blackwood) 1859.

Opie   Mrs [Amelia] Opie, *Adeline Mowbray* (1804), London (Pandora Press) 1986.

Orme   Robert Orme, *History of the Military Transactions of the British Nation in Indostan* (1763–78), 2 vols, 4th edn revised, London (F. Wingrave) 1803.

Osborn   Sherard Osborn, *The Past and Present of British Relations with China*, Edinburgh and London (W. Blackwood) 1860.

Osborne   Peter Osborne (ed.), *Socialism and the Limits of Liberalism*, London (Verso) forthcoming.

Ouchterlony   Lieut. John Ouchterlony, *The Chinese War: An Account of All the Operations of the British Forces from the Commencement to the Treaty of Nanking*, London (Sanders and Otley) 1844.

Page   H. A. Page, *Thomas De Quincey: His Life and Writings. With Unpublished Correspondence* (1877), 2nd edn, 2 vols, London (John Hogg) 1879.

Park   Mungo Park, *Travels in the Interior of Africa* (1799), reprinted as *The Life and Travels of*

Mungo Park, Edinburgh (W. P. Nimmo, Hay and Mitchell) 1897.

Parry
Benita Parry, 'Problems in Current Theories of Colonial Discourse', *Oxford Literary Review*, vol. 9, nos. 1–2, (1987) 27–58.

Percival, R.
Robert Percival, *An Account of the Island of Ceylon* (1803), 2nd edn, London (C. and R. Baldwin) 1805.

Percival, T. 1788
Thomas Percival, *A Father's Instructions: consisting of Moral Tales, Fables, and Reflections* (1775), 7th edn, Warrington and London (for J. Johnson) 1788.

Percival, T. 1807
The Works, Literary, Moral, and Philosophical of Thomas Percival, new edn, 2 vols, London (J. Johnson) 1807.

Philips
C. H. Philips (ed.) *Historians of India, Pakistan and Ceylon*, London (Oxford University Press) 1961.

Pieris
P. E. Pieris, *Tri Sinhala*, Colombo (Colombo Apothecaries Co.) 1939.

Powell
Geoffrey Powell, *The Kandyan Wars: the British Army in Ceylon, 1803–1813*, London (Leo Cooper) 1973.

Rees
Abraham Rees et al., *The Cyclopaedia; or, Universal Dictionary of Arts, Sciences, and Literature*, 39 vols, London (for Longman, Hurst, Rees, Orme and Brown) 1819.

Robertson
William Robertson, *An Historical Disquisition concerning the Knowledge which the Ancients had of India* (1791), 3rd edn, London (for A. Strahan, et al.) 1799.

Ronan
Colin A. Ronan, *Discovering the Universe: A History of Astronomy*, New York (Basic Books) 1971.

Rousseau
Pierre Rousseau, *Man's Conquest of the Stars*, trans. Michael Bullock, New York (Norton) 1961.

Rush
Benjamin Rush, *Medical Inquiries and Observations*, 2 vols, Philadelphia (T. Dobson) 1793.

Russell, J.
Joshua Russell, *Journal of a Tour in Ceylon and India undertaken at the request of the Baptist Missionary Society*, London (Houlston and Stoneman) 1852.

Russell, M.
The Right Rev. M. Russell, *View of Ancient and Modern Egypt; with an Outline of its Natural History* (1831), 6th edn, Edinburgh (Oliver and Boyd) 1844.

Russell, W. H.

My Diary in India, in the Year 1858–9, 2 vols, London (Routledge, Warne and Routledge) 1860.

Said

Edward W. Said, *Orientalism* (1978), London and Harmondsworth (Penguin Books) 1985.

Sale

Lady [Florentia] Sale, *A Journal of the Disasters in Affghanistan*, London (John Murray) 1843.

Schaffer

Simon Schaffer, 'The Nebular Hypothesis and the Science of Progress', in James R. Moore (ed.) *History, Humanity and Evolution: Essays for John C. Greene*, Cambridge (Cambridge University Press) 1990.

Shelley 1887.

The Wandering Jew. A Poem by Percy Bysshe Shelley, ed. Bertram Dobell, London (Reeves and Turner; The Shelley Society), 1887.

Shelley 1967

Shelley: Poetical Works, ed. Thomas Hutchinson, London (Oxford University Press) 1967.

de Silva

K. M. de Silva (ed.) *History of Ceylon*, 3 vols, Colombo (Colombo Apothecaries Co. for University of Ceylon) 1973.

Sleeman

W. H. Sleeman, *The Thugs or Phansigars of India*, Philadelphia (Carey and Hart) 1839.

Smith

The Works of the Rev. Sydney Smith (1839), 4th edn, 2 vols, London (Longman, Brown, Green and Longmans) 1848.

Snyder

Robert Lance Snyder, *Thomas De Quincey: Bicentenary Studies*, Norman and London (University of Oklahoma Press) 1985.

Spivak 1985a

Gayatri C. Spivak, 'Can the Subaltern Speak? Speculations on Widow-Sacrifice', in *Wedge*, nos. 7–8, Winter/Spring 1985.

Spivak 1985b

'Overdeterminations of Imperialism: David Ochterlony and the Ranee of Sirmoor', in *Europe and Its Others*, vol. 1, Colchester (Univerity of Essex) 1985.

Staunton

Remarks on the British Relations with China and the Proposed Plans for Improving them. By Sir George Thomas Staunton, Bart., London (Edmund Lloyd and Simpkin and Marshall) 1836.

Stevenson

Seth W. Stevenson, *A Dictionary of Roman Coins (Republican and Imperial)*, revised by C. Roach Smith, London (George Bell) 1889.

Suetonius

Gaius Suetonius Tranquillus, *The Twelve Caesars*, trans. Robert Graves, revised and ed.

Michael Grant, Harmondsworth (Penguin Books; Penguin Classics) 1979.

Tales　　*Tales of the Wild and Wonderful*, London (for Hurst, Robinson) 1825.

Taylor　　Philip Meadows Taylor, *Confessions of a Thug* (1839), London (Henry S. King) 1873.

Tennent　　Sir James Emerson Tennent, *Ceylon, An Account of the Island Physical, Historical, and Topographical*, 2 vols, London (Longman, Green, Longman and Roberts) 1859.

Thackeray　　W. M. Thackeray, *Notes of a Journey from Cornhill to Grand Cairo by way of Lisbon, Athens, Constantinople, and Jerusalem* (1846), vol. 5 in *The Works of William Makepeace Thackeray*, 13 vols, London (Smith, Elder) 1900.

Thompson E.　　Edward J. Thompson, *The Other Side of the Medal*, London (Hogarth Press) 1925.

Thompson J.　　J. M. Thompson, *Napoleon Bonaparte; his Rise and Fall*, Oxford (Basil Blackwell) 1958.

Tieck　　Ludwig Tieck, *Werke*, 4 vols, Munich (Winkler-Verlag) 1963–6.

Tolfrey　　[William Tolfrey], *A Narrative of Events which have recently occurred in the Island of Ceylon, written by a Gentleman on the Spot*, London (T. Egerton) 1815.

Turner　　Michael Turner (ed.) *Parlour Poetry*, London (Michael Joseph) 1967.

Urquhart　　D. Urquhart, *The Spirit of the East* (1838), 2nd edn, 2 vols, London (Henry Colburn) 1839.

Vibart　　Colonel H. M. Vibart, *Richard Baird Smith: The Leader of the Delhi Heroes in 1857*, Westminster (Archibald Constable) 1897.

Vigne 1840　　G. T. Vigne, *A Personal Narrative of a Visit to Ghuzni, Kabul, and Affghanistan, and of a Residence at the Court of Dost Mohamed, &c.*, London (Whittaker) 1840.

Vigne 1842　　*Travels in Kashmir, Ladak, Iskardo, &c.*, 2 vols, London (Henry Colburn) 1842.

Volney　　[Constantin-François Chasseboeuf comte de Volney] *A New Translation of Volney's Ruins; or Meditations on the Revolution of Empires* (1791), 2 vols, Paris (for Levrault) 1802.

Walvin　　James Walvin, *England, Slaves and Freedom, 1776–1838*, London (Macmillan) 1986.

Warburton   Eliot Warburton, *The Crescent and the Cross*
                   (1845), 2 vols, Leipzig (Bernhard Tauchnitz;
                   Collection of British Authors vol. ccxxxix)
                   1852.

Whale   John C. Whale, *Thomas De Quincey's Reluctant
                   Autobiography*, London and Sydney (Croom
                   Helm) 1984.

Wilks   Mark Wilks, *Historical Sketches of the South of
                   India, in an Attempt to Trace the History of
                   Mysoor*, 3 vols, London (Longman, Hurst,
                   Rees, Orme and Brown) 1810–17.

Wood   Robert Wood, *The Ruins of Palmyra, Otherwise
                   Tedmor, In The Desert*, London (for the author)
                   1753.

Wordsworth   *The Prelude, or Growth of a Poet's Mind, by
                   William Wordsworth*, ed. Ernest de Selincourt,
                   2nd edn, revised by Helen Darbishire, Oxford
                   (Oxford University Press; Clarendon Press)
                   1959.

Index